IMAGES
of America

HAMILTON

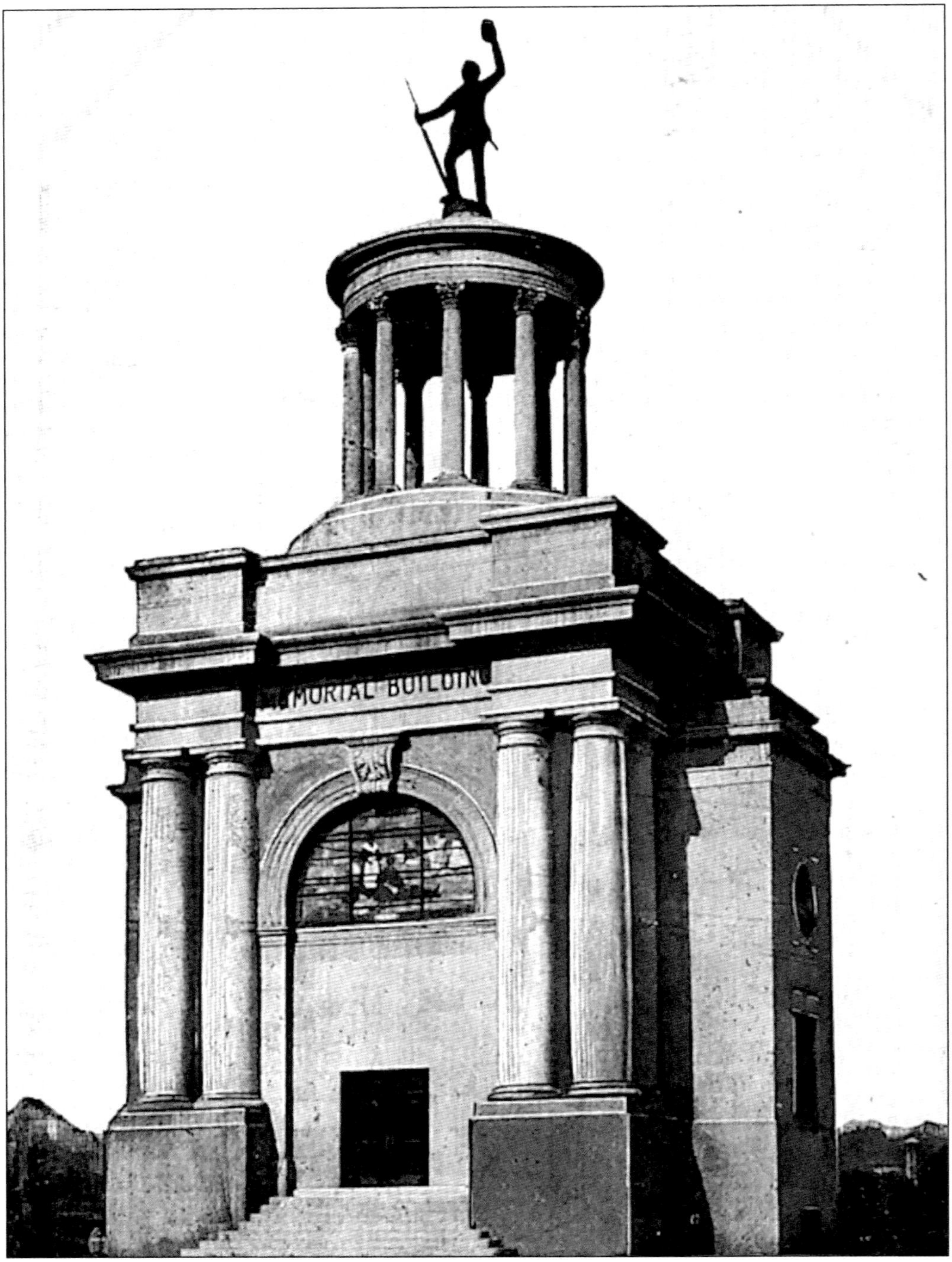

Appropriately, a 17-foot Civil War soldier nicknamed Billy Yank stands atop Hamilton's Soldiers, Sailors, and Pioneers Monument. The early-1900s memorial is open to the public as a museum, which includes war memorabilia such as a tiny Civil War cannon, military uniforms, weapons, historic flags, a replica of Fort Hamilton, and a piece of the *U.S.S. Maine*. The building is used in the city's logo. (Courtesy the authors.)

IMAGES
of America

HAMILTON

Randy McNutt and Cheryl Bauer

ARCADIA
PUBLISHING

ISBN 978-0-7385-3400-8

Published by Arcadia Publishing
Charleston, South Carolina

Printed in the United States of America

Library of Congress Catalog Card Number: 2005922430

For all general information contact Arcadia Publishing at:
Telephone 843-853-2070
Fax 843-853-0044
E-mail sales@arcadiapublishing.com
For customer service and orders:
Toll-Free 1-888-313-2665

Visit us on the Internet at www.arcadiapublishing.com

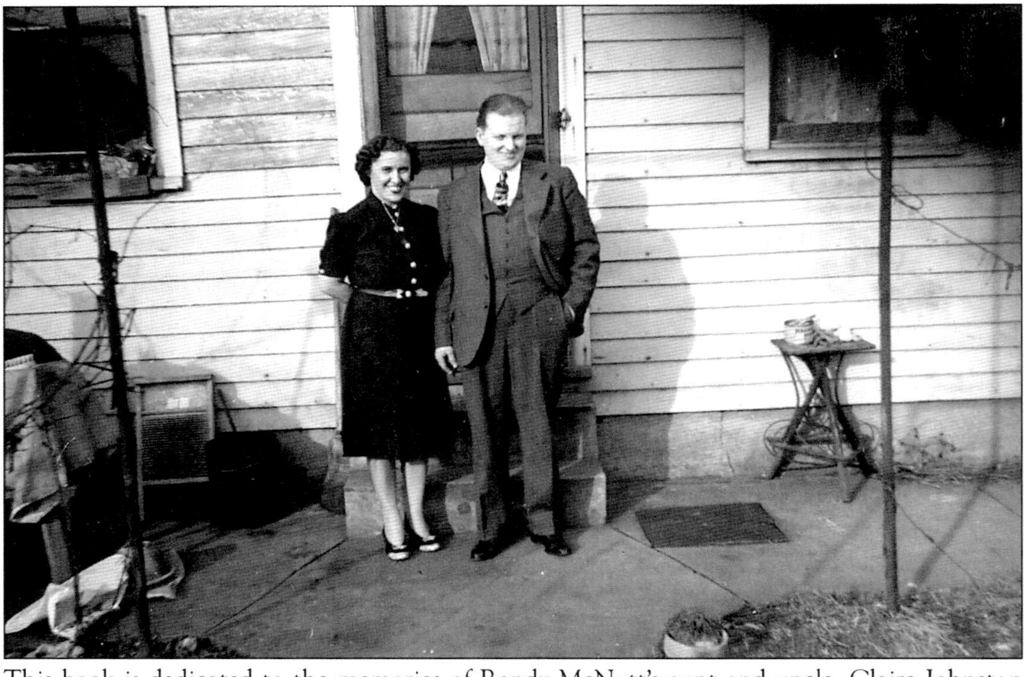

This book is dedicated to the memories of Randy McNutt's aunt and uncle, Claire Johnston Hornung and Vernon Hornung, who gave him a lifetime of wonderful experiences while growing up in the Lindenwald neighborhood. Mr. Hornung worked there with his father and brothers at Hornung Meats. Mrs. Hornung grew up in the neighborhood. The couple lived on Laurel Avenue for nearly a half century. (Courtesy the authors.)

Contents

Acknowledgments

Most of the photographs in this book came from the archives of the Butler County Historical Society, whose staff generously provided their time, resources, and good cheer.

The authors especially thank Betty Maham, the society's administrative assistant at the Benninghofen House museum, who helped dig out many old photographs and information; Mildred Holland, who assisted; and Carol Gabriel, the society's director and the museum curator.

Without their help and perseverance, this project would have been far less effective. We thank these kind women for their friendship and love of history.

Thanks also go to Joni Copas, the director of communications for the Hamilton City School District. She helped find other old photos and took an interest in the project from the start. In addition, Gerry Hammond of the City of Sculpture also helped identify sculptures and provided much-needed details. A good friend, David Belew of Historic Hamilton Inc., also lent his knowledge of Hamilton and its people. So did our friend and author James Blount, a native who has done so much to preserve the city's history.

Finally, Don Schollenbarger, curator of the Memorial Building, also helped.

For more information on Hamilton's past and present, write to the Butler County Historical Society, 327 North Second Street, Hamilton, Ohio, 45011. Or view its Web site at http://freepages.history.rootsweb.com/~butlercounty. The City of Sculpture may be reached at its offices at One High Street, Hamilton, Ohio, 45011, or through its Web site, www.cityofsculpture.org.

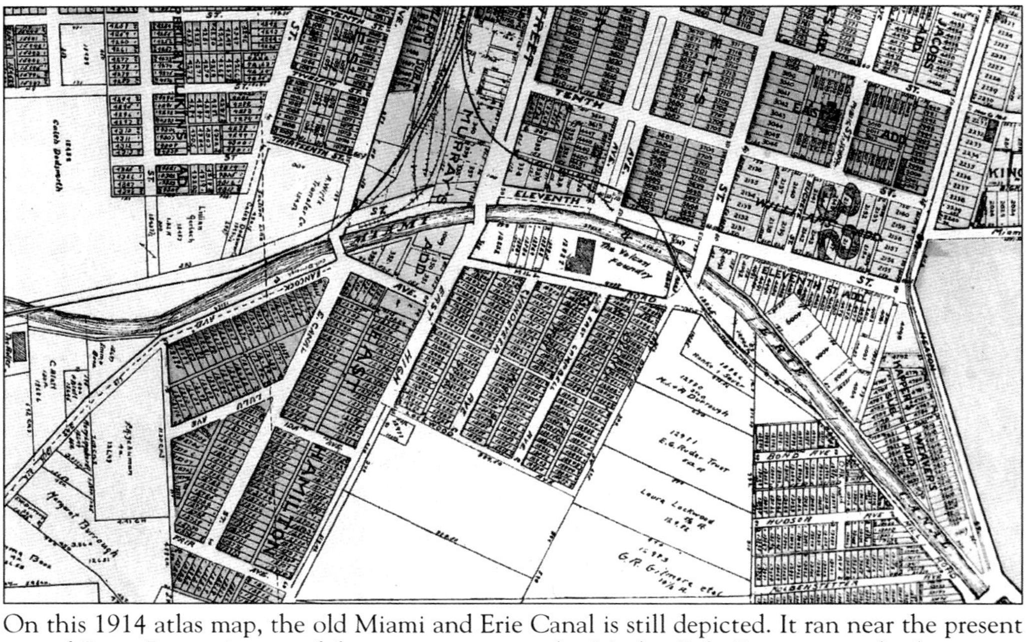

On this 1914 atlas map, the old Miami and Erie Canal is still depicted. It ran near the present site of State Route 4, east of downtown, passing the Mosler Safe Company and other major industries that took advantage of the watery route. By then, however, the canal's days were coming to an end. The Miami and Erie's heyday had come decades earlier, before trains and trucks established themselves as transportation alternatives. (Courtesy the authors.)

INTRODUCTION

Since its founding as Fort Hamilton in 1791, the city of Hamilton has continued to renew itself and change focus, from frontier outpost to major Midwest industrial center to the internationally known City of Sculpture.

The Butler County seat began as an army supply depot on the Great Miami River in 1791. General Arthur St. Clair, governor of the Northwest Territory, named the wooden fort in honor of Alexander Hamilton, an American founding father and George Washington's secretary of the treasury. It served its purpose well but saw no battles.

When General "Mad" Anthony Wayne's soldiers defeated an Indian coalition at the Battle of Fallen Timbers in what is now northwest Ohio in 1794, and the subsequent Treaty of Greenville finally assured peace throughout the Ohio Country in 1795, the army abandoned Fort Hamilton. In the late 1790s, a town started growing around the site, and new residents used some of the fort's structures for building materials. In 1803, Ohio became the 17th state and legislators formed the surrounding Butler County. Hamilton became the seat of local government, a distinction it continues to hold.

Israel Ludlow laid out the town on December 17, 1794. Initially named Fairfield, the community quickly reverted to the name of the fort. Residents were mostly former soldiers who had served there. A two-story frame house, formerly used by the fort commanding general when he was visiting, opened as a tavern operated by William McClellan. Soon, other taverns, houses, and stores popped up, and the town grew along the river and across it.

An industrial leader by the mid-1800s, Hamilton was the home of wealthy factory owners who lived in mansions on Dayton Street and in other areas. For years, their factories helped make Hamilton nearly a self-contained unit. So many different products were made in the city in those days that it lived up to its impressive nickname: the Greatest Manufacturing City of its Size in the World.

By 1875, Hamilton was home to 12,800 people, including 4,000 immigrants who brought much-needed industrial skills to Ohio. A few years later, the city would produce 250 products in 140 manufacturing plants.

When construction of the city's most recognizable symbol, the Soldiers, Sailors, and Pioneers Monument—also known as the Memorial Building—started in 1902 along the Great Miami, Hamilton could do about anything. The building was erected and designed exclusively by Hamilton residents (except for its massive and magnificent stained glass windows, which came from Cincinnati). Rudolph Thiem, a German immigrant, sculpted the building's *Billy Yank*, a 17-foot bronze Civil War soldier, and local artisans chiseled the names of Butler County veterans on the interior marble walls.

The Memorial Building represented Hamilton's hopes for a peaceful tomorrow as well as the abilities of its diverse and growing population of immigrants and original residents. They worked in large factories and small businesses that gave Hamilton a reputation for quality craftsmanship. At Hamilton's industrial peak in the early 1900s, thousands of residents worked in local factories, including Champion Coated Paper Co., Estate Stove Co., Niles Tool Works, Ford Motor Co., Mosler Safe Co., and Beckett Papers. "Known in World Markets" was the city's motto.

Its dozens of factories survived changing markets, new fads, and Mother Nature. In March 1913, during a time of heavy rains, Hamilton faced its greatest challenge as the Great Miami flooded again. In only two days, more than 200 people died and 300 homes and buildings were destroyed. Property damage exceeded $10 million. Four buildings were swept away in the raging waters.

Yet Hamilton overcame the destruction and participated in a large-scale flood-prevention program that has restrained the Great Miami since those days.

Through the 1970s, Hamilton was pure Middle America—friendly, hospitable, open. It produced important people in sports (Cincinnati Reds pitcher Joe Nuxhall), music (composers Johnny Black and Wayne Perry), literature (William Dean Howells and Fannie Hurst), and comedy (Ray Combs). The population peaked at about 67,000 people. Today, they number more than 60,000.

Not surprisingly, Hamilton industries turned out tens of thousands of pieces of military equipment during World War II. When the Korean War ended in 1953, nearly 21,000 people worked in 125 Hamilton factories. A decade later, things had changed. Some larger industries had moved, merged, and closed. By the early 1960s, the city had lost 25 to 43 percent of its industrial jobs. Among the last to go was the internationally known Mosler Safe Co., which since the 1890s had helped to give Hamilton a reputation as "The Safe Capital of America."

In 2000, the city rebounded from a long period of industry closures by receiving official state designation as the City of Sculpture and establishing a plan to become a leading center for international, regional, and local sculptors. The city even named its first sculptor-in-residence, Dennis Baker. Hamilton now focuses heavily on the arts, and encourages the development of smaller businesses.

"People feel they can make an impact both economically and socially for Hamilton through a relationship with the arts," said Mike Dingeldein, a City of Sculpture Committee member. "Ultimately, we hope to begin to attract a new economic base through arts-related activities." Board President Trudy Marcum added, "Industry comes and goes, but art is forever."

Until the early 2000s, Hamilton was the home of two large hospitals, Fort Hamilton and Mercy. Mercy closed in 2003 but Fort Hamilton expanded. The city continues to have an award-winning daily, the *Journal-News*, a respected regional arts center, a university (the Hamilton Campus of Miami University, founded in 1968), and modern downtown buildings such as the Government Services Center and One Renaissance Plaza, which contrast nicely with the old Dixon Opera House, the Butler County Courthouse, and other nineteenth-century buildings.

Fittingly, in October 2004 the nation's largest sculpture of Alexander Hamilton was erected in a median on High Street at Journal Square. It greets visitors who have come to see a city that is renewing itself in body, spirit, and history.

One

FORT HAMILTON

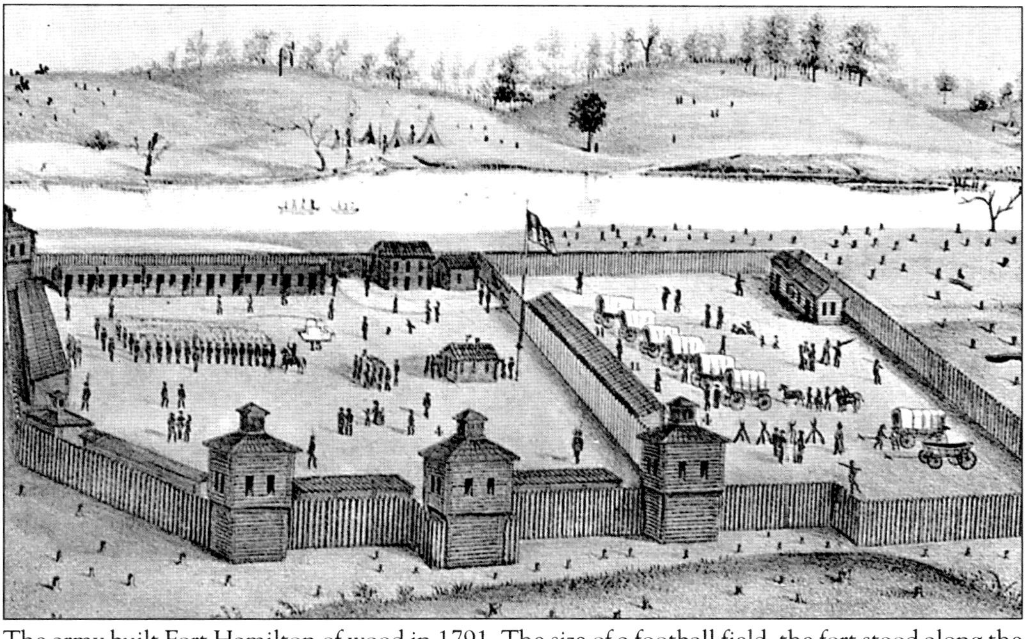

The army built Fort Hamilton of wood in 1791. The size of a football field, the fort stood along the east bank of the Great Miami River. Some historians believe it was rectangular; others believe it came to a point on one end. In those days, grassy prairies around the fort yielded 300 tons of hay in good years. Soldiers abandoned the supply post in 1797. (Courtesy the BCHS.)

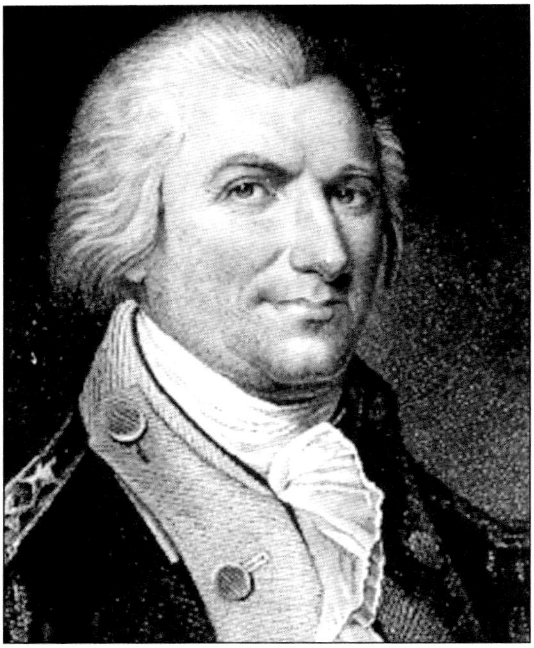

General Arthur St. Clair, governor of the Northwest Territory, built Fort Hamilton to supply his new American army, which marched north to confront an Indian coalition. The tribes killed and wounded about 900 of 1,300 soldiers in what is now Mercer County. St. Clair fought heroically but ultimately was relieved of his command. Despite the outcome, St. Clair's name is prominently displayed around Hamilton today. (Courtesy the Morristown National Historical Park.)

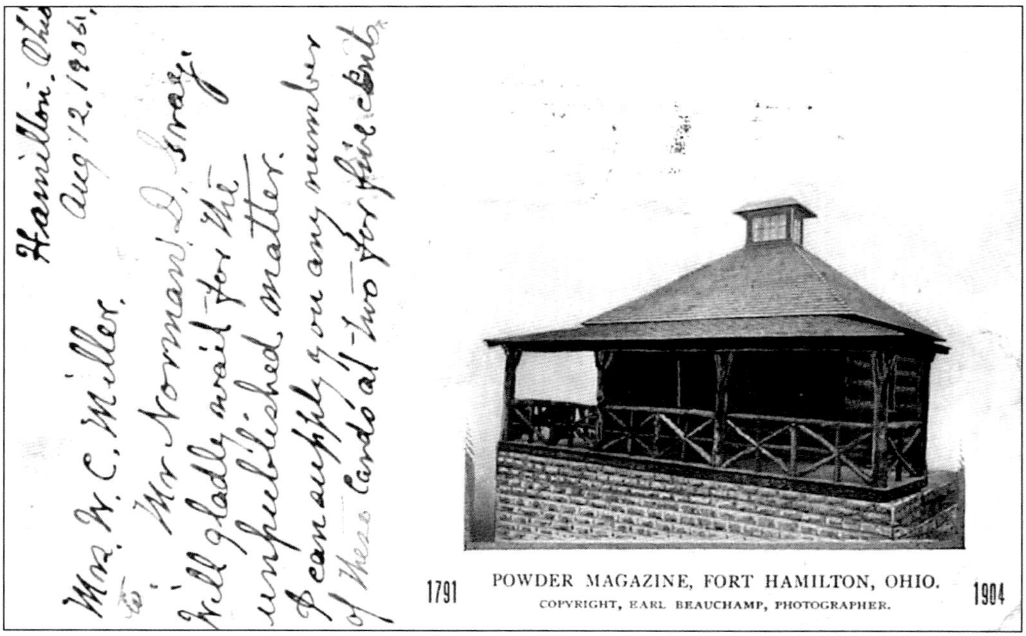

Fort Hamilton's last remaining component, the powder magazine, was abandoned in the late 1790s and later used as Hamilton's first school building. When the city's first school opened in 1818, the powder magazine was no longer needed. It was destroyed in the 1913 flood. The magazine stood near where the Soldiers, Sailors, and Pioneers Monument stands today, along the Great Miami. The most famous soldier to be stationed at the fort was a young William Henry Harrison, who in later years proudly told stories of serving at Fort Hamilton. Indians never attacked it. (Courtesy the authors.)

General "Mad" Anthony Wayne's soldiers improved Fort Hamilton in 1793. The Revolutionary War veteran assumed command of the frontier army after St. Clair's Defeat in 1791, and went on to defeat an Indian coalition at the Battle of Fallen Timbers, near present-day Toledo. After Wayne signed the Treaty of Greenville in 1795, Ohio teemed with settlers. Statehood followed in 1803. The victory gave Wayne immortality in Hamilton. (Courtesy the Independence National Historical Park.)

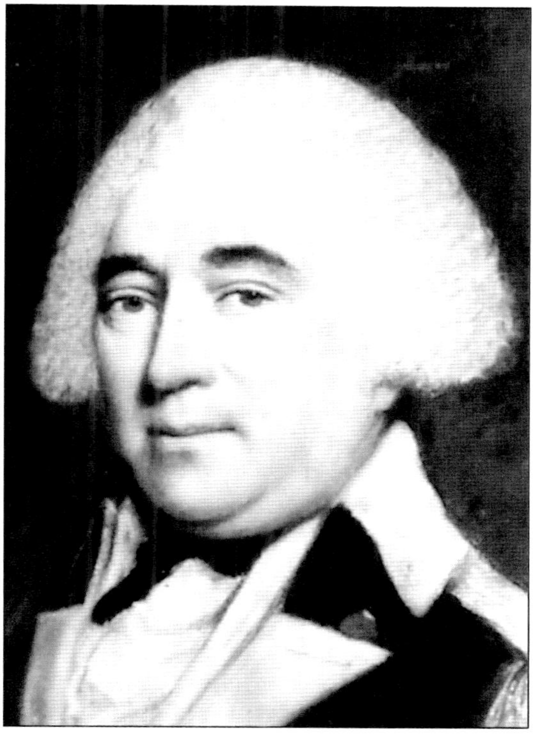

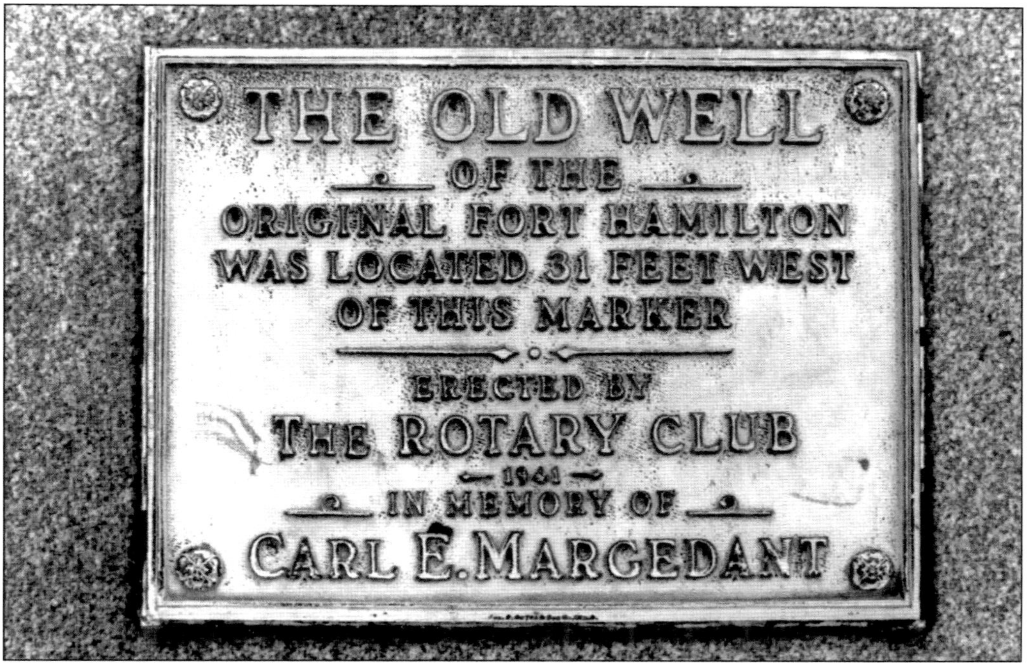

A bronze tablet marks the site of Fort Hamilton's well, located 31 feet west of the tablet. The memorial is in front of the Anthony Wayne Hotel on Monument Avenue, near the Memorial Building. The Hamilton Rotary Club erected the marker in 1941. (Courtesy the authors.)

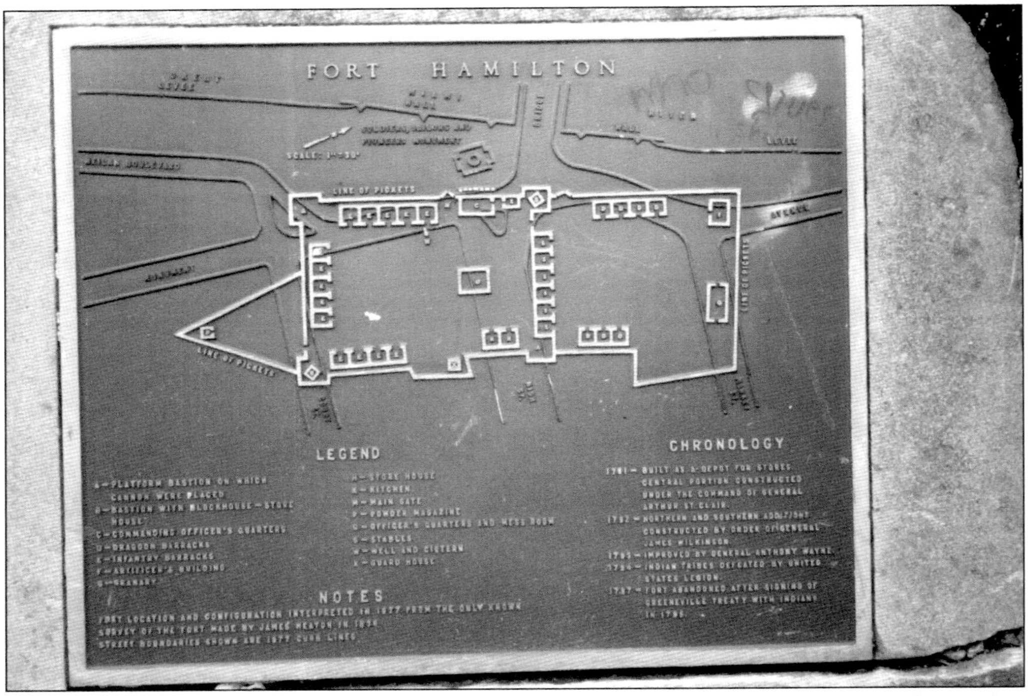

In a grassy area on which Fort Hamilton once stood, visitors can read a bronze plaque that shows the boundaries of the fort and the Great Miami. The fort included a platform bastion on which cannon were placed. Blockhouses protected the soldiers. (Courtesy the authors.)

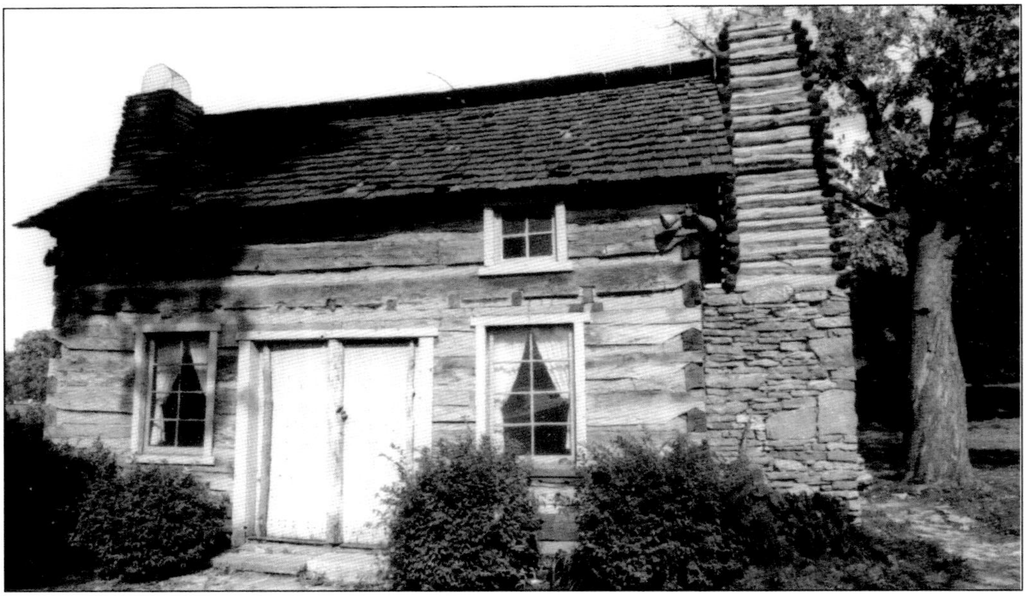

Built *c.* 1804 on the west side of the city, Hamilton's log cabin is one of city's oldest buildings. In 1964, it was relocated to the original Fort Hamilton grounds on Monument Avenue as a gift from R.B. Hershner of Hamilton. Walter A. and Thomas B. Rentschler provided restoration money. On December 18, 2004, the Hershner family helped rededicate the cabin. (Courtesy Randy McNutt.)

Two

CITY SCENES

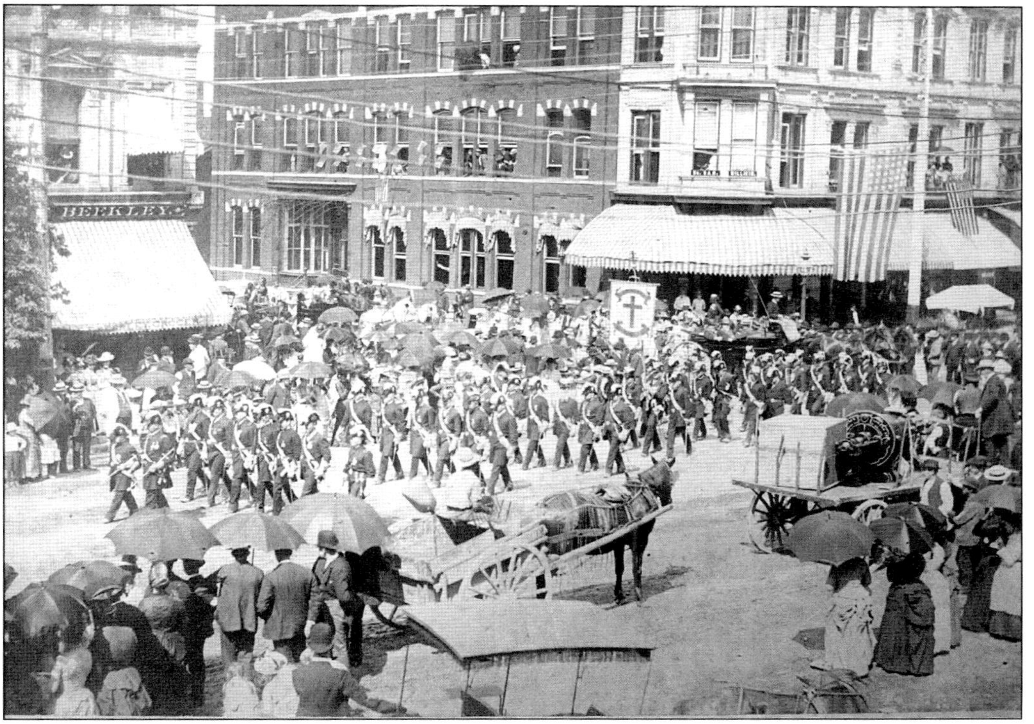

Hamilton celebrated its centennial in 1891 with a large parade downtown. Surviving for a century was a major accomplishment for any community. By 1890, the city was a thriving community of 48,597 people. (Courtesy the BCHS.)

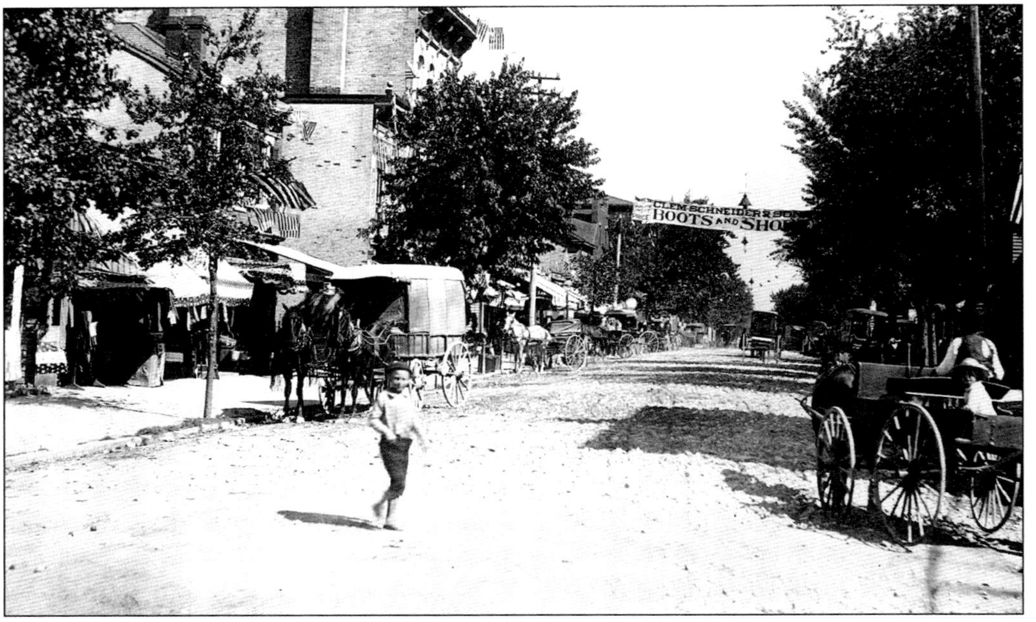

In 1891, many of Hamilton's small businesses thrived and some of its streets were still dirt roads. In this picture, taken that year on North Third Street, a large banner proclaimed "boots and shoes" for sale at a local store. (Courtesy the BCHS.)

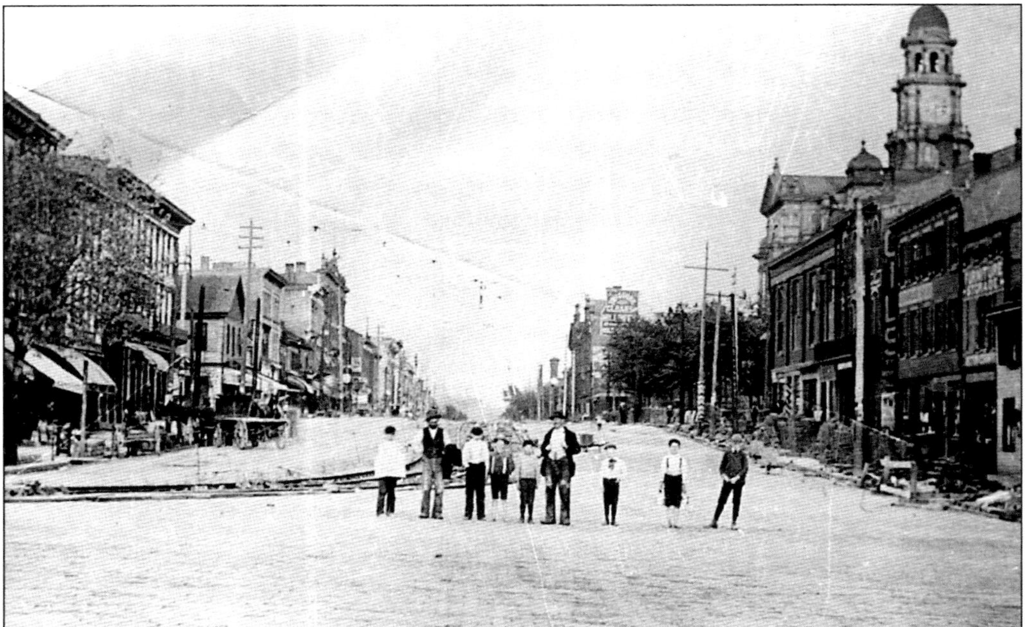

In Hamilton in 1897, High Street was paved with bricks. In this photograph, looking east toward the courthouse, newly built traction car tracks can be seen in the middle of the street. The tracks ran across the High Street Bridge, turned right on "B" Street, and led north to Trenton and Middletown. (Courtesy the BCHS.)

Where's Billy Yank? In this photograph of the Memorial Building, taken before its recognizable sculpture was erected, work crews prepared the pedestal for the arrival of the 17-foot bronze statue. The Butler County Courthouse steeple is behind the Memorial Building, to the left. In front is a replica of a Fort Hamilton blockhouse. The Memorial Building was dedicated on July 4, 1906. (Courtesy the BCHS.)

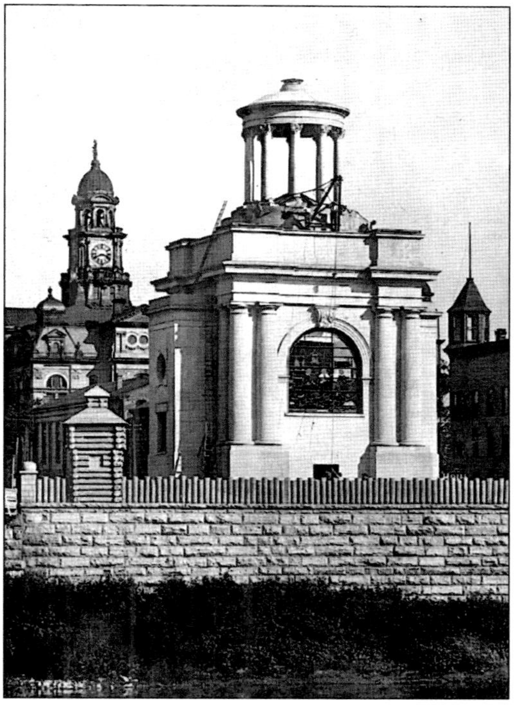

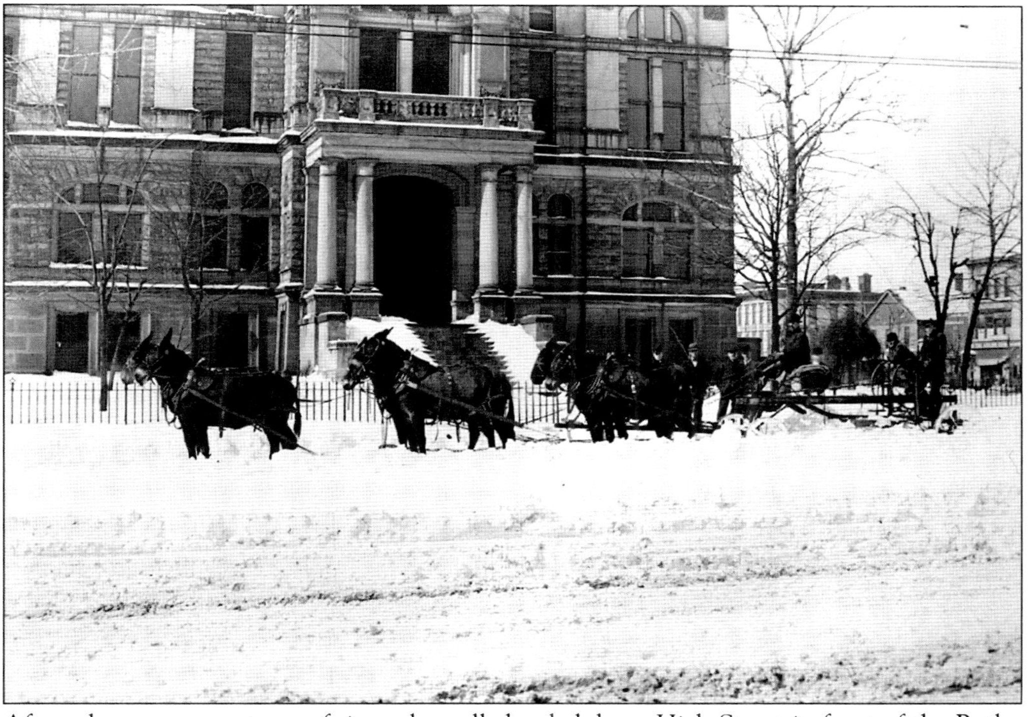

After a heavy snow, a team of six mules pulled a sled down High Street in front of the Butler County Courthouse. This scene was from February 18, 1910. (Courtesy the BCHS.)

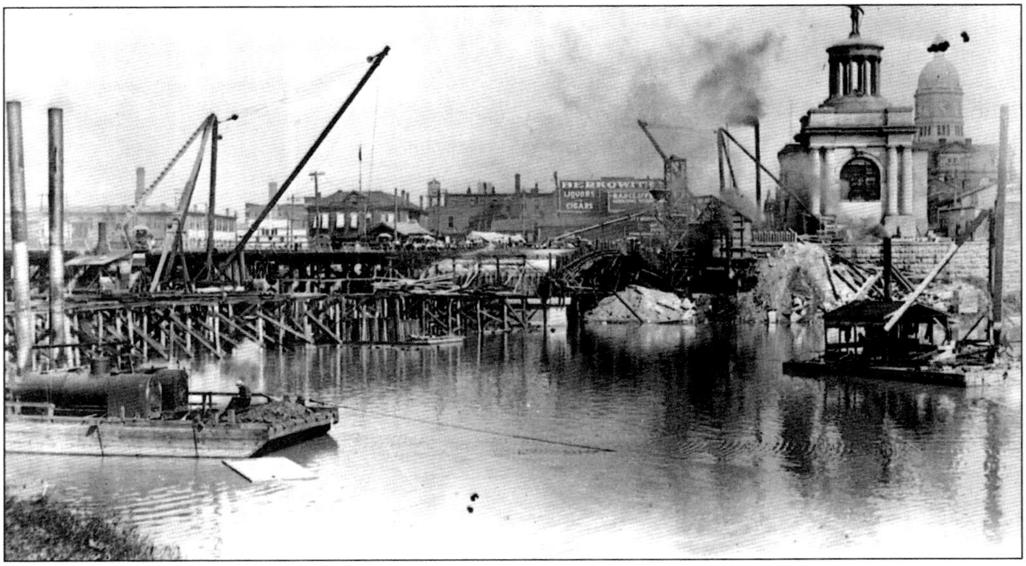

On the Great Miami River, workers used boats to build the new High Street-Main Street Bridge, c. 1914. The old steel truss bridge was washed away in the Flood of 1913. (Courtesy the BCHS.)

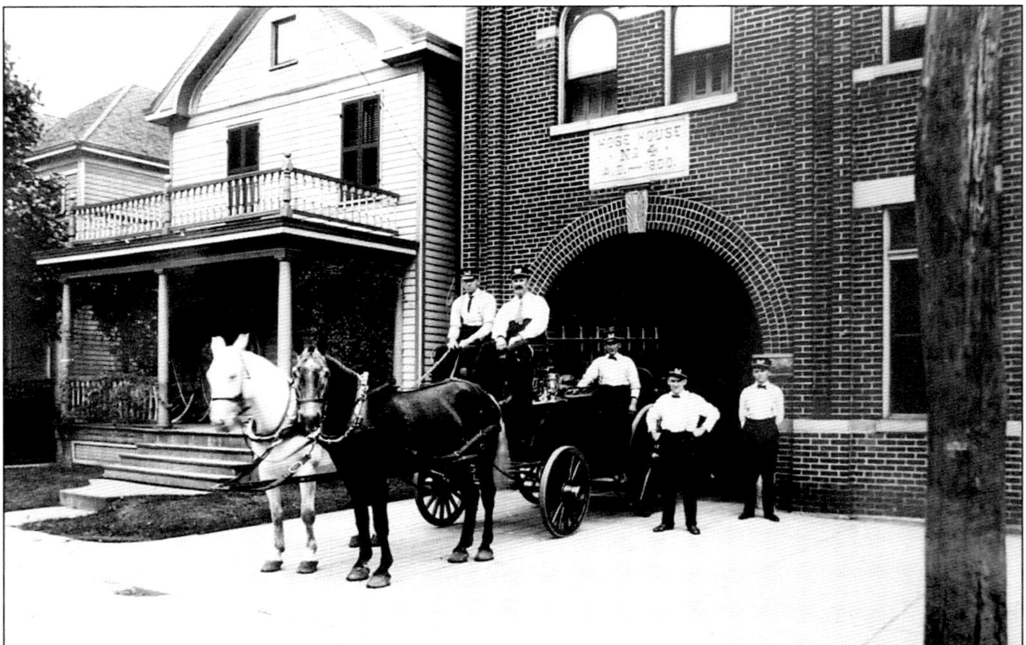

In the early 1900s, five professional firefighters posed with their horse-drawn fire wagon at Hose House No. 4, erected in 1900 on East Avenue in Hamilton. The firehouse protected the residential and industrial northeast side of the city. (Courtesy the BCHS.)

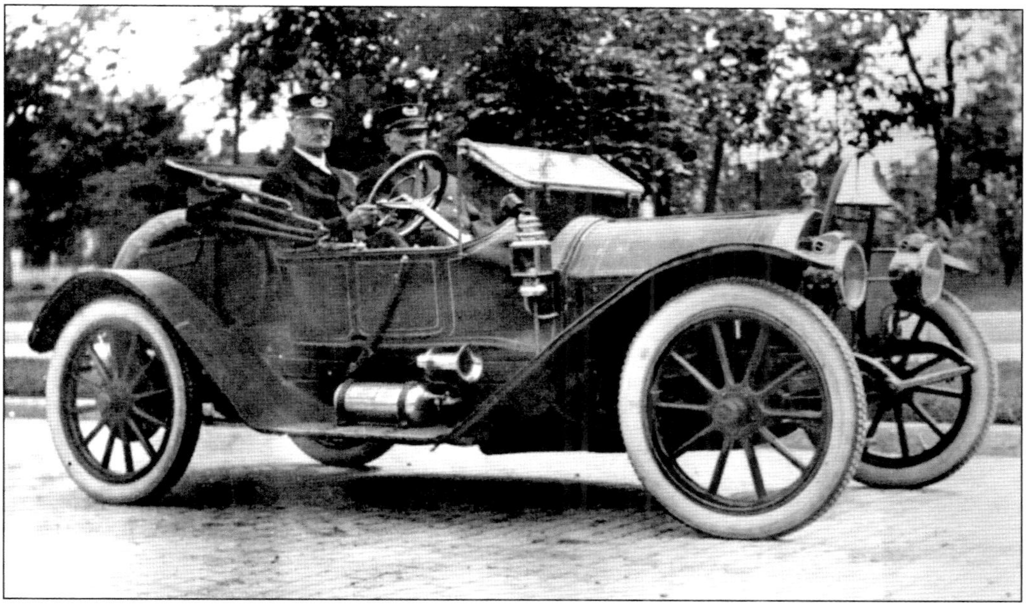

Hamilton Fire Chief William C. Dowty and Fire Marshal W. McGlung drove to the scene of fires in style. Neither man was identified specifically in this photograph taken on South Third Street, *c*. 1914. Dowty started with the department in 1879 as a hoseman. McGlung started in 1905 as Dowty's assistant. (Courtesy the BCHS.)

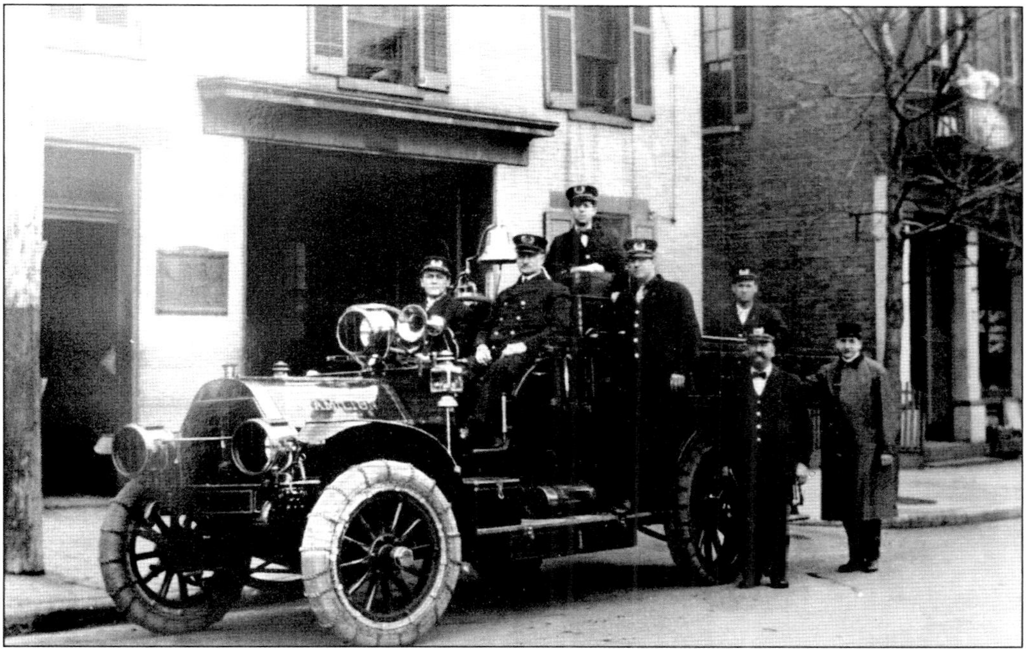

Seven members of Fire Company No. 1, at Main and "B" Streets on Hamilton's west side, posed in this 1912 photograph. Notice the snow chains wrapped around the truck's tires and the woman standing on the balcony to the right. Company No. 1 was organized in 1839. (Courtesy the BCHS.)

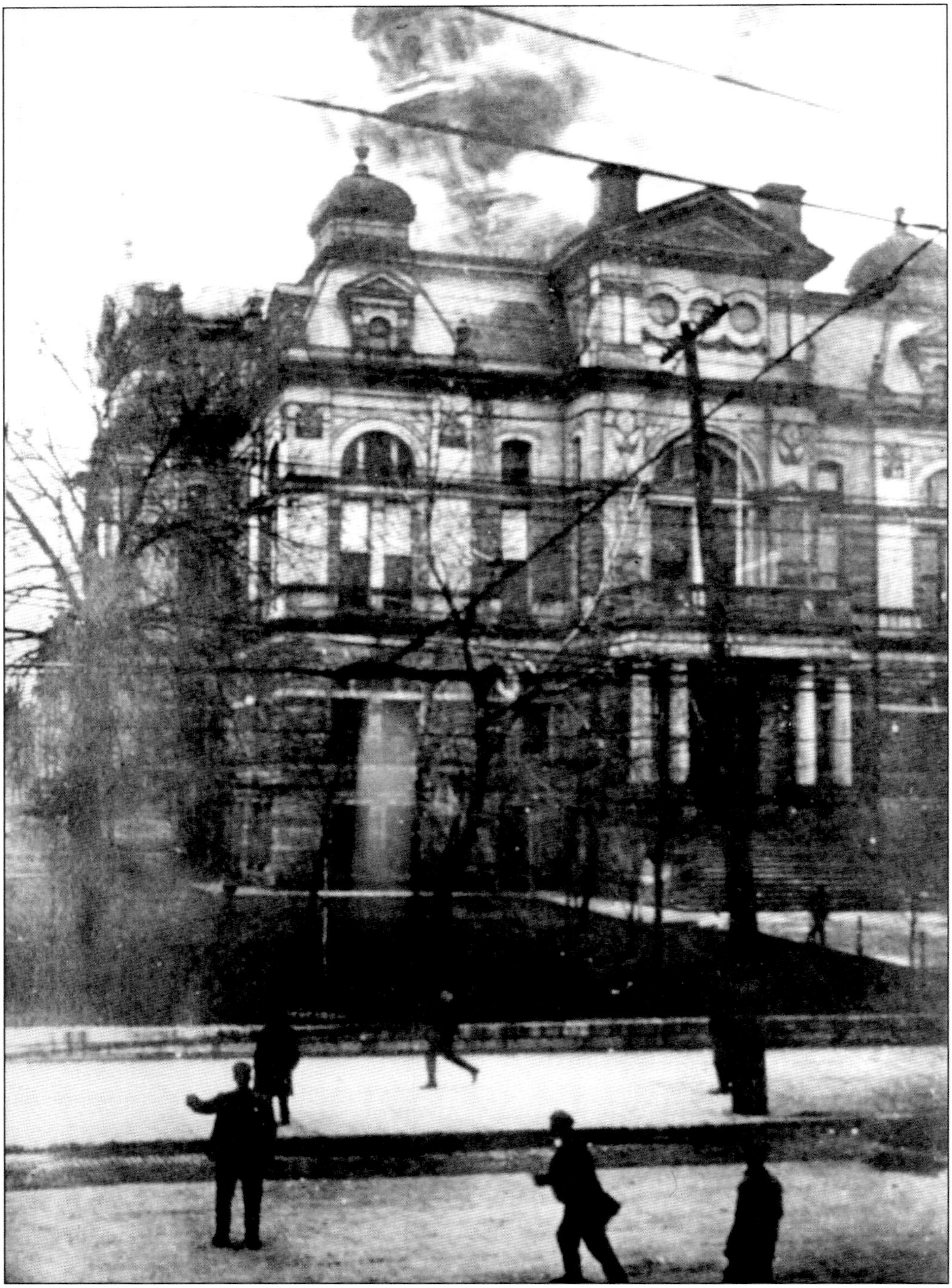

The dome and tower at the Butler County Courthouse in Hamilton fell during a fire on March 14, 1912, about a year before the city suffered through the devastating flood on the Great Miami River. Fortunately, the fire did not destroy the sandstone courthouse (which opened on February 4, 1889, at a cost of $305,000) and its rich interior woodwork. (Courtesy the BCHS.)

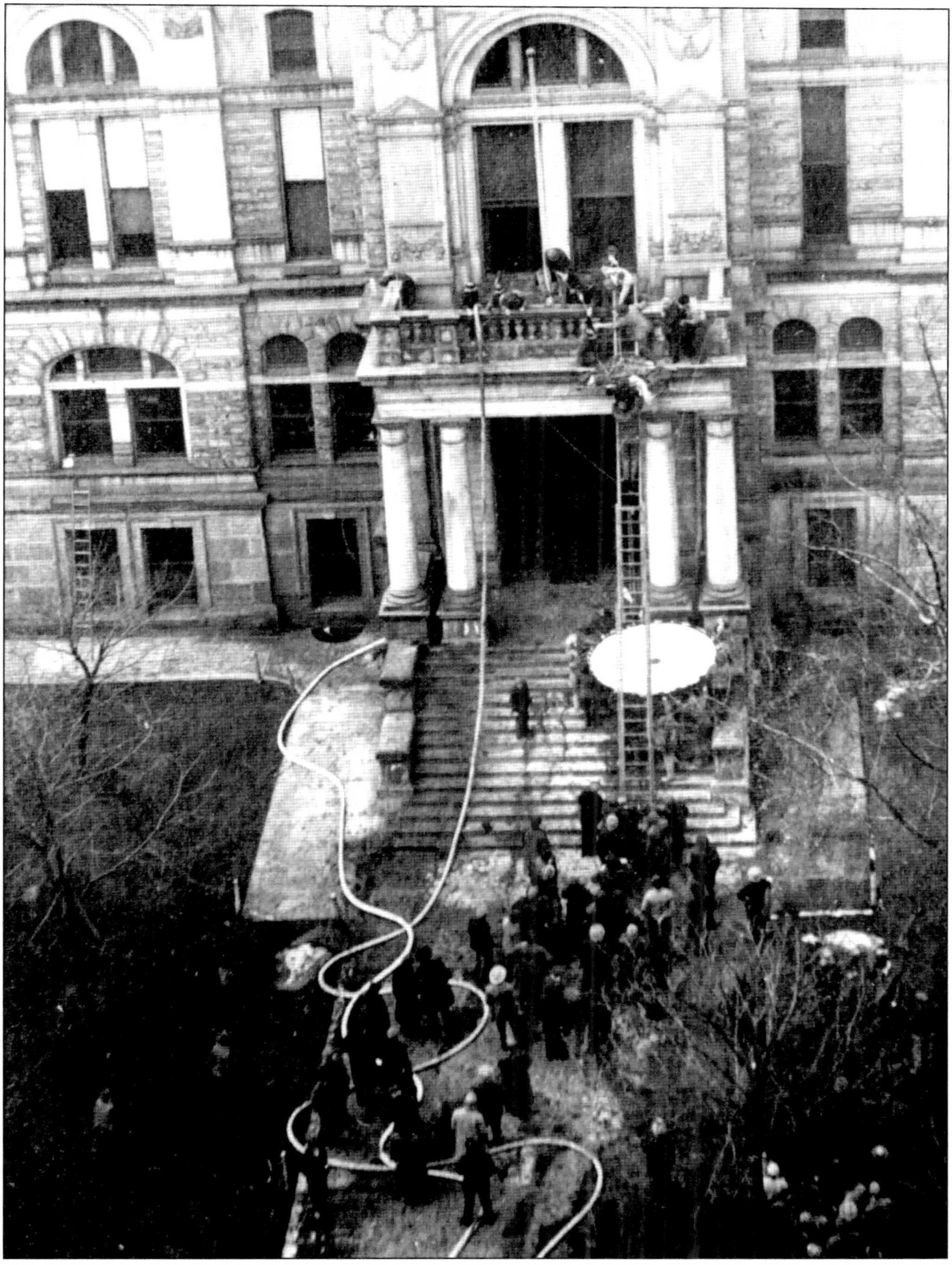

On March 14, 1912, firefighters rescued injured comrades on the second floor of the four-story Butler County Courthouse. Notice the circular life-saving device held by several men on the courthouse steps. While fighting the blaze, however, three firefighters—John M. Hunker, William M. Love, and George P. Fritz—died, and some county records were destroyed. (Courtesy the BCHS.)

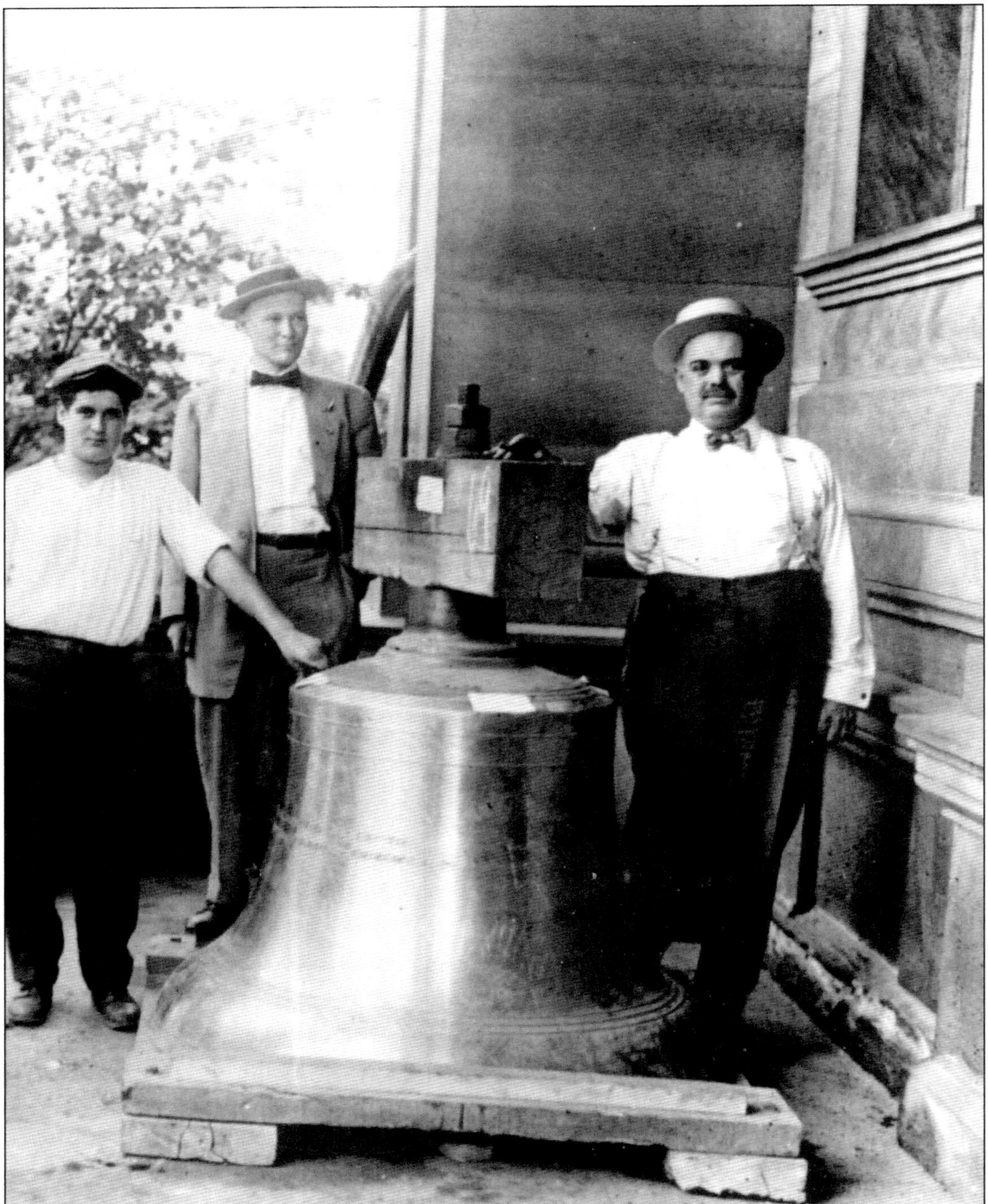

On August 9, 1913, a new bell for the Butler County Courthouse tower arrived—all 2,880 pounds of it—to finally complete the courthouse restoration. Thomas C. Smith, Charles Kehm, and Thomas A. Smith helped roll the bell into the building. Several days later, the bell was raised to the tower. Unfortunately, the photographer did not specifically identify the men. (Courtesy the BCHS.)

On December 6, 1926, scaffolding surrounded the tower of the restored Butler County Courthouse as workers prepared the new dome. Because of excessive weight, the dome and high tower—renovated after the fire of 1912—would later have to be removed, leaving the flat-roofed dome that exists today. (Courtesy the BCHS.)

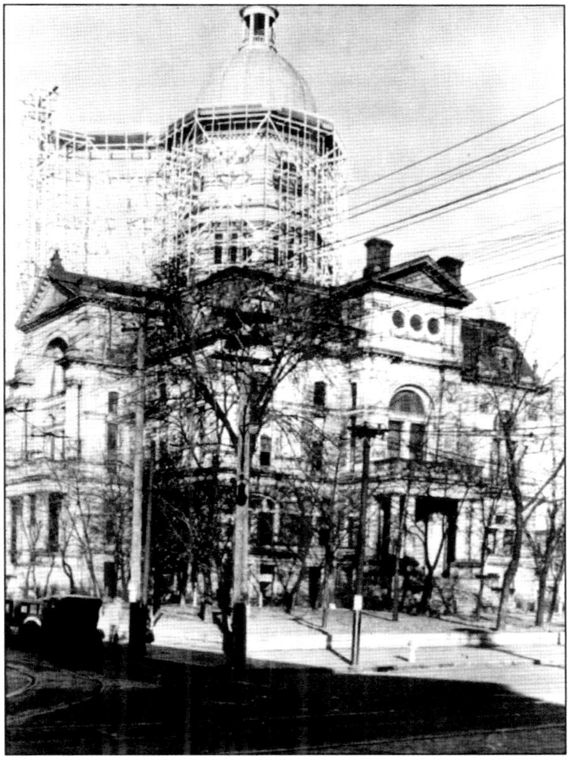

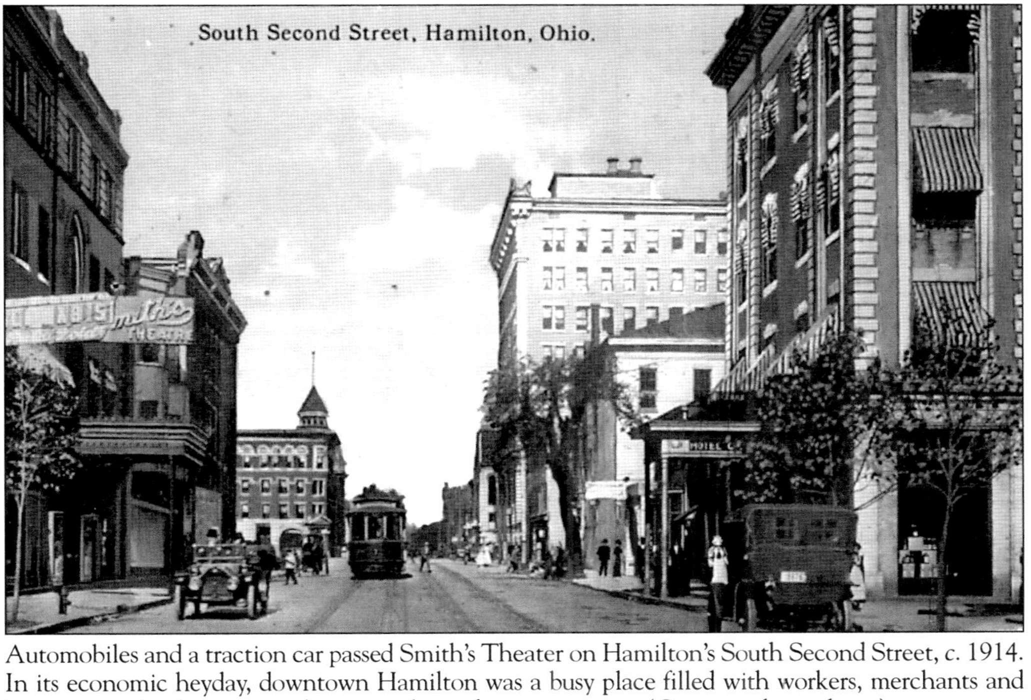

Automobiles and a traction car passed Smith's Theater on Hamilton's South Second Street, *c.* 1914. In its economic heyday, downtown Hamilton was a busy place filled with workers, merchants and businesspeople, shoppers, and many seekers of entertainment. (Courtesy the authors.)

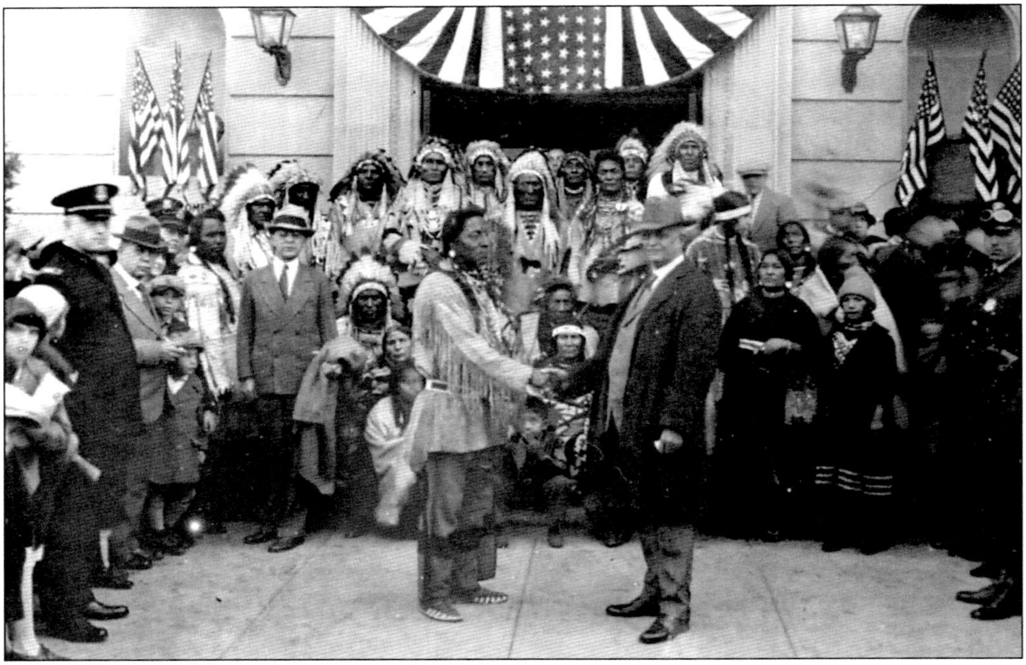

When Hamilton's newest, largest, and finest hotel, the Anthony Wayne, was dedicated in October of 1927, many dignitaries and curious people participated in the ceremonies, including a group of Native Americans. In the center, Ernest Reider shook hands with the chief, who was in full headdress. The police officer to the far right was identified as James O'Conner. (Courtesy the BCHS.)

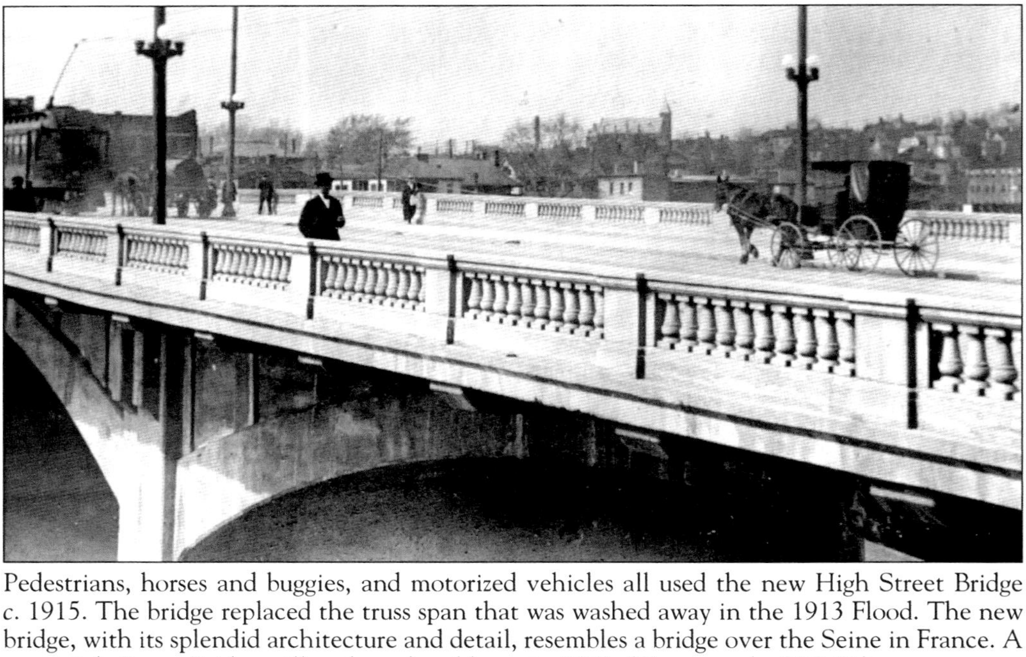

Pedestrians, horses and buggies, and motorized vehicles all used the new High Street Bridge c. 1915. The bridge replaced the truss span that was washed away in the 1913 Flood. The new bridge, with its splendid architecture and detail, resembles a bridge over the Seine in France. A new High Street Bridge will replace the old one in 2006. (Courtesy the BCHS.)

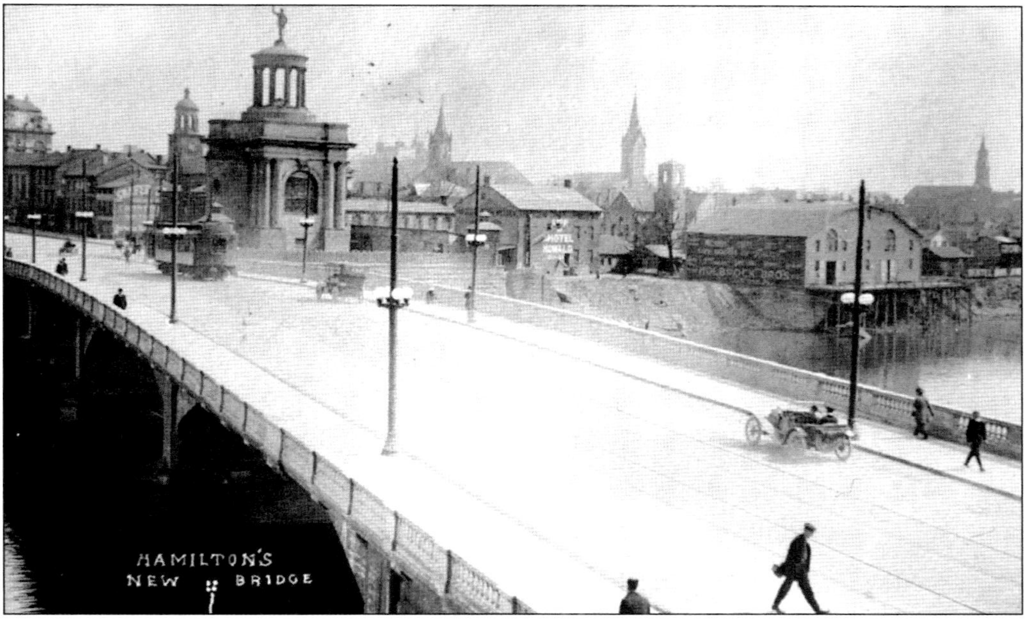

In 1915, Hamiltonians must have truly thought they had arrived in the twentieth century as they crossed their new, modern, secure bridge leading from High Street to Main Street on the west side. The 576-foot span, which cost $142,440, came with electric lamps, reinforced concrete, and a wide berth. It was dedicated May 6, 1915. (Courtesy the BCHS.)

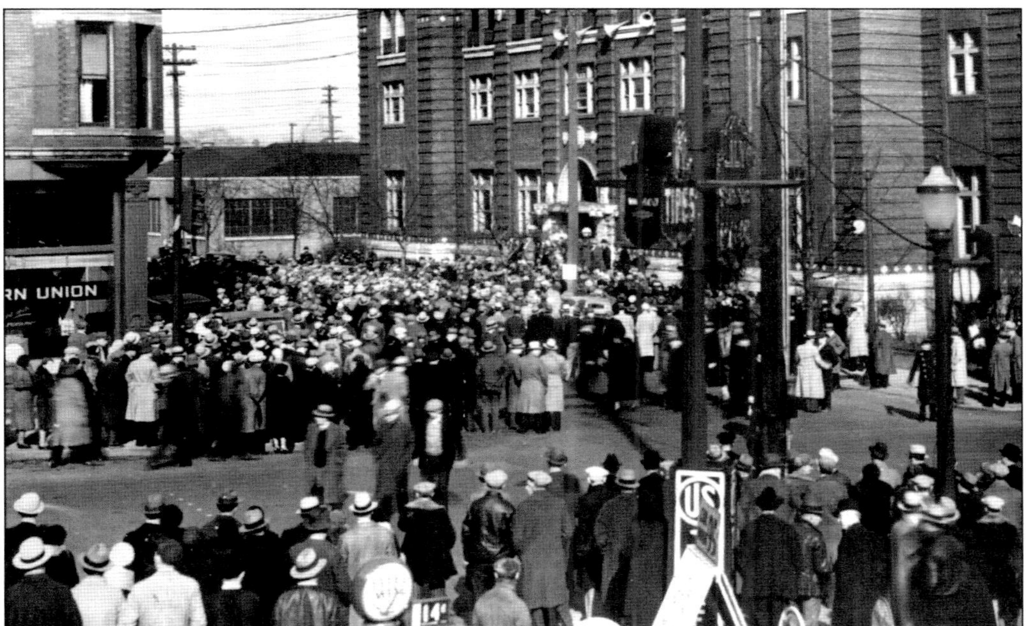

In this photograph, taken sometime during the early Depression era, a group of Hamiltonians gathered around communist speakers in front of the YMCA on Market Street near Second Street. The turbulent economic time was a fertile period for fringe political groups. (Courtesy the BCHS.)

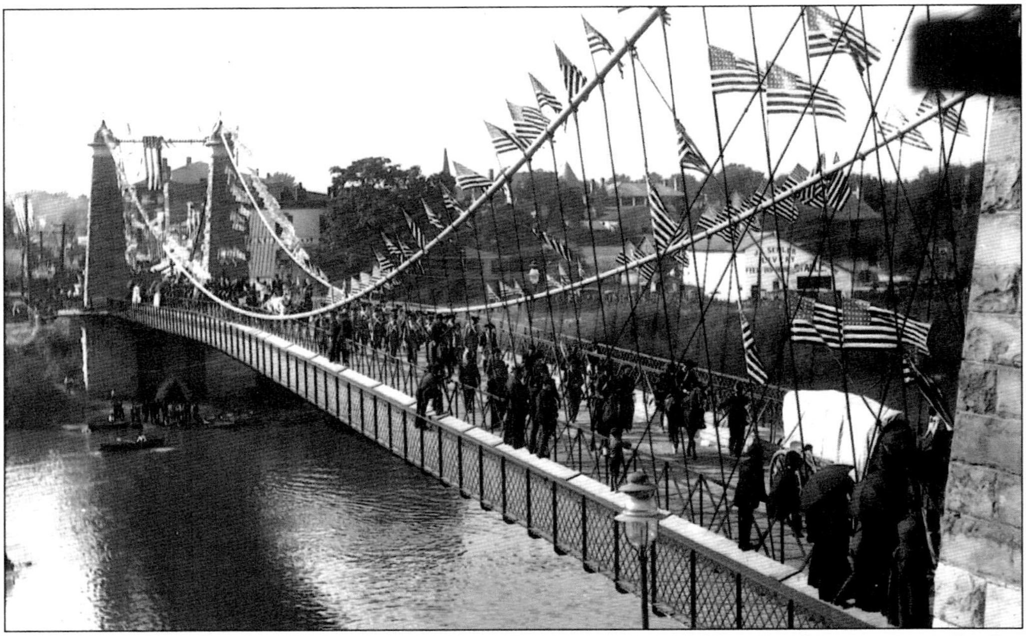

Hamilton residents celebrated the city's bicentennial with a parade across the suspension bridge over the Great Miami River in 1891. Reaching the 100-year mark was a major achievement for any town, and by then Hamilton was a fast-growing industrial center. (Courtesy the BCHS.)

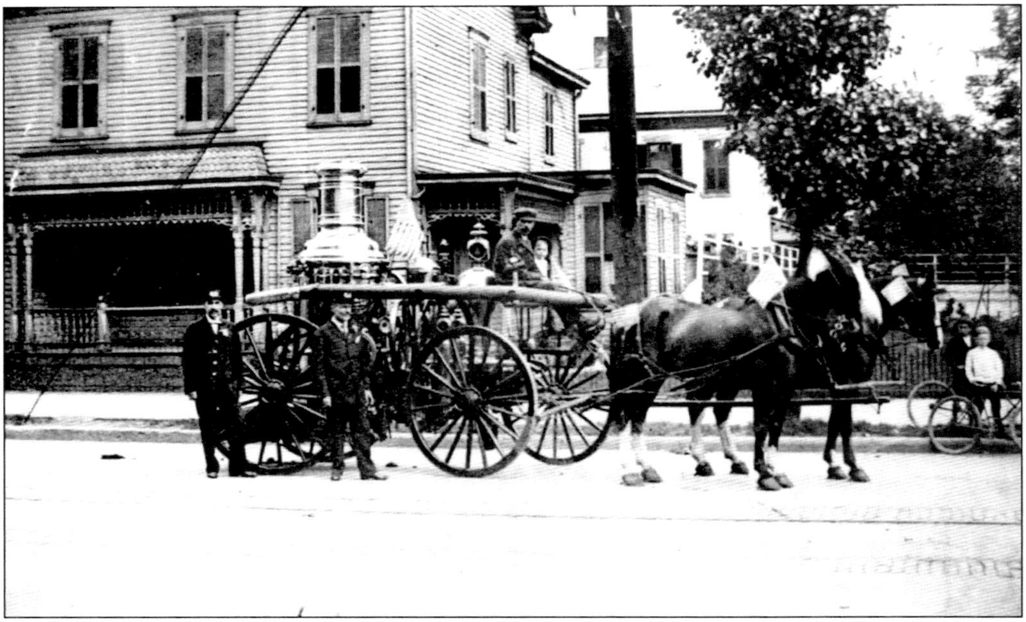

In this 1907 photograph, firefighters proudly displayed their fire engine for some unidentified boys on North Third Street in Hamilton. From left to right, the firefighters were Captain Philip Erb, Engineer Joseph Webster, and driver John Steel. Today, Neptune, an 1873 Ahrens-Fox steam-powered pumper, is on display at the Hal Sheperd Firehouse at South Second Street and Pershing Avenue. (Courtesy the BCHS.)

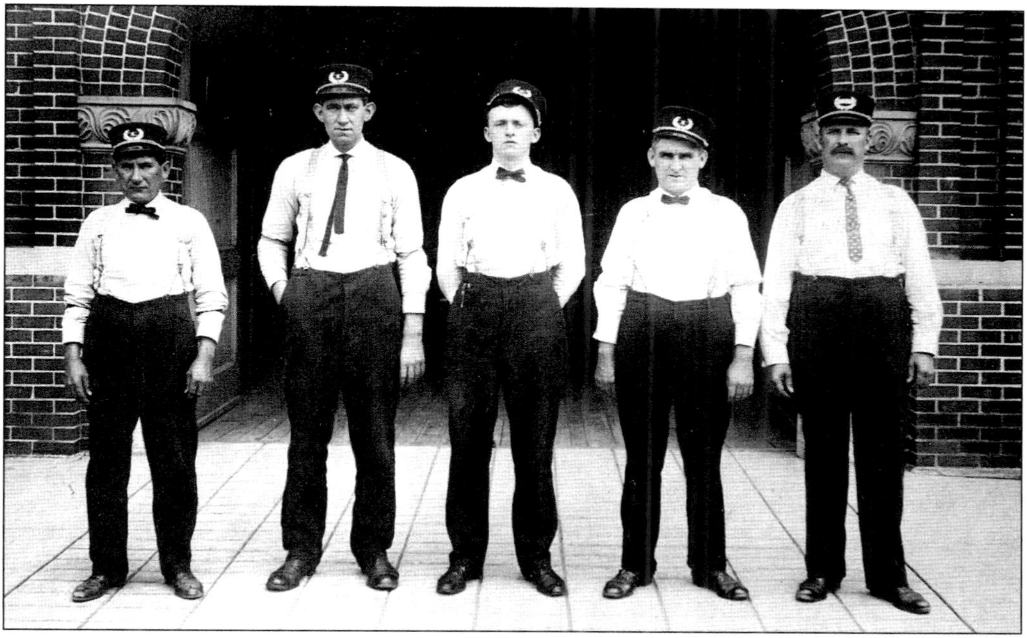

These unidentified firefighters stand in front of their fire station, probably on Hamilton's west side, in the early 1900s. By then, the city had long employed a paid, professional fire force. Its last horse-drawn fire engine was put aside in 1919. (Courtesy the BCHS.)

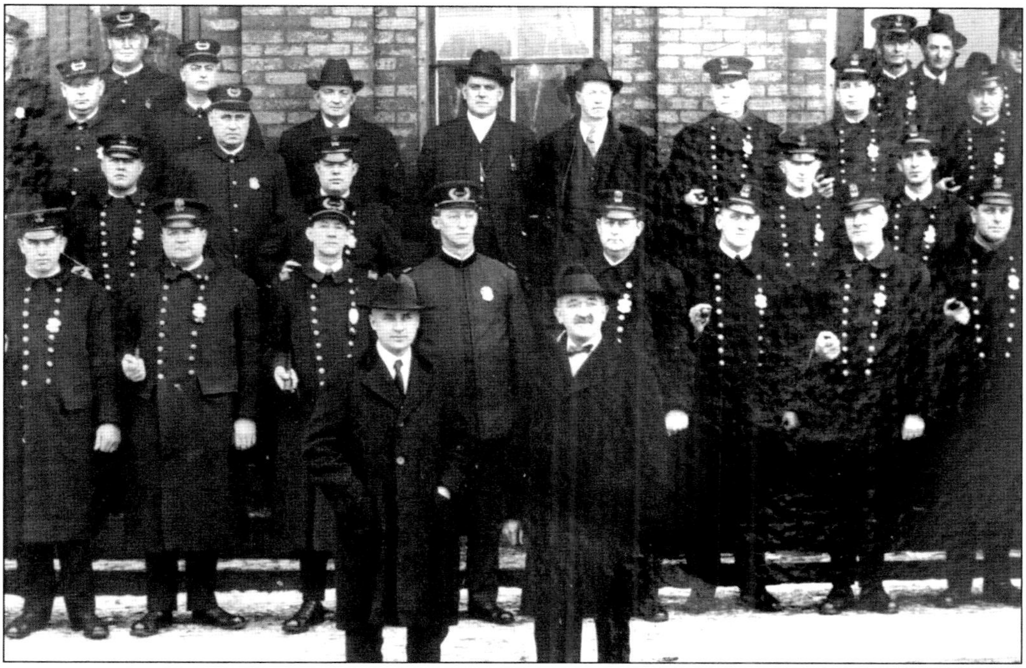

Unidentified members of the Hamilton Police Department posed for this photograph in December of 1917. Hamilton was a rough-and-tumble town in those days, with plenty of neighborhood taverns and a tough reputation. (Courtesy the BCHS.)

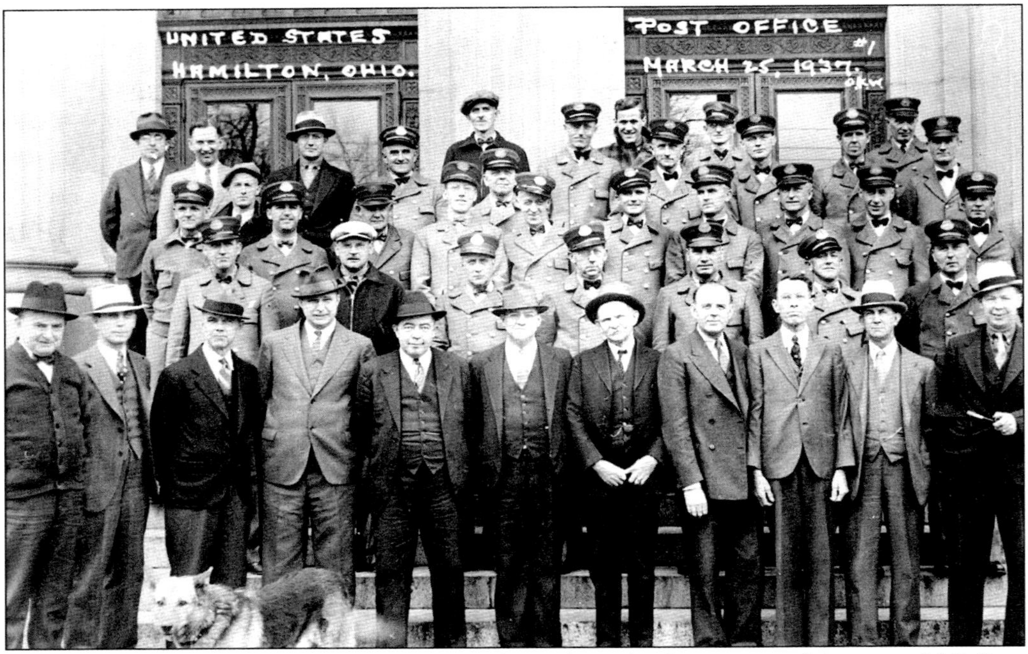

Hamilton's letter carriers and office personnel stand on the front steps of the main U.S. Post Office on March 25, 1937. (Courtesy the BCHS.)

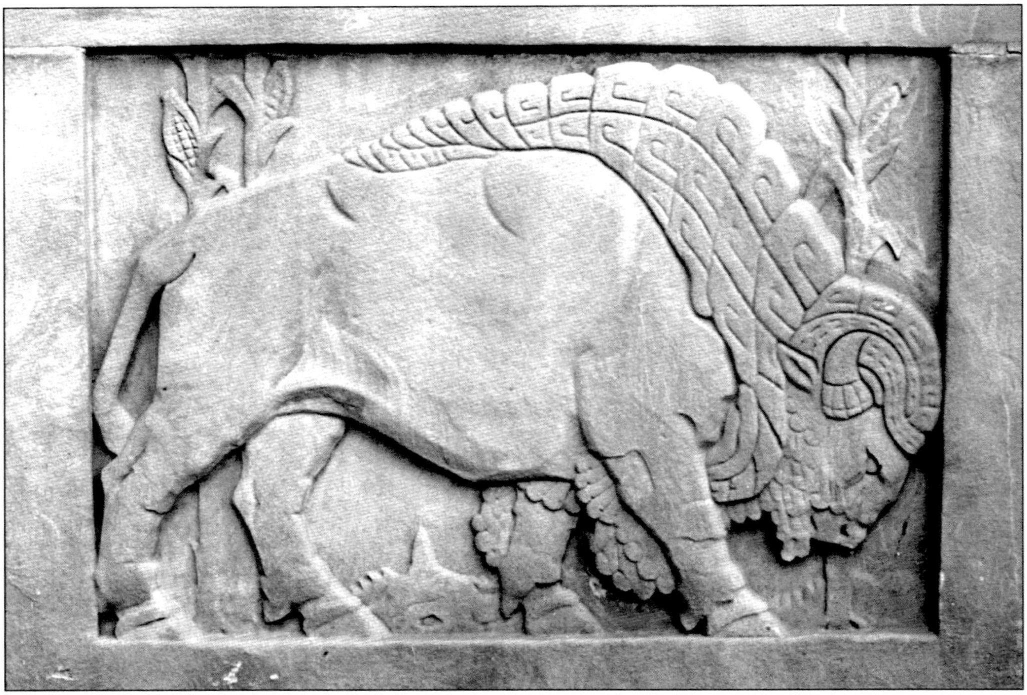

A buffalo is carved in the stone of Hamilton's Municipal Building on High Street. Young artist Robert McCloskey, who would later write children's books, helped carve the artwork when the building was erected in the 1930s. (Courtesy Randy McNutt.)

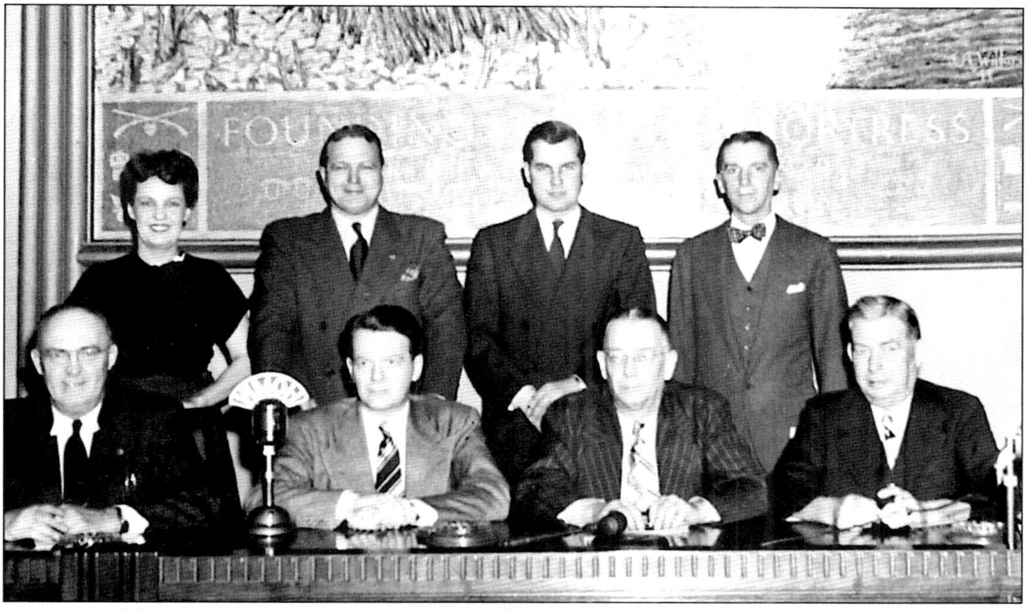

Members of the Hamilton City Council prepared for their swearing-in session in their chambers in 1948. Clerk Adel Edmonds stood on the left. Councilmen George Radcliff and Ed Beckett sat at left and right. Meetings were broadcast on radio by WMOH. Behind them was the *Foundation of the Fortress* mural, painted by Hamilton artist Jack Willard to depict the pioneers Richard Butler, Israel Ludlow, and William Wells around Fort Hamilton. (Courtesy the BCHS.)

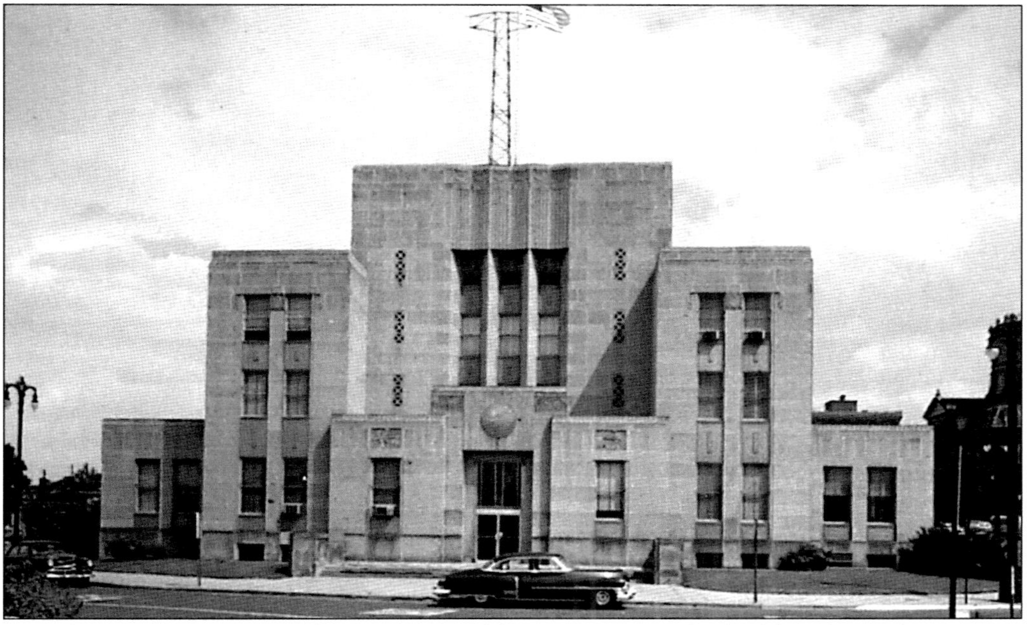

Hamilton's Municipal Building is pictured here, *c.* 1950. The building housed most city offices and council chambers until these were moved to the new One Renaissance Center on High Street *c.* 2000. The old Municipal Building is now used as a small-business incubator. (Courtesy the authors.)

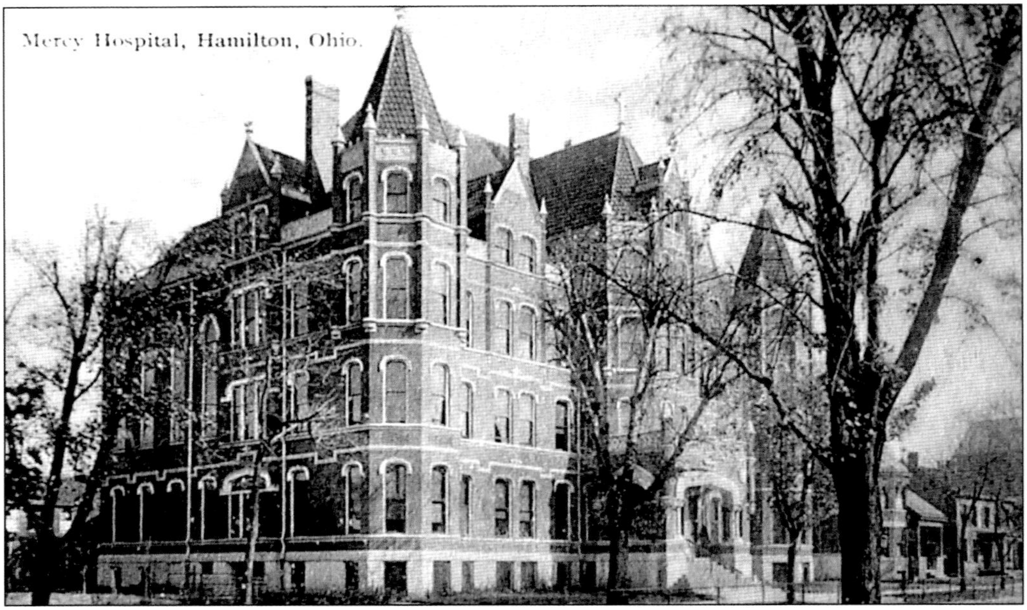

Mercy Hospital, Hamilton's first hospital, opened on October 5, 1892. A new addition was built off of Second Street in 1904. Operated by the Sisters of Mercy, the hospital served the city until it was closed on June 1, 2001. (Courtesy the authors.)

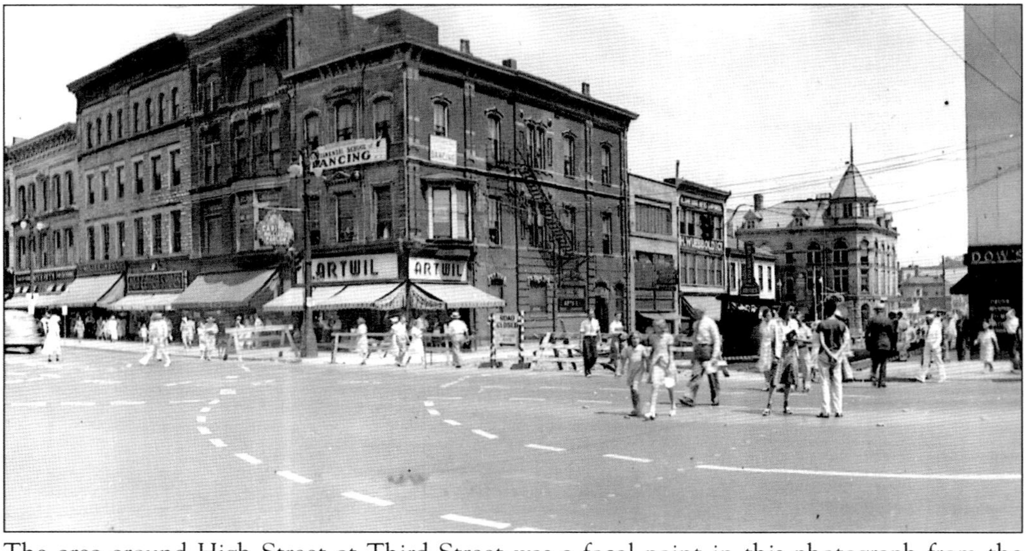

The area around High Street at Third Street was a focal point in this photograph from the 1940s. Even today, the area's importance is not lost. Working closely with the city, developers plan to renovate and reopen the three old commercial buildings on the immediate left. The early twenty-first century brings architectural change and rehabilitation to downtown Hamilton. (Courtesy the BCHS.)

Three

TRANSPORTATION

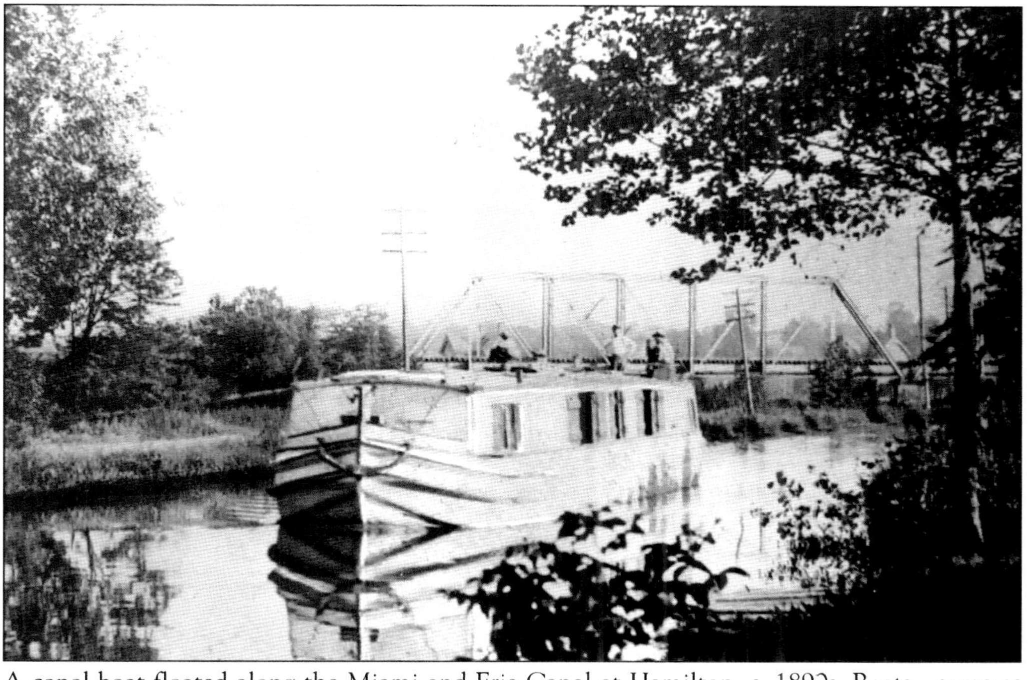

A canal boat floated along the Miami and Erie Canal at Hamilton, c. 1890s. Boats—some as long as 78 feet—carried freight and passengers from Cincinnati, Dayton, and other towns from the late 1820s to the 1880s. Mules and horses pulled the boats by rope from a towpath, along what is now State Route 4. The top speed was three to four miles per hour. Trains killed the canals. (Courtesy the BCHS.)

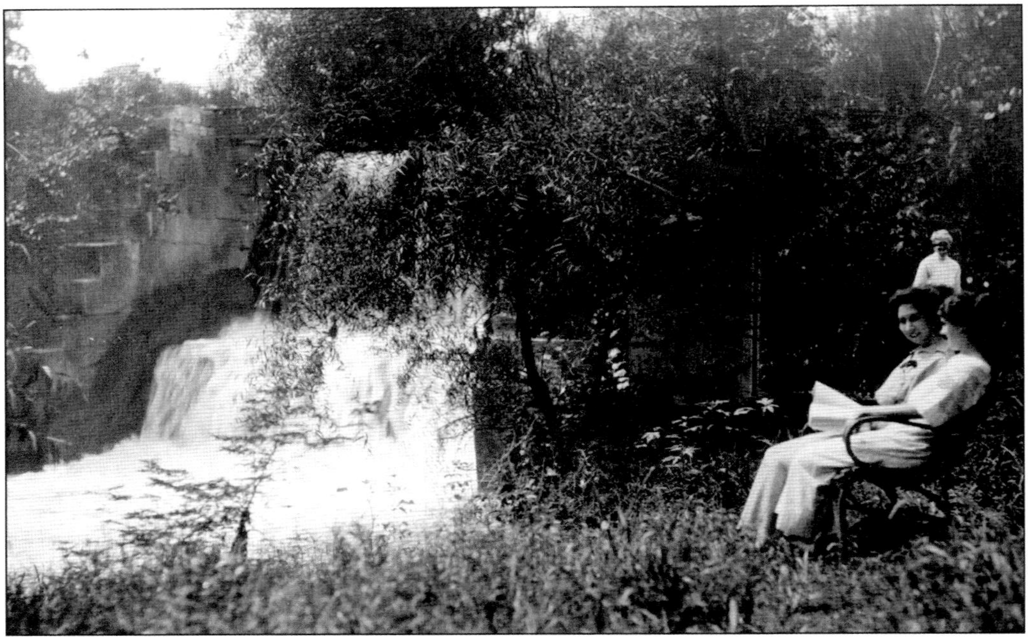

Women read and relaxed on a bench at the lock and spillway of the Miami and Erie Canal, c. 1890s. Twelve stone locks operated between Hamilton and Middletown in Butler County, about one per mile. (Courtesy the BCHS.)

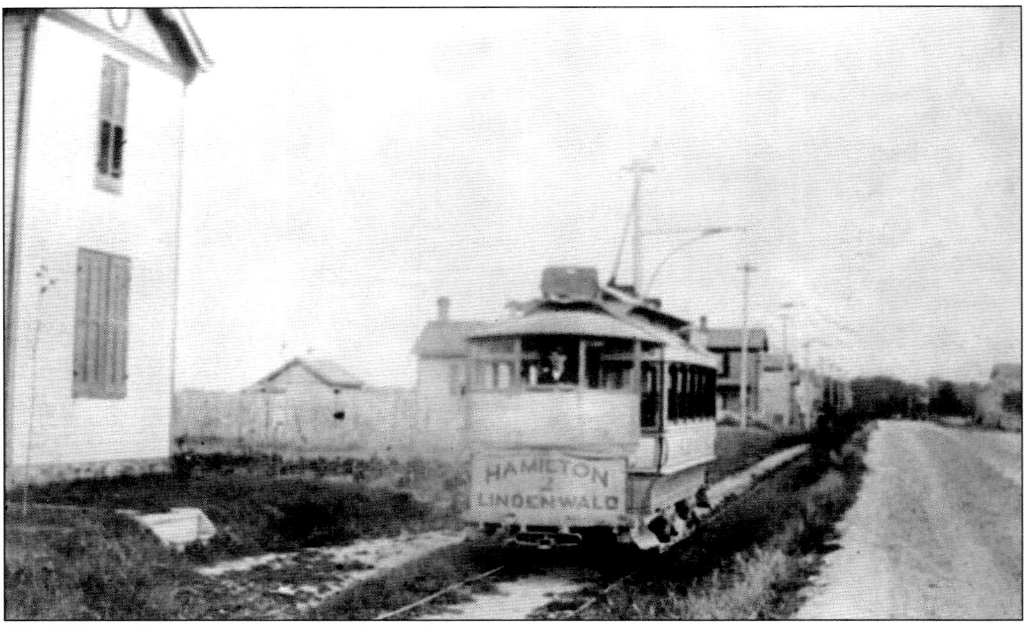

In 1895, this trolley car ran from downtown Hamilton to Lindenwald, a new neighborhood on the city's south side. Such traveling convenience helped Lindenwald grow. Its residents could hop on a trolley car and arrive in the busy downtown in 15 minutes. Later, the rails on High Street were used by city trolleys and the Cincinnati and Lake Erie interurban cars. (Courtesy the BCHS.)

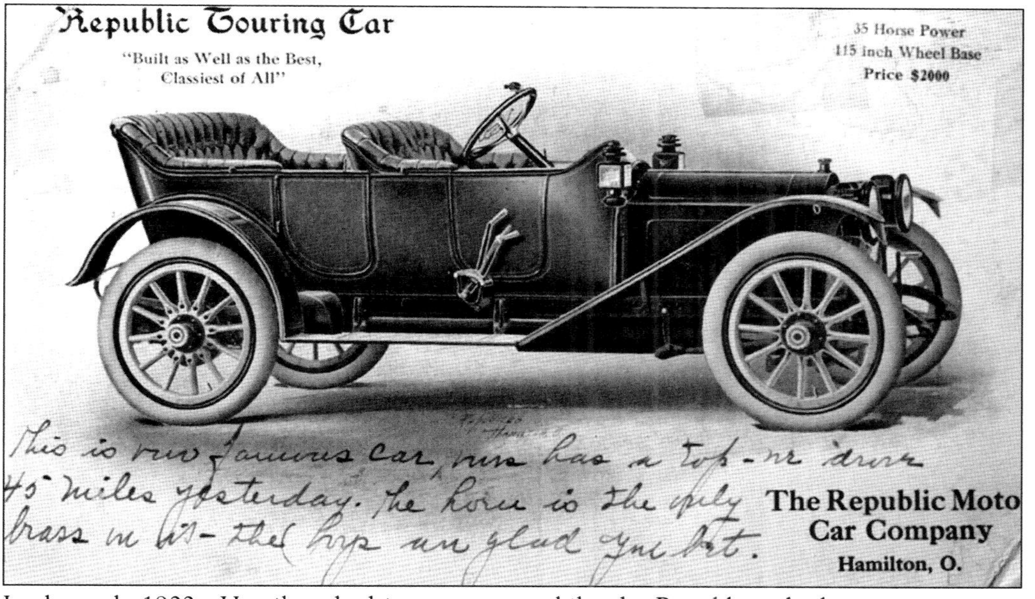

In the early 1900s, Hamilton had its own automobile, the Republic, which was not a major seller. The Republic Motor Car Company manufactured touring cars with a 35-horsepower motor and a 115-inch wheelbase. The company's motto was "Built as Well as the Best, Classiest of All." Unfortunately, the Republic didn't survive the initial wave of new car companies. (Courtesy the BCHS.)

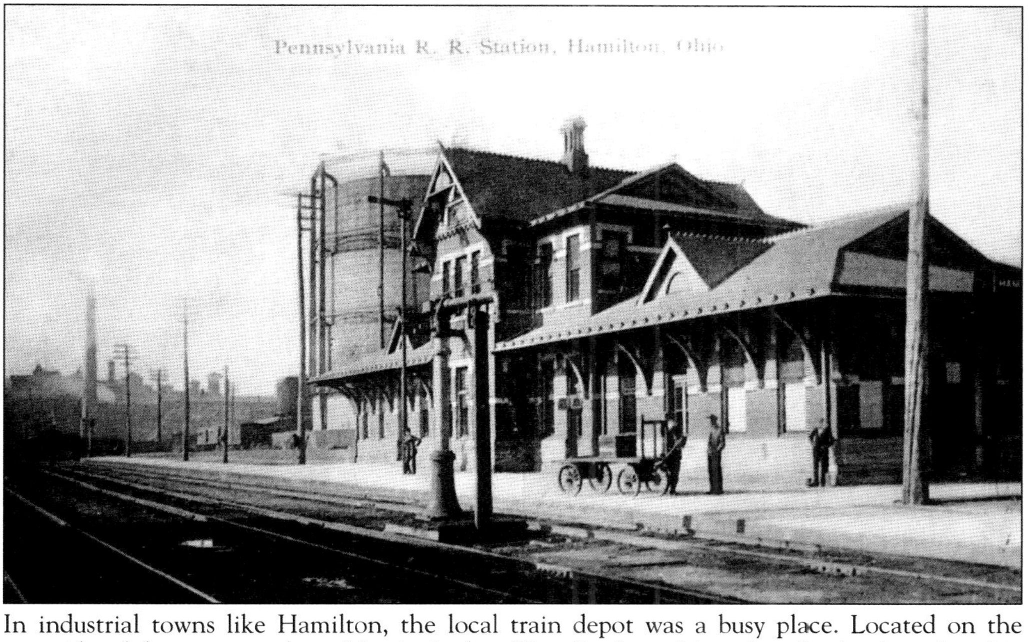

In industrial towns like Hamilton, the local train depot was a busy place. Located on the east side of downtown, where Martin Luther King Boulevard is today, the brick and gothic Pennsylvania Railroad Station served hundreds of passengers a day. In this 1912 picture, a large water tower stood next to the station. Water was poured over engines and cars to prevent sparks from igniting fires from friction. (Courtesy the authors.)

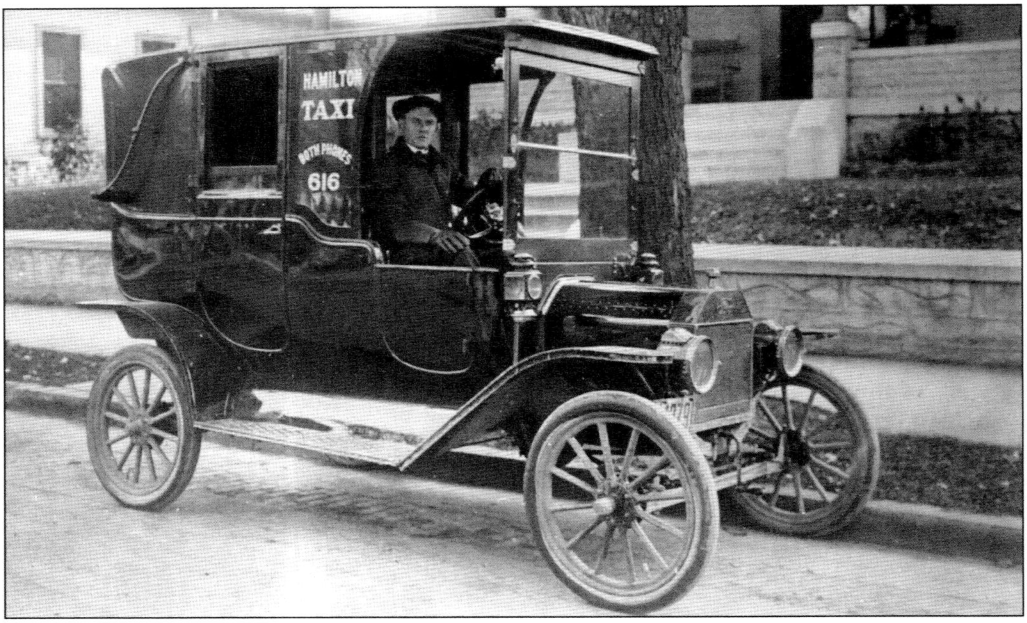

Thad Hoffman sat behind the wheel of Hamilton's first taxi at 417 Main Street on the west side in 1912. His partner in the Hamilton Taxi venture was Reuben Hoffman. All you had to do was call the company's telephone number, 616, and pray that the skies didn't snow. (Courtesy the BCHS.)

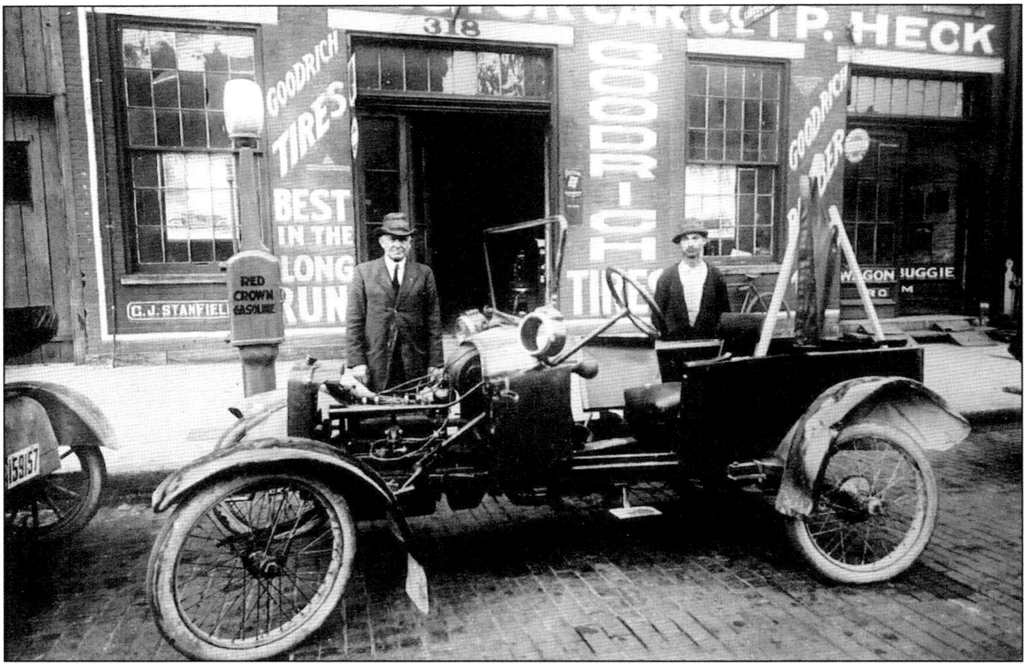

The Heck Motor Car Company, located on Court Street in Hamilton's downtown, started manufacturing wagons and buggies as early as 1802, then started selling motorized cars in the early 1900s. The big Flood of 1913 helped put the company out of business. (Courtesy the BCHS.)

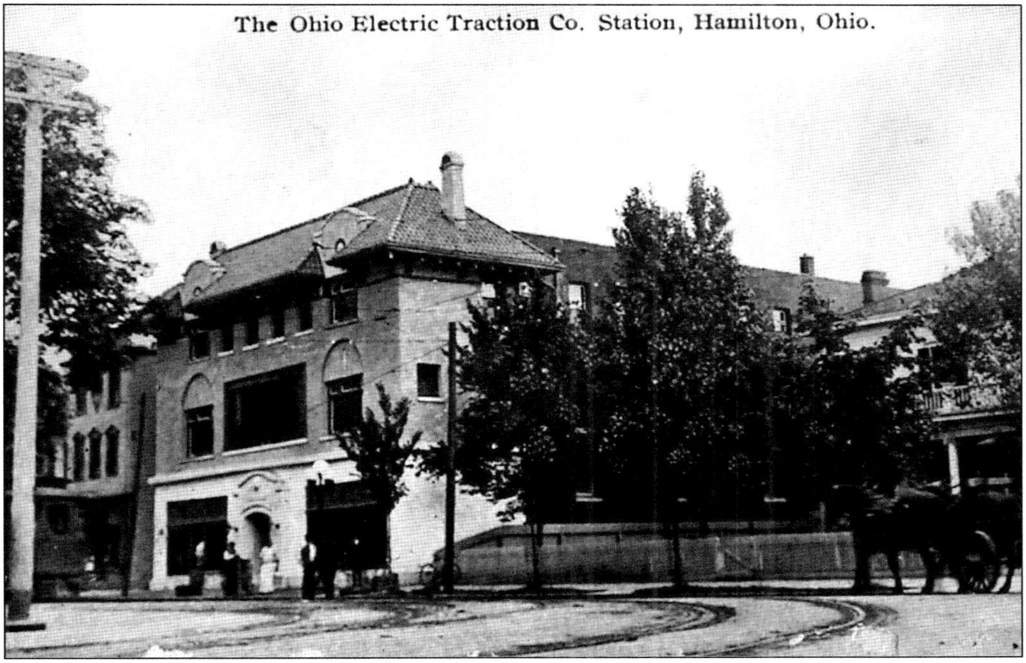

The Ohio Electric Traction Company's station in downtown Hamilton looked more like a building from the southwest in this photograph from the early part of the twentieth century. Passengers caught the traction cars there. On regular commutes, passengers could ride all the way south to Symmes Corner in Fairfield Township and to Cincinnati. (Courtesy the BCHS.)

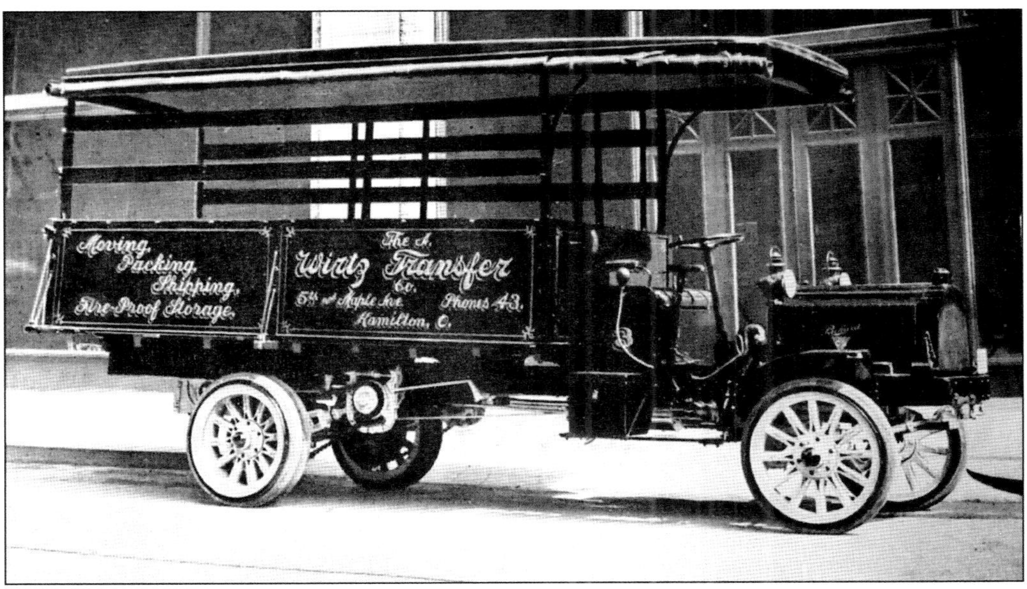

The Wirtz Transfer Company operated a large moving truck in Hamilton in 1913. Workers could pile a lot of furniture onto the bed of their new vehicle. (Courtesy the authors.)

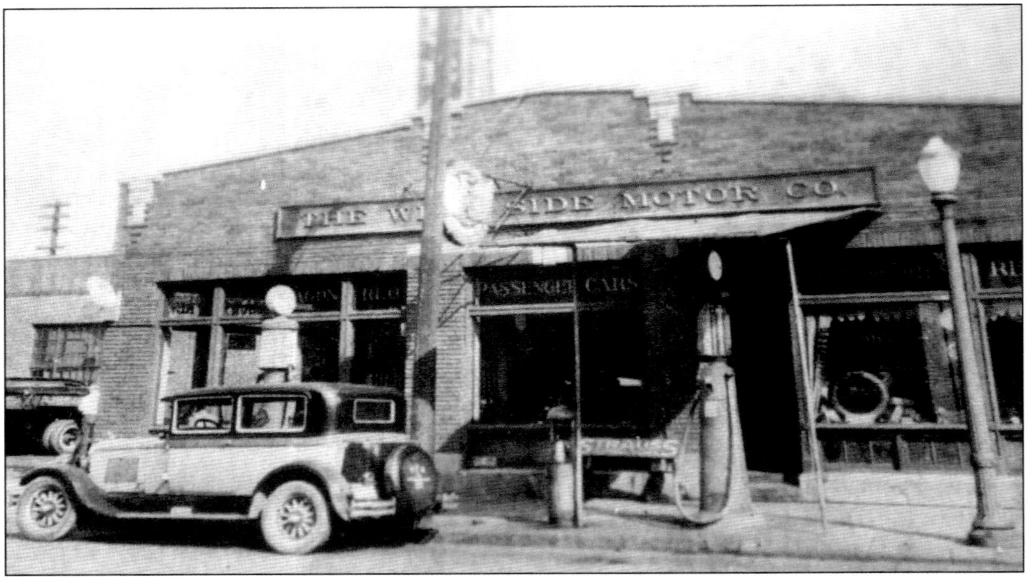

The West Side Motor Company was among Hamilton's oldest auto dealerships, starting in 1891 as Schmitt Brothers at 118–120 West Main Street and later at 216 West Main. The company was the only REO dealership in Butler County. By 1936, the firm was the oldest operating dealership in the city. Its mechanics could fill a car up with gas right at the curb. The headquarters offered a sales room, garage, offices, and repair shop in one building. (Courtesy the BCHS.)

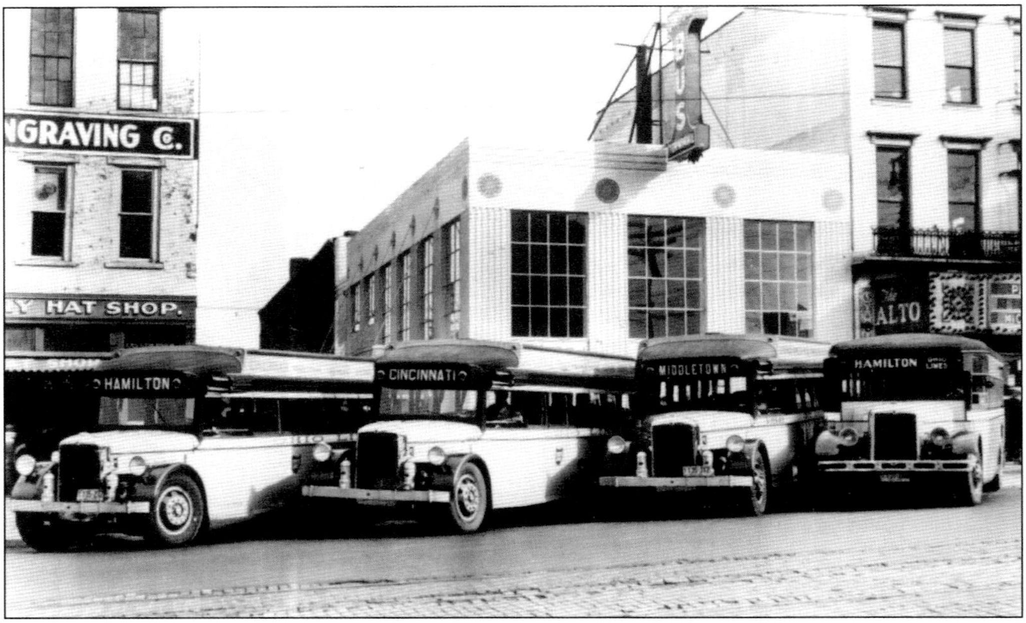

Using the Hamilton-Cincinnati Bus Company, passengers could go to Cincinnati on State Route 4, a 25-mile, one-way trip. This 1931 photograph showed new buses owned by Ohio Bus Line Company, which provided service on U.S. Route 127. That year, Ohio Bus bought Hamilton-Cincinnati Bus, built a small, modern terminal at 40 High Street, and offered rides from Hamilton to Cincinnati, Middletown, and other communities. (Courtesy the BCHS.)

Four

FAITH, CHARITY, AND EDUCATION

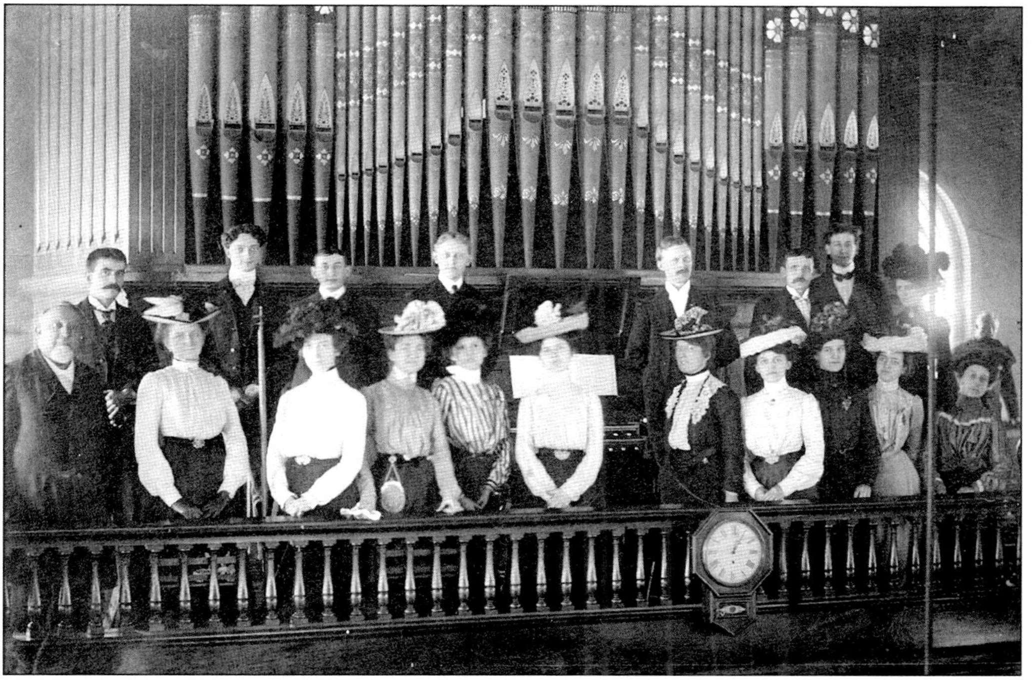

In 1900, the ladies' hats matched the grandeur of their surroundings at St. John's Reformed Church. Members of the choir were, from left to right: (top) Henry Houzler, Otto Liebrich, Gus Phillips, E. Masmann, John Lotz, August Haid, William Kepler, and Junnette Stephens; (bottom) Reverend C.A. Hermann, Margarethe Hufnagle, Gussie Stephan, Caroline Lingler, Anna Buetner, Katherine Braun, Helen Lingler, Frieda Ludeke, Maggie Schmuck, Irma Ludeke, and Frieda Kuhn. (Courtesy the BCHS.)

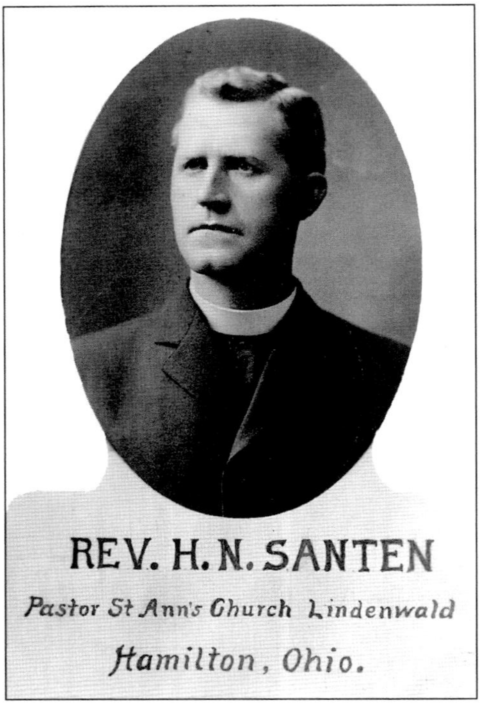

The Reverend H.N. Santen's photograph appeared on a postcard in the early 1900s. He was the pastor of St. Ann's Catholic Church on Pleasant Avenue in Lindenwald. In those days, the church was new and so was the neighborhood it served. (Courtesy the authors.)

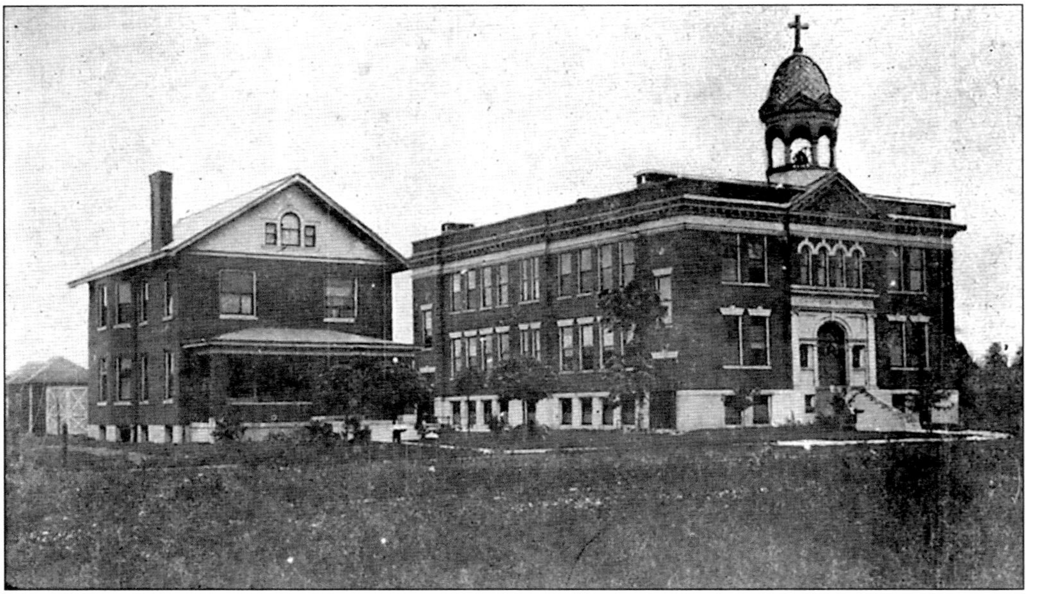

An early twentieth-century postcard showed the original St. Ann's Catholic Church, school, and rectory in Lindenwald, on Hamilton's south side. The combination school and church building was built in 1911. The old school building still operates and St. Ann's church bells resonate throughout the neighborhood every day. (Courtesy the authors.)

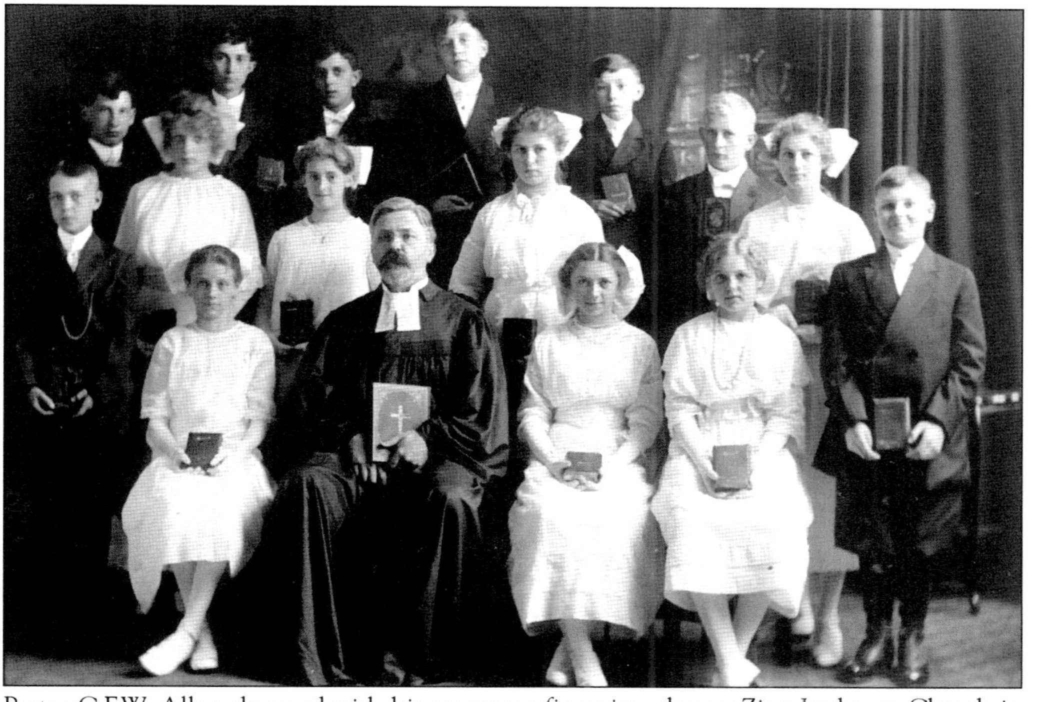

Pastor C.F.W. Allwardt posed with his young confirmation class at Zion Lutheran Church in downtown Hamilton in 1914. As World War I broke out across Europe, the times were difficult for Southwest Ohio's thousands of German Americans. (Courtesy the BCHS.)

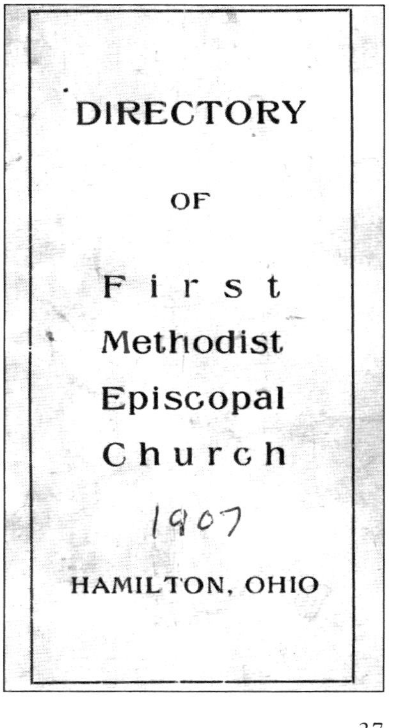

DIRECTORY

OF

First Methodist Episcopal Church

1907

HAMILTON, OHIO

The First Methodist Episcopal Church, on Ludlow Street downtown between Second and Third Streets, issued a small church directory in 1907. It included a brief history of the church (organized in 1818); a list of pastors and church officers; Epworth League, resident, and nonresident members; probationers; and a "Necrology of 1906"—the church members who had died that year. (Courtesy the authors.)

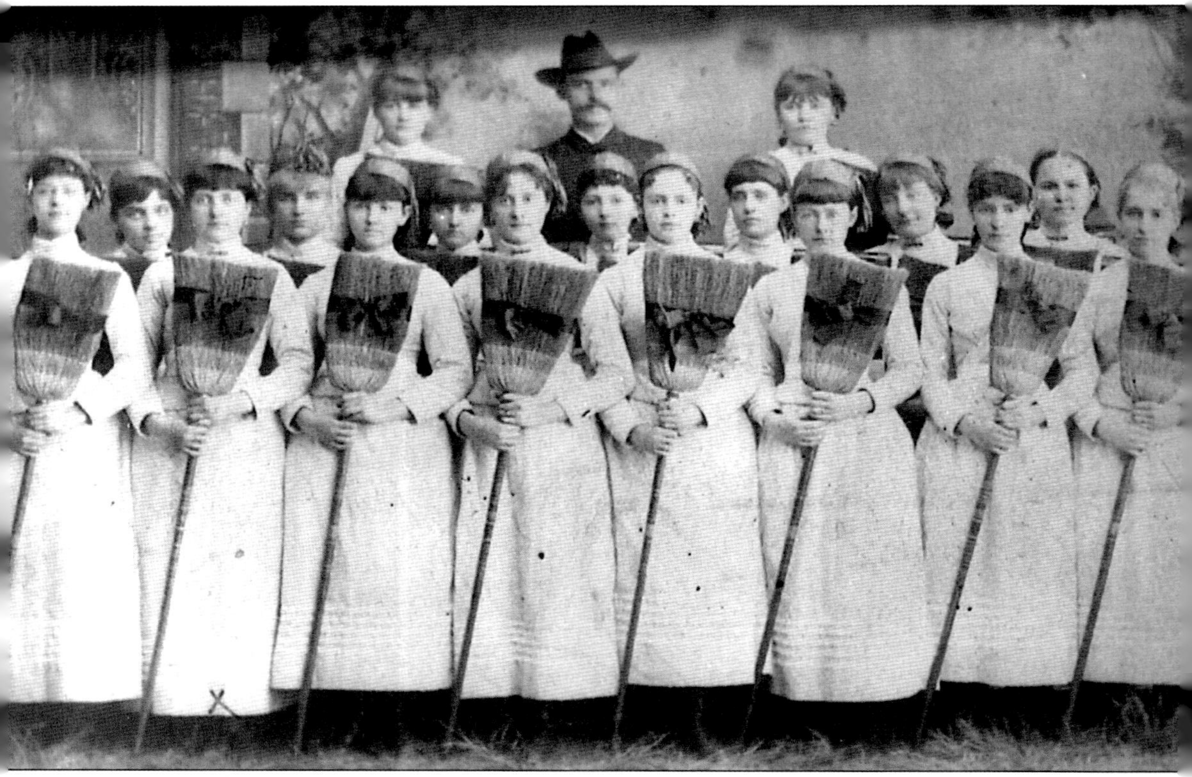

In 1884, the Grand Army of the Republic sponsored a Broom Brigade under the command of Captain R.A. Schotts. The photograph identified the 17 young women as being in a Relief Corps, but researchers at the Butler County Historical Society aren't certain what job the corps performed. Perhaps its members helped clean up the city after high waters and strong winds. (Courtesy the BCHS.)

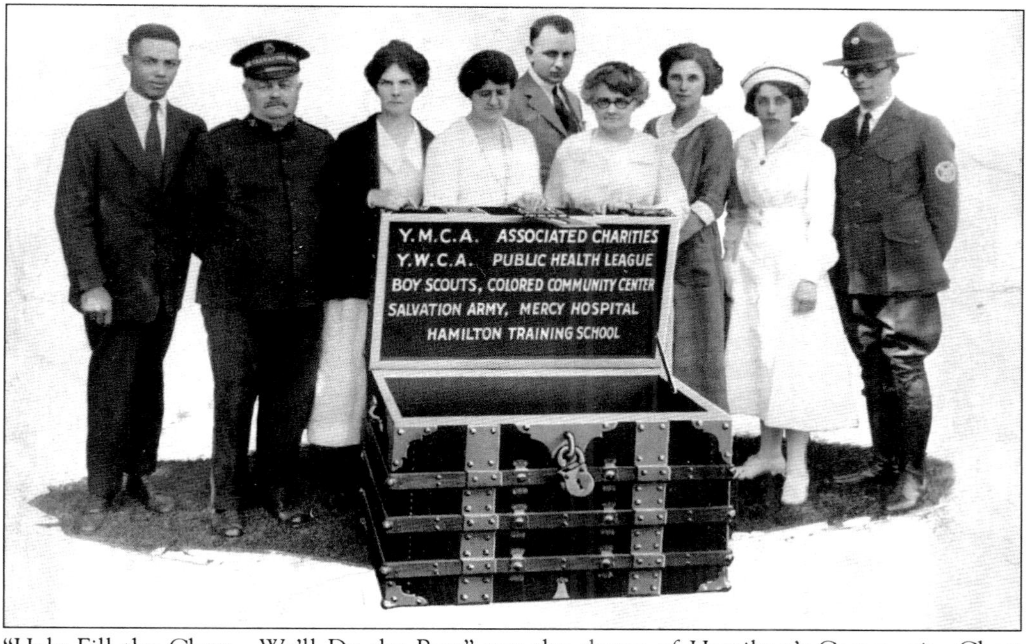

"Help Fill the Chest—We'll Do the Rest" was the slogan of Hamilton's Community Chest Collection drive of July 10–12, 1922. Shown from left to right are Horace Preston, Commander William Hyde, Ellen McCarthy, Jennie Dodds, John L. Prosser, Birdie Ashbury Gories, Isabelle Beardsley, nurse Antoinette Droege, and Jim Stimson. (Courtesy the BCHS.)

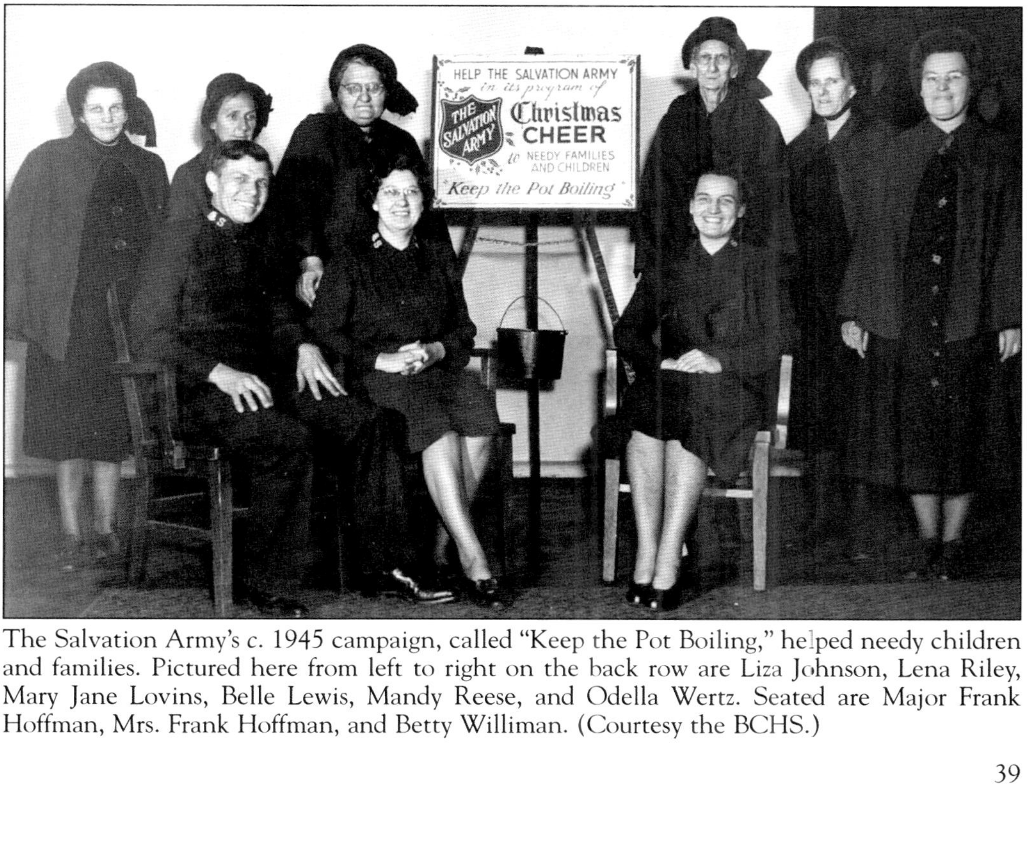

The Salvation Army's *c.* 1945 campaign, called "Keep the Pot Boiling," helped needy children and families. Pictured here from left to right on the back row are Liza Johnson, Lena Riley, Mary Jane Lovins, Belle Lewis, Mandy Reese, and Odella Wertz. Seated are Major Frank Hoffman, Mrs. Frank Hoffman, and Betty Williman. (Courtesy the BCHS.)

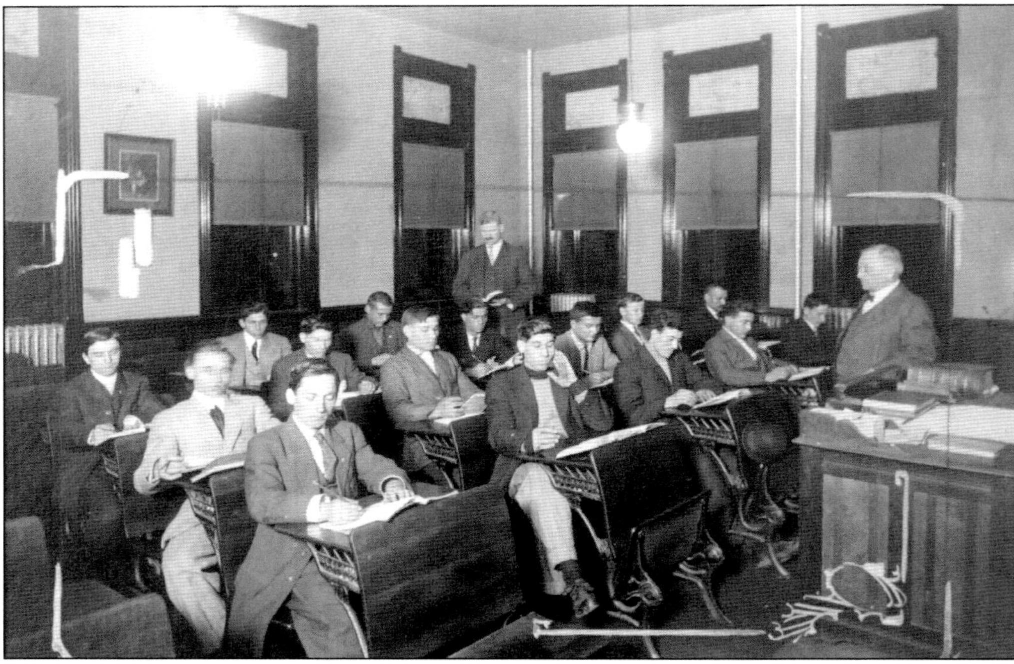

In the 1920s, the YMCA sponsored an English class for foreigners to accommodate the large number of immigrants still entering Hamilton and greater Ohio. The teacher and his students were not identified. In those days, the YMCA was a meeting place for many Hamilton groups and people. (Courtesy the BCHS.)

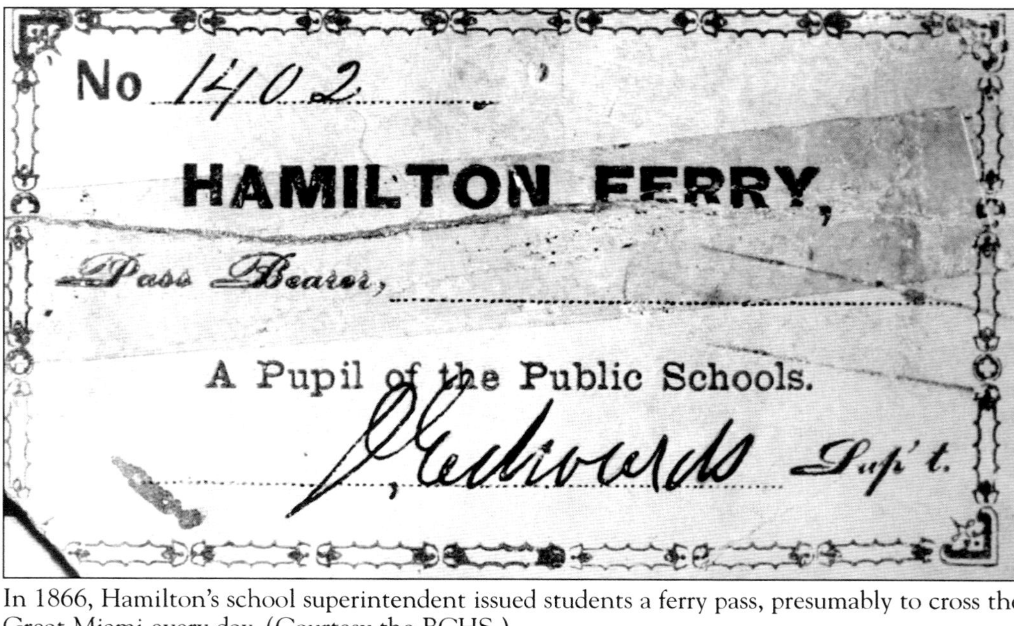

No 1402

HAMILTON FERRY,

Pass Bearer,

A Pupil of the Public Schools.

Edwards Sup't.

In 1866, Hamilton's school superintendent issued students a ferry pass, presumably to cross the Great Miami every day. (Courtesy the BCHS.)

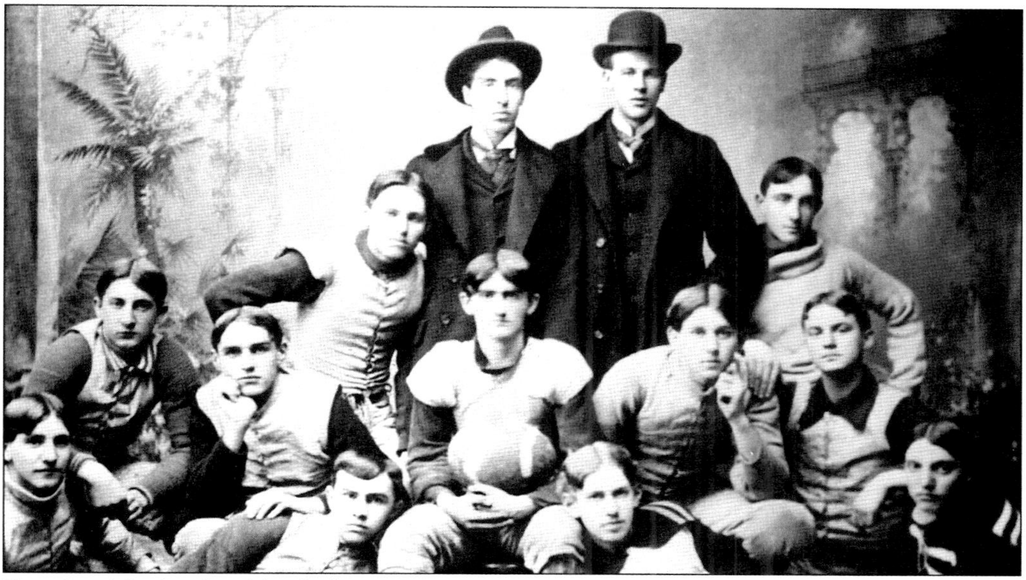

Hamilton's high school football team played the hard way in 1897—with little padding. Players pictured here are, from left to right: (bottom row) Louis Trapp, Murray Snider, Edward Abbey, and Harry Rogers; (middle row) Carl Eberling, Flenner Rooke, Lee Schell, Louis Frechtling, and Calvin Skinner; (top row) H. Lee Good, Manager Walton Bowers, ? Newell, and George James. (Courtesy the BCHS.)

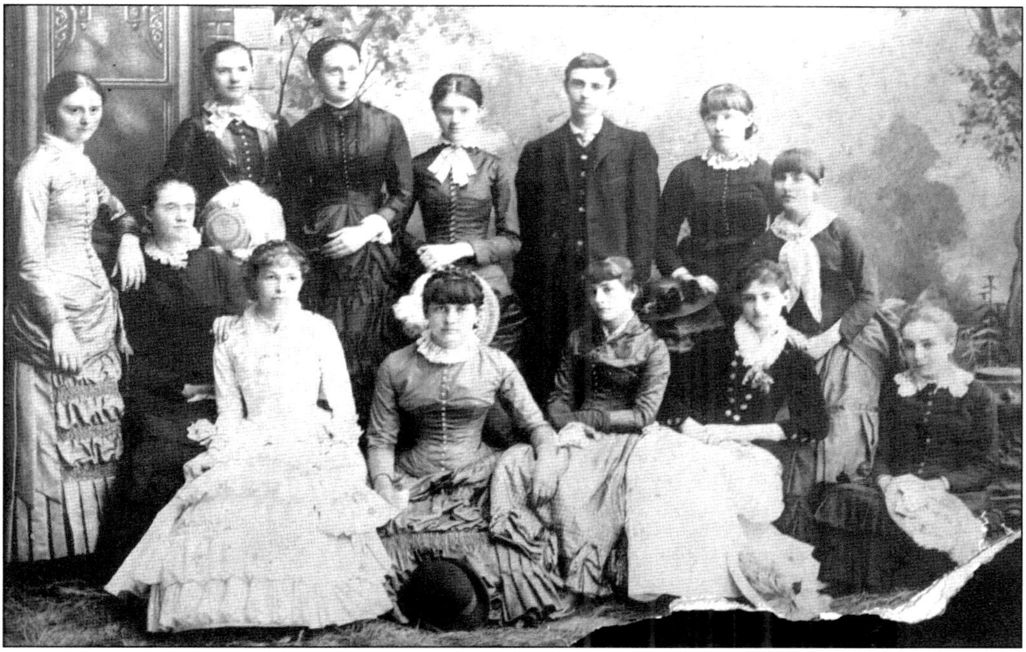

When these 13 students graduated from Hamilton's high school in 1883, earning a high school diploma was a big achievement. Notice the preponderance of females in the class. Perhaps this was because the young men often quit school early to find full-time jobs to help their families. (Courtesy the BCHS.)

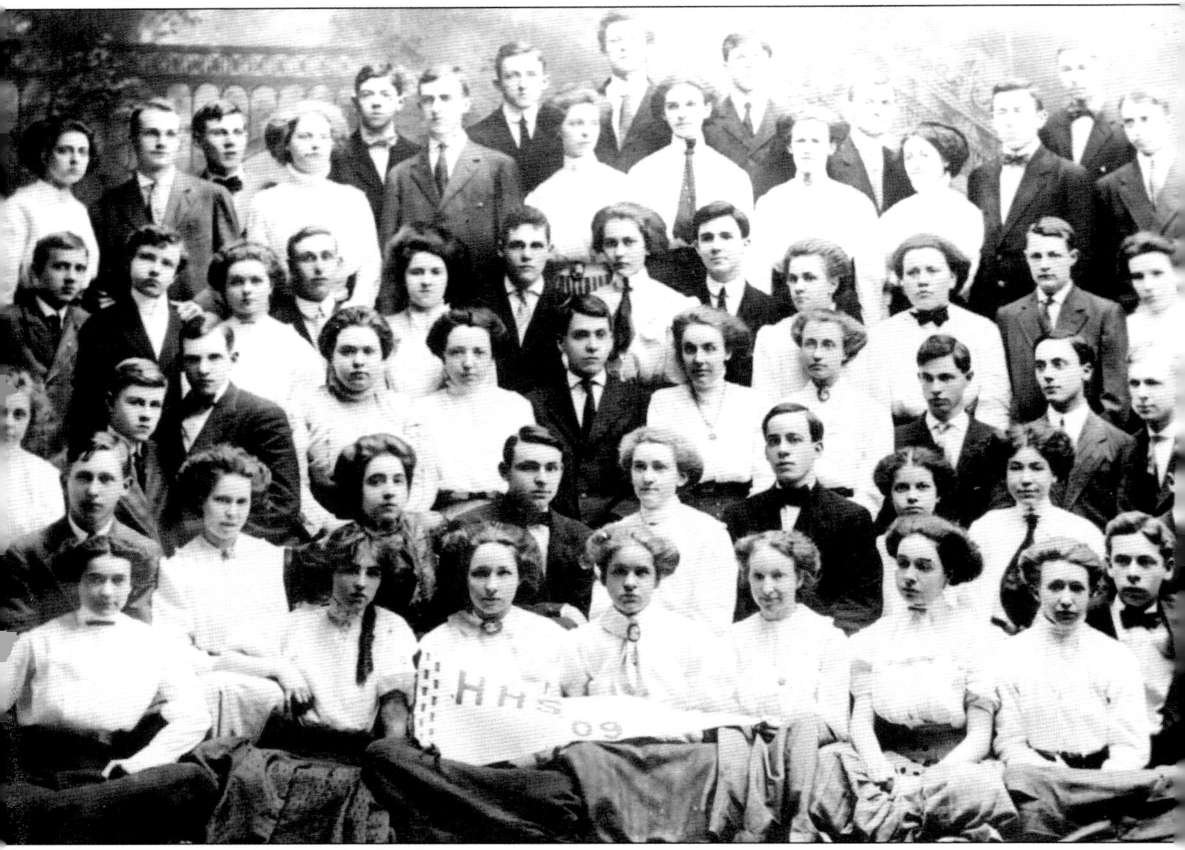

By 1909, the class of Hamilton High School had grown to 57 students, including a larger number of boys. Here, the unidentified class members posed for the photographer and held their HHS 1909 pennant. They were ready to make their mark on a new decade in a young century. (Courtesy the BCHS.)

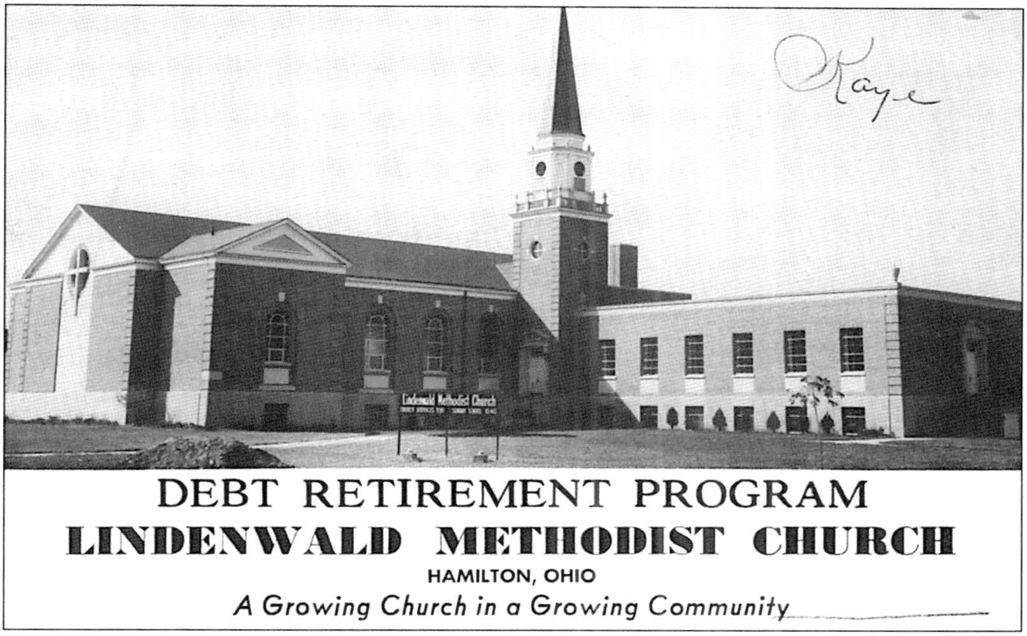

Lindenwald United Methodist Church conducted its first formal service in its Pleasant Avenue building on Palm Sunday in 1955. After six years of fundraising, the congregation, which formed in 1903, built the new church and moved from its Fairview Avenue location. Initial membership was 1,075; school enrollment was nearly 1,000. For this debt retirement campaign, the victory goal was $75,000. (Courtesy the authors.)

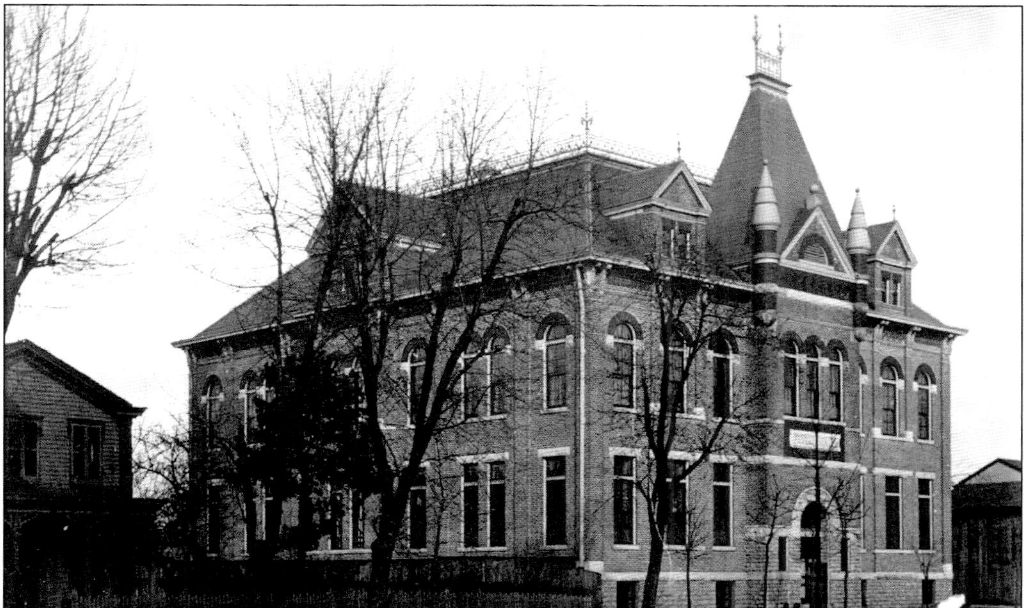

Hamilton's Third Ward School on Dayton Street is seen as it appeared in the early 1900s. The building continues to enjoy a long life in Hamilton's education scene. For decades it has been an office for the Hamilton Board of Education. (Courtesy the BCHS.)

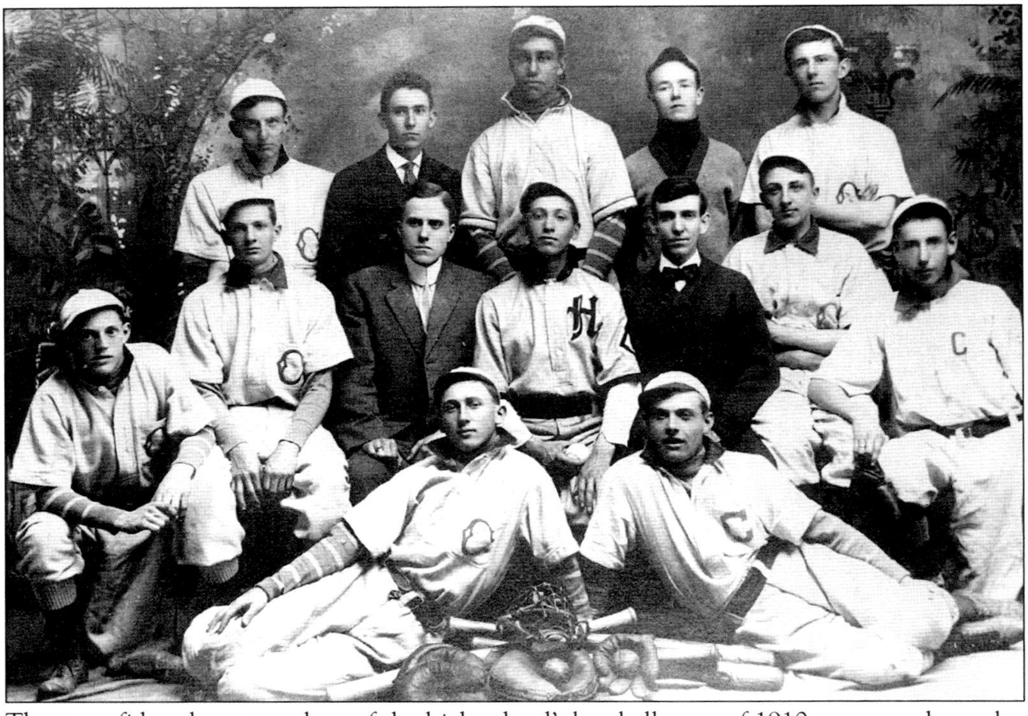

These confident boys, members of the high school's baseball team of 1910, came ready to play some old-fashioned hardball. The letter "C" on their uniforms stood for Central High School, the name of Hamilton's high school then. By the looks on their faces, they could defeat the Cincinnati Redlegs. Team member Lee Hobbs later played in the minors for the Reds. Note their small baseball gloves, balls, and bats. (Courtesy the BCHS.)

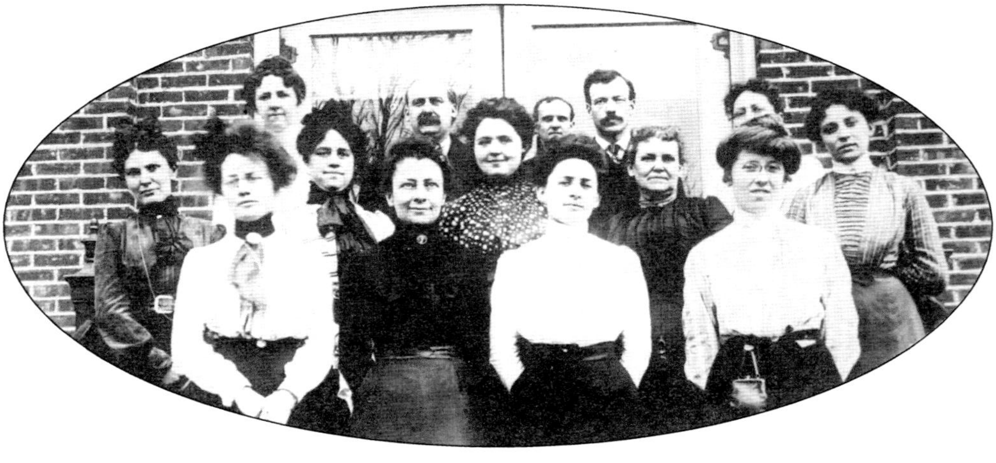

Most of the teachers at Hamilton's Second Ward School were fairly young in this early-1900s photograph. No doubt they needed some youthful vigor to keep up with their students. In those days, women were often expected to stop teaching after marriage and were generally required to resign when they became pregnant. (Courtesy the BCHS.)

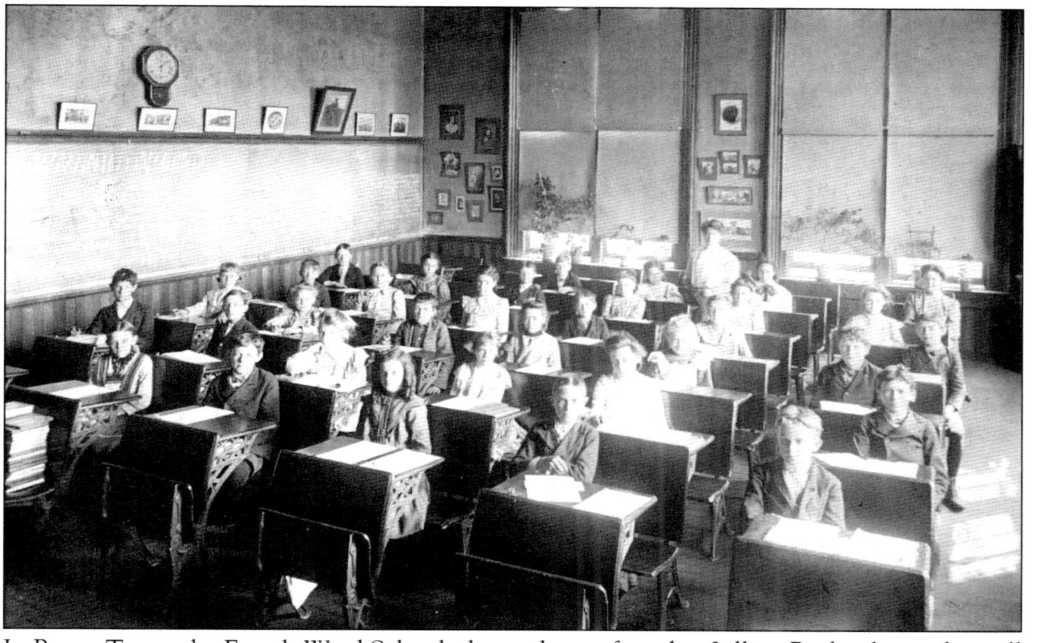

In Room Ten at the Fourth Ward School, the students of teacher Lillian Becker learned to tell the time by reading a schoolhouse clock on the wall to the left. Her students were neatly dressed and ready to learn. (Courtesy the BCHS.)

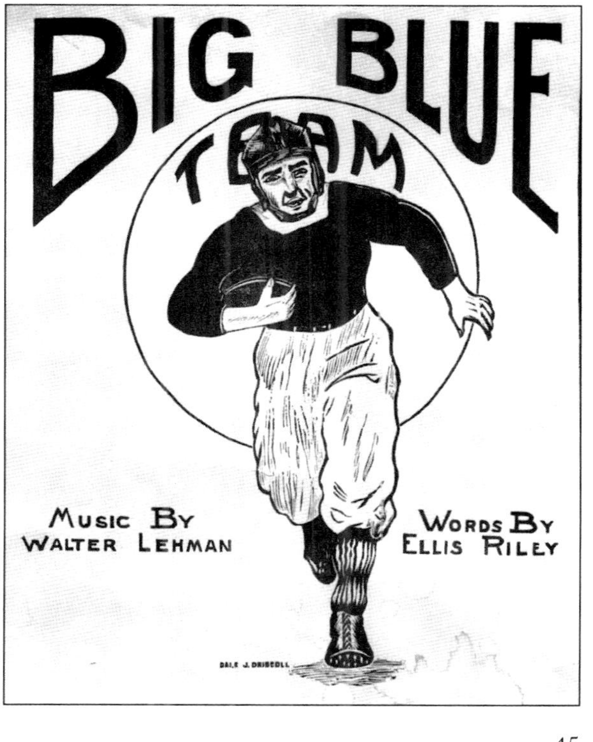

Hamilton High has been known as Big Blue for as long as anyone can remember. In this commemorative sheet, a rah-rah song composed by Walter Lehman and lyricist Ellis Riley, the "Big Blue Team" lives on in history. (Courtesy the BCHS.)

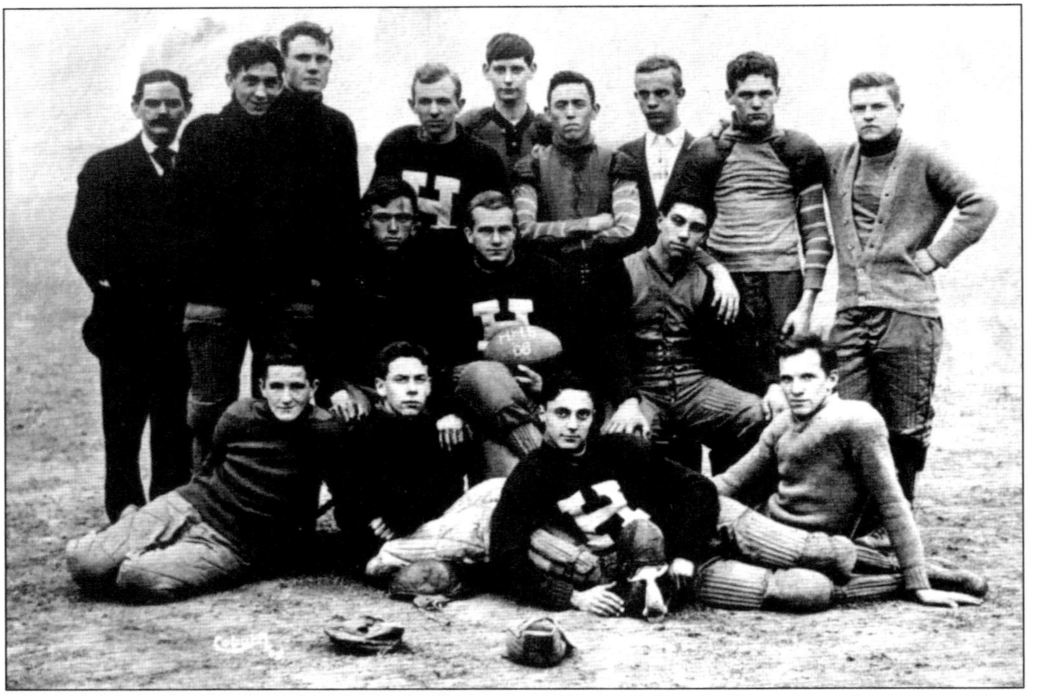

In 1908, Hamilton High School's football team was the undefeated champion of southern Ohio. The team was starting a tradition of expectation that continues today. (Courtesy the BCHS.)

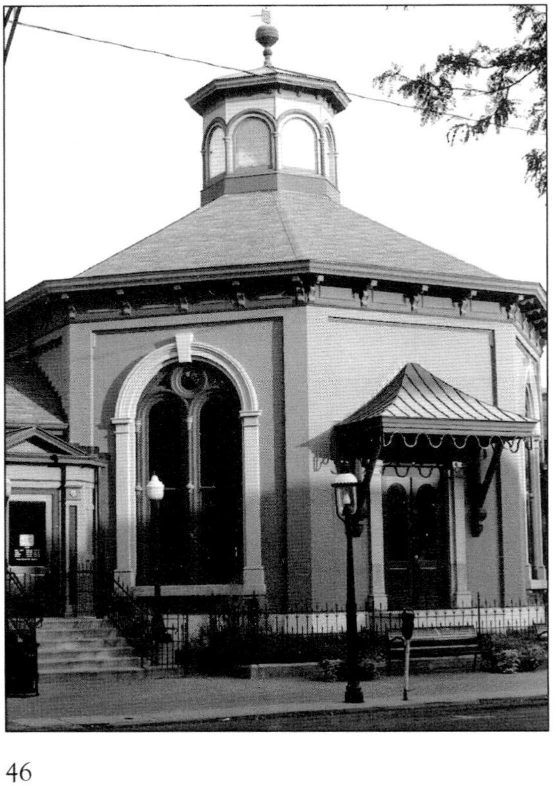

Clark Lane, an industrialist and philanthropist, built the octagonal Lane Public Library in 1866 and bought 3,000 books. It became the first free public library west of the Alleghenies. Additional rooms were later built. Across the street (the library is at North Third and Buckeye Streets), Lane designed and built the octagonal brick Lane-Hooven House. Both buildings have been restored. (Courtesy Randy McNutt.)

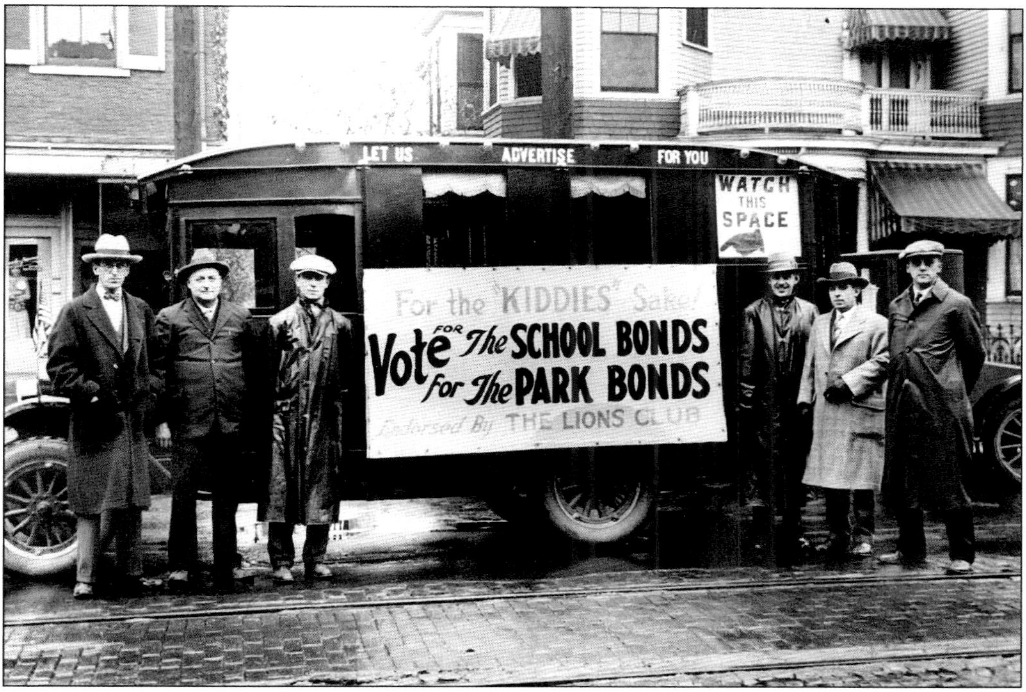

On a rainy day in the early 1930s, in front of a home on North Third Street, a group of city bonds supporters gathered to promote their dual causes—school and park bond levies. From left to right the men were identified as Roy Warndorf, "Sockey" Treibel, a Mr. ? Hines, Dr. ? Beckett, Dr. ? Baker, and Ed Warndorf. (Courtesy the BCHS.)

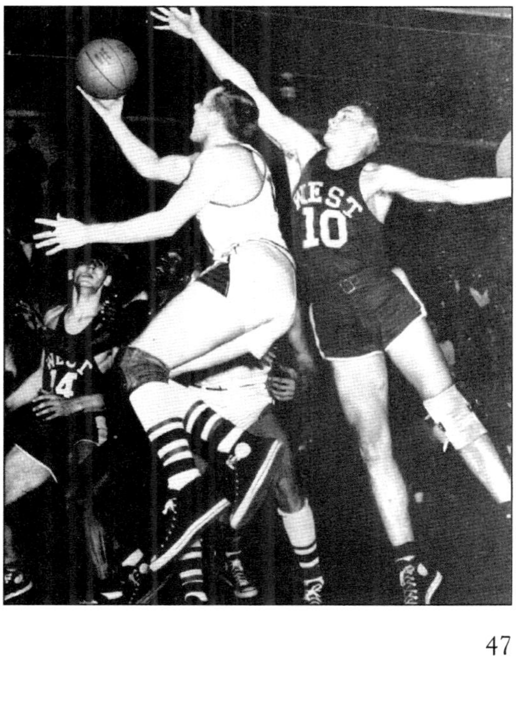

Hamilton High School's 1949 basketball team, led by all-state captain Bill Wilks, won the state championship, defeating Toledo Central Catholic 70–52 in March at the fairgrounds' coliseum in Columbus. That season Hamilton defeated such strong teams as Middletown, Lancaster, Portsmouth, and Niles. (Courtesy Hamilton City Schools.)

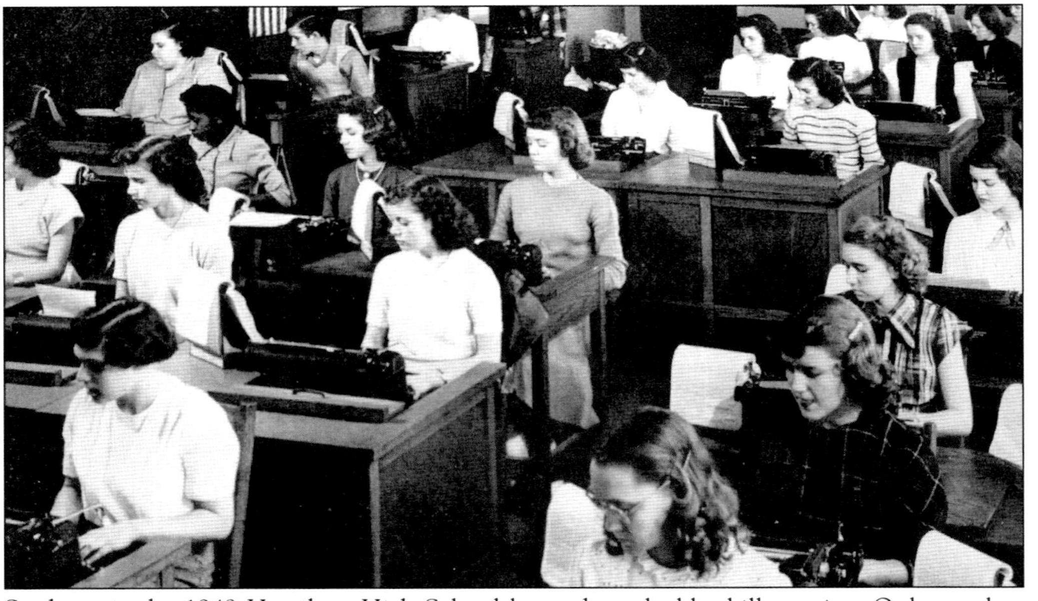

Students in the 1949 Hamilton High School learned a valuable skill—typing. Only one boy was visible, to the back left. Typing skills helped many young women enter the job market after high school at Hamilton industries such as Ohio Casualty, Champion Paper, and Mosler Safe Company. If these students look well-groomed, consider one of the yearbook's slogans: "Good homes make good schools." (Courtesy the Hamilton City Schools.)

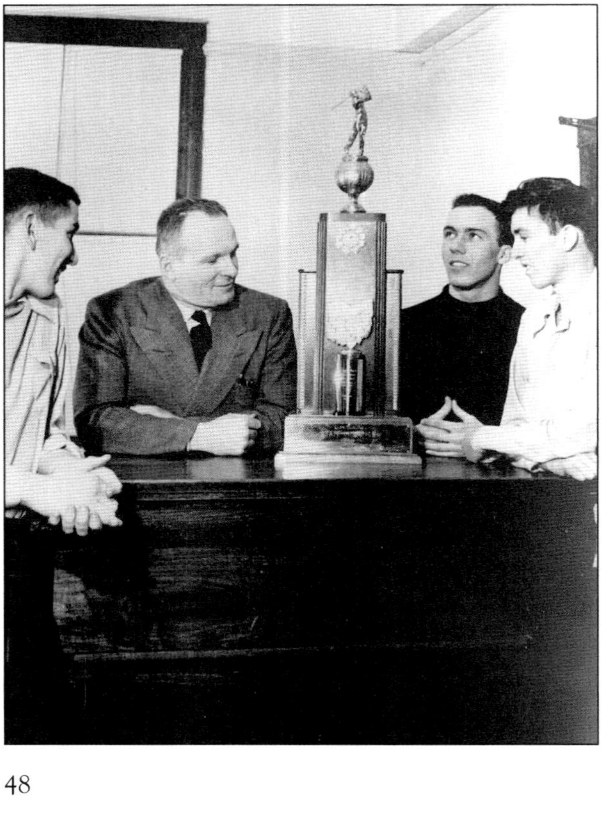

The 1948–1949 academic year saw the Hamilton High golf team winning a state championship. Here, several members stand with their trophy at the school offices. Golf team members, in no particular order, were Coach Dick Goos, Wayne Barrett, Jim Tewart, Clifford Griffith, and Hugh Quinn. (Courtesy the Hamilton City Schools.)

Five

NEIGHBORHOOD BUSINESSES

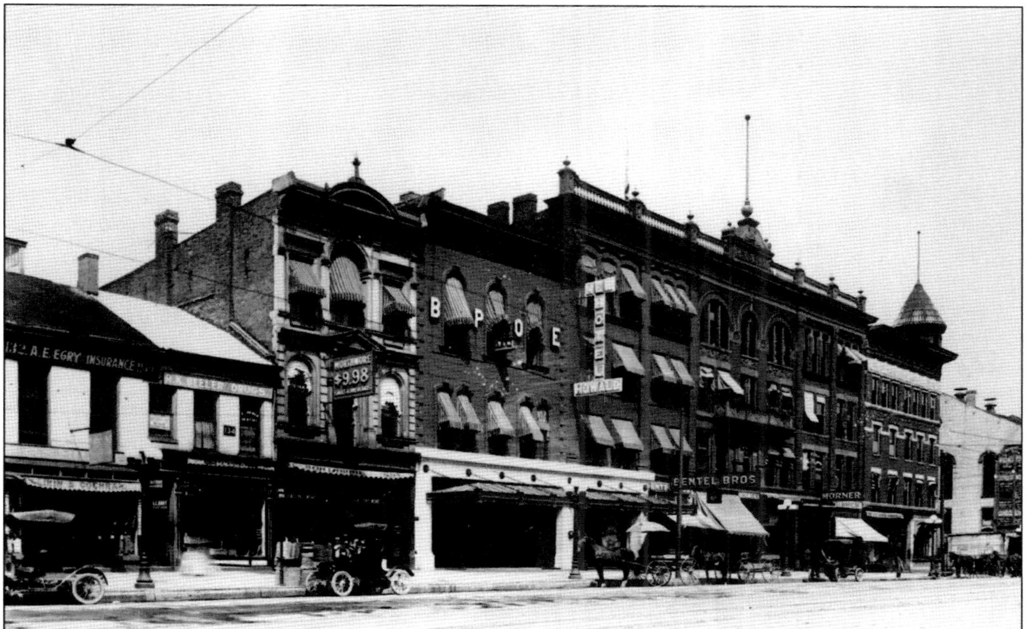

High Street in 1909 was small-city America at its zenith: a collection of locally-owned businesses, sidewalks lined with white globe lamps, traction-car lines crisscrossing the sky like spider webs, new automobiles belching black exhaust, and spires and lightning rods poking their way to the heavens. (Courtesy the BCHS.)

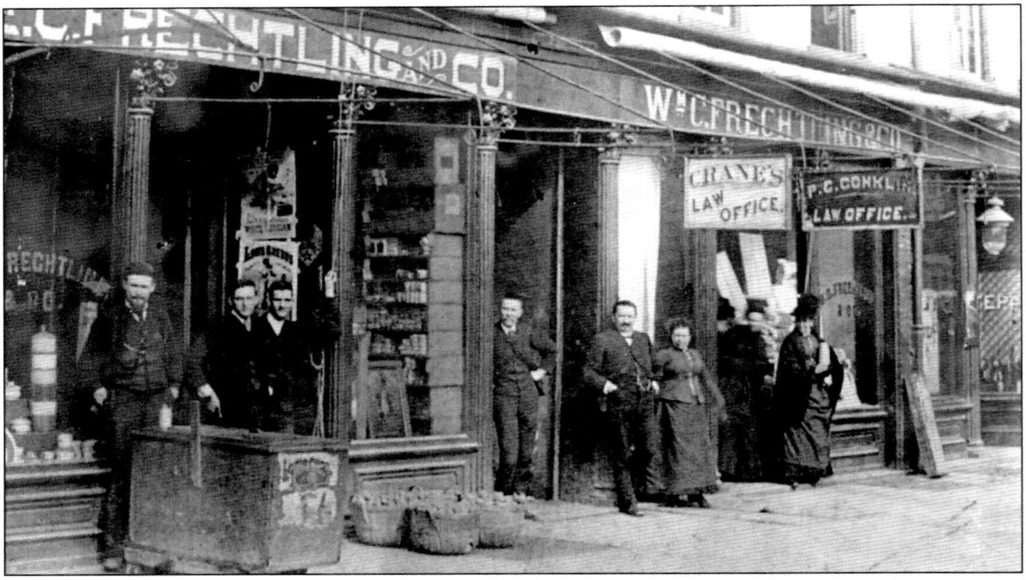

As the county seat, Hamilton had its share of lawyers in the early 1900s. Their offices blended with those of shopkeepers and other small business people. At first glance, this picture made it appear that lawyers were waiting on the High Street sidewalk, ready to grab any business that comes along. Actually, they were people walking near W.C. Frechtling & Co., a popular store that sold a little of everything. (Courtesy the BCHS.)

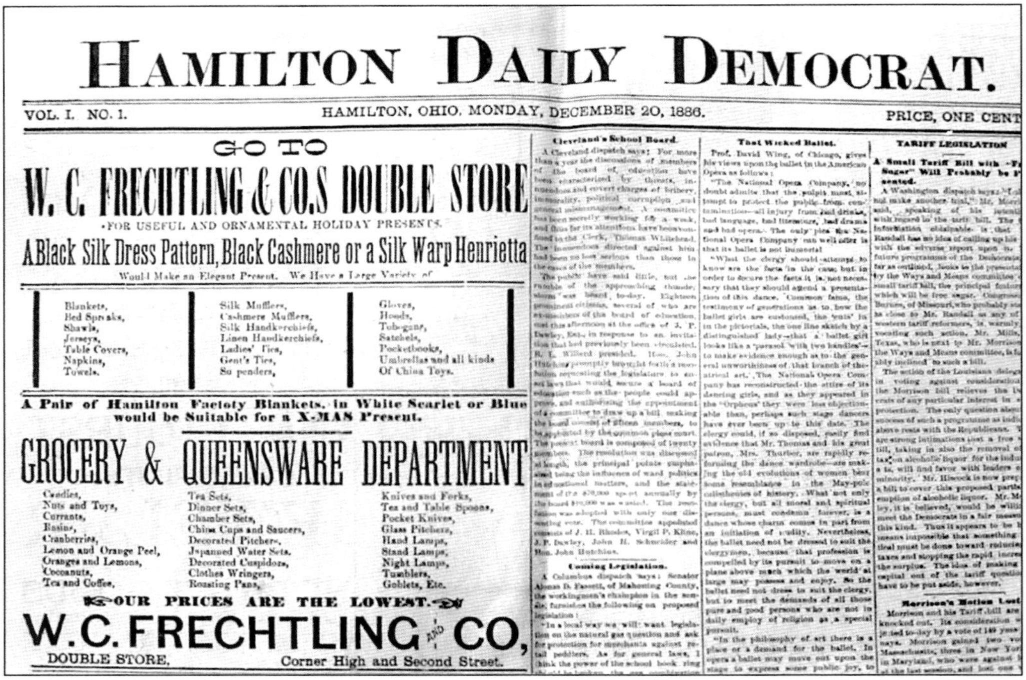

HAMILTON DAILY DEMOCRAT.

VOL. I. NO. 1. HAMILTON, OHIO, MONDAY, DECEMBER 20, 1886. PRICE, ONE CENT

GO TO

W. C. FRECHTLING & CO.S DOUBLE STORE

FOR USEFUL AND ORNAMENTAL HOLIDAY PRESENTS.

A Black Silk Dress Pattern, Black Cashmere or a Silk Warp Henrietta

Would Make an Elegant Present. We Have a Large Variety of

Blankets, Bed Spreads, Shawls, Jerseys, Table Covers, Napkins, Towels.

Silk Mufflers, Cashmere Mufflers, Silk Handkerchiefs, Linen Handkerchiefs, Ladies' Ties, Gent's Ties, Suspenders,

Gloves, Hoods, Toboggans, Satchels, Pocketbooks, Umbrellas and all kinds Of China Toys.

A Pair of Hamilton Factory Blankets, in White Scarlet or Blue would be Suitable for a X-MAS Present.

GROCERY & QUEENSWARE DEPARTMENT

Candies, Nuts and Toys, Currants, Raisins, Cranberries, Lemon and Orange Peel, Oranges and Lemons, Cocoanuts, Teas and Coffee.

Tea Sets, Dinner Sets, Chamber Sets, China Cups and Saucers, Decorated Pitchers, Japanned Water Sets, Decorated Cuspidors, Clothes Wringers, Roasting Pans,

Knives and Forks, Tea and Table Spoons, Pocket Knives, Glass Pitchers, Hand Lamps, Stand Lamps, Night Lamps, Tumblers, Goblets, Etc.

OUR PRICES ARE THE LOWEST.

W.C. FRECHTLING AND CO,

DOUBLE STORE, Corner High and Second Street.

Cleveland's School Board.

That Wicked Ballet.

TARIFF LEGISLATION

Coming Legislation.

Morrison's Motion Lost

The *Hamilton Daily Democrat* sold for a penny in December 1886. Next to national stories on page one is a large advertisement for W.C. Frechtling & Co., which sold night lamps, pitchers, and knives, among other sundries. (Courtesy the BCHS.)

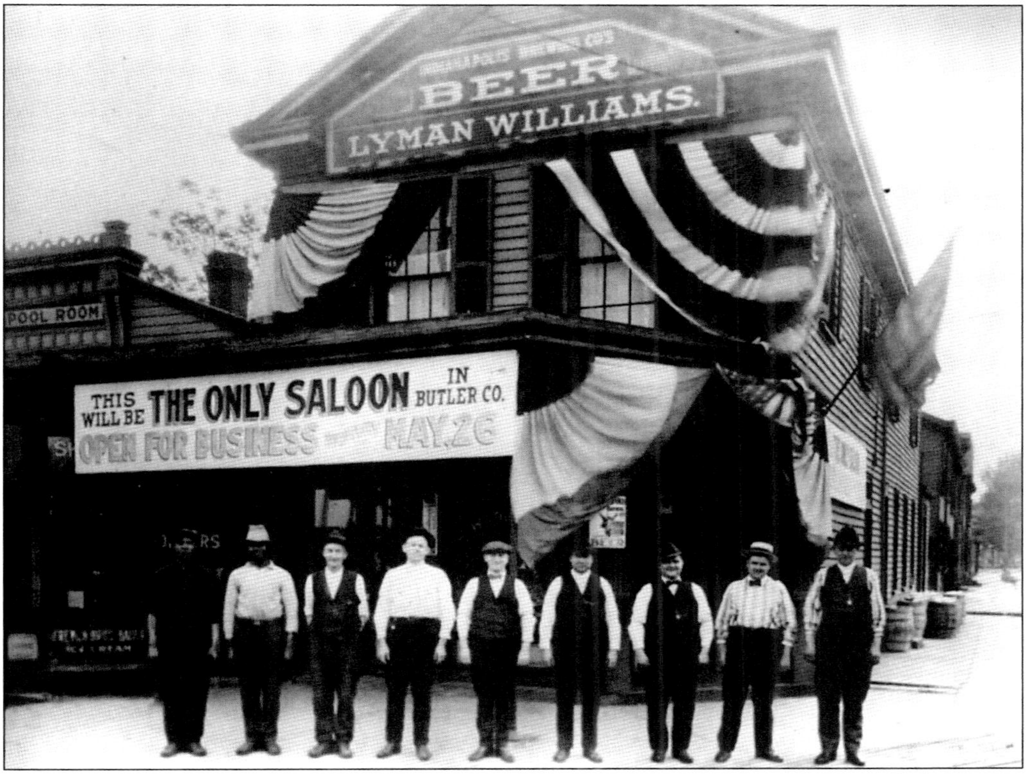

Saloon owner Lyman Williams and eight other men stand in front of his establishment at 433–435 South Fifth Street to promote his resolve. The sign in the front explained that the saloon would be the only one open in Butler County on May 26, 1919, on the outset of Prohibition. The men were not identified. (Courtesy the BCHS.)

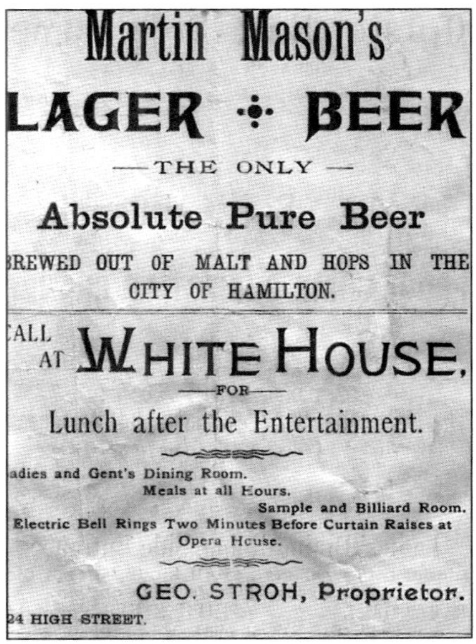

This advertisement promoted Martin Mason's lager beer, brewed in Hamilton. The city was home to several breweries at the turn of the twentieth century. By the middle of the century, they were gone, due in part to the Prohibition and later to competition from larger Cincinnati breweries. (Courtesy the BCHS.)

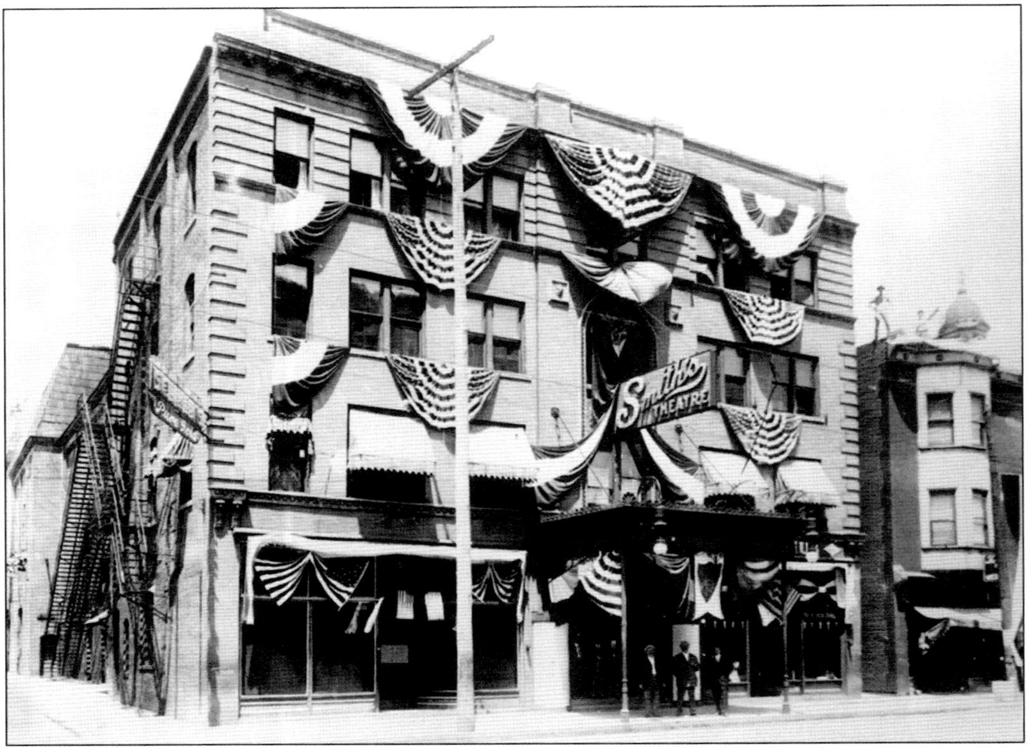

In the early 1900s, Smith's Theater was one of several downtown movie houses that attracted Hamiltonians with the latest "talkies" and other forms of entertainment. (Courtesy the BCHS.)

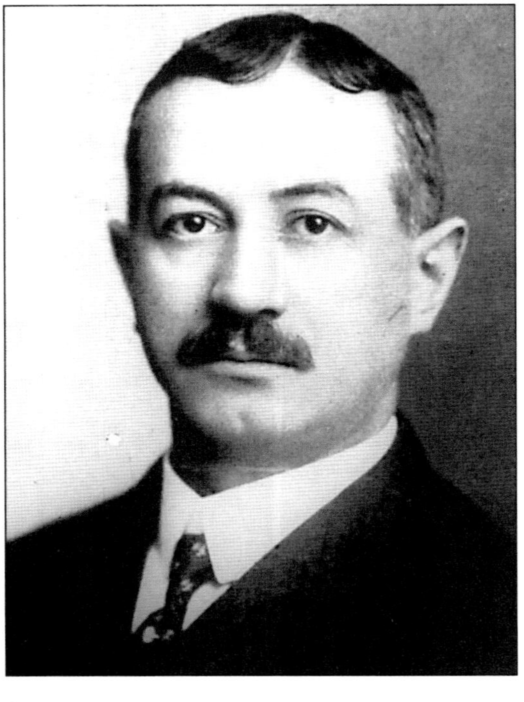

Pictured here is Charles Howald, a well-known city resident in 1914 and proprietor of the Hotel Howald. His establishment on High Street was "recognized as the finest in a city the size of Hamilton . . . a mecca for the traveling public, conservatively managed and modern in all its appointments," according to the *Butler County Atlas and Pictorial Review*. (Courtesy Hamilton City Schools.)

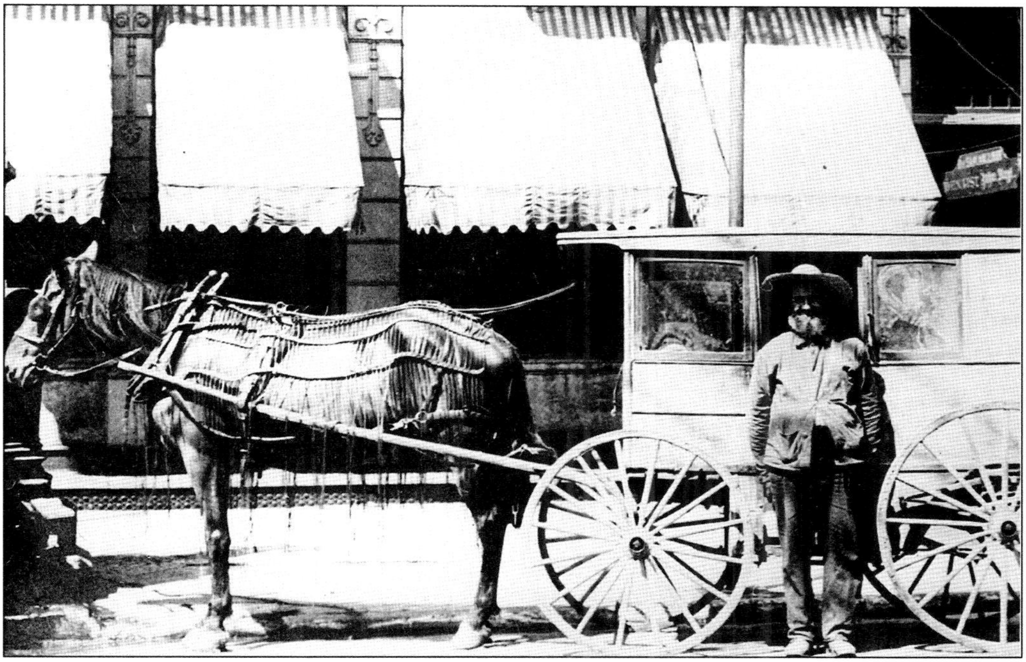

Eldon Purdy stood with his horse, Topsy, while on their milk route at the corner of Third and High Streets in 1916. Homemakers only had to go to their back doors to retrieve fresh milk, cream, cottage cheese, and butter for breakfast. Purdy continued a proud tradition of house-to-house milk delivery in Hamilton that finally died in the 1980s. (Courtesy the BCHS.)

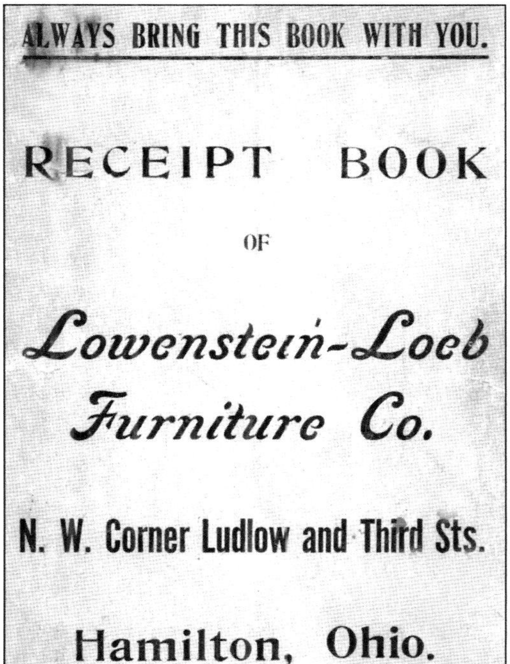

ALWAYS BRING THIS BOOK WITH YOU.

RECEIPT BOOK

OF

Lowenstein-Loeb

Furniture Co.

N. W. Corner Ludlow and Third Sts.

Hamilton, Ohio.

In the early part of the twentieth century, Lowenstein-Loeb was one of several downtown furniture stores. It operated at the corner of Ludlow Avenue and Third Street. The store gave customers small receipt books with removable covers in which to record their monthly payments. Although Lowenstein-Loeb no longer operates, Hamilton still has several locally-owned furniture stores. (Courtesy the authors.)

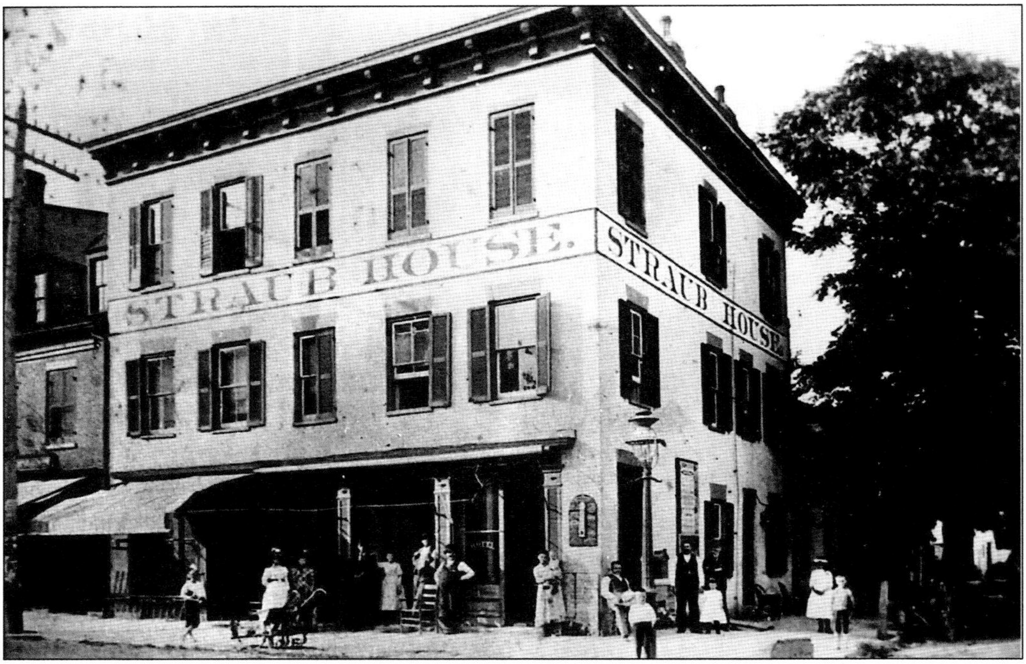

The Straub House operated on Main Street on Hamilton's west side. This photograph shows the three-story hotel in 1891. (Courtesy the BCHS.)

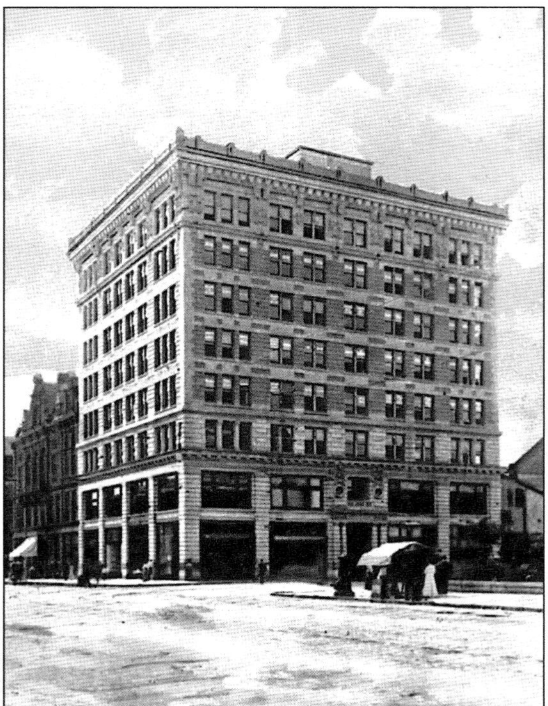

The Rentschler Building, 6 South Second Street at High, opened in 1906. Construction started in 1903 on what was once Hamilton's tallest building. Owner George Adam Rentschler, a Hamilton entrepreneur, used the first floor as the headquarters of his Citizens Bank (later Key Bank). He rented the remainder of the offices. In 2003, a brass plaque was added: "The Rentschler Building—A Hamilton Landmark since 1903." (Courtesy the authors.)

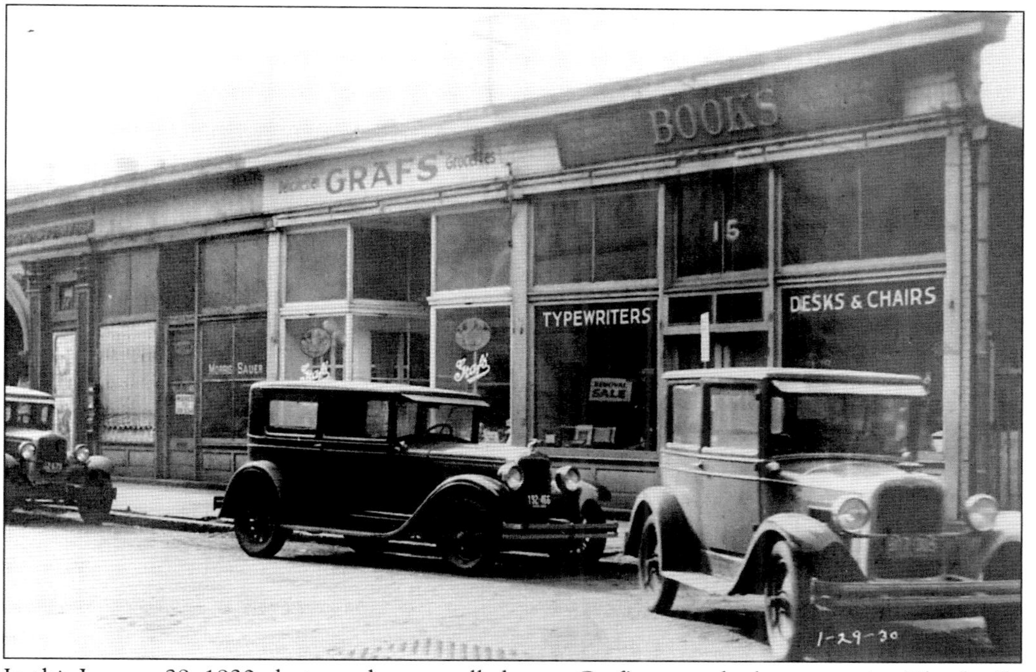

In this January 29, 1930 photograph, cars pulled up to Graf's to get the best groceries. The family store is flanked by an office supply store and other small shops downtown. (Courtesy the BCHS.)

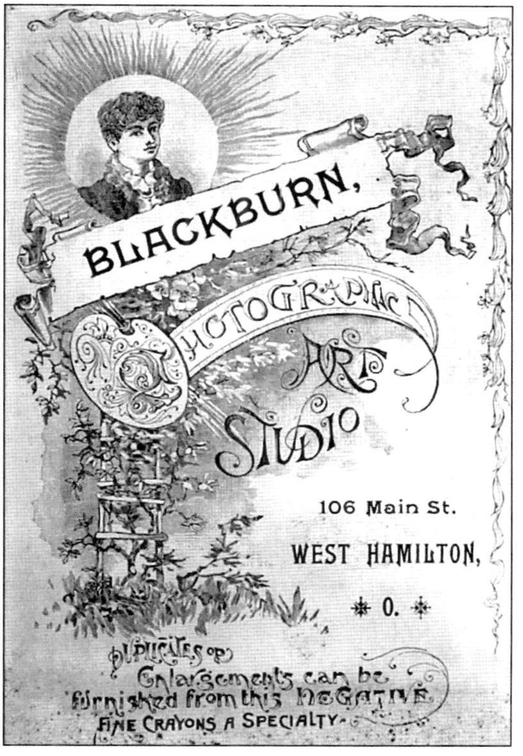

In the 1890s, the Blackburn Photographic Art Studio operated at 106 Main Street in "West Hamilton." Fine crayons were a specialty. Having a photograph taken was still a solemn event for many people, often done only to commemorate an important occasion such as a wedding or birth of a child. Judging by the artistic nature of the advertisement, Blackburn provided high-quality service. (Courtesy the BCHS.)

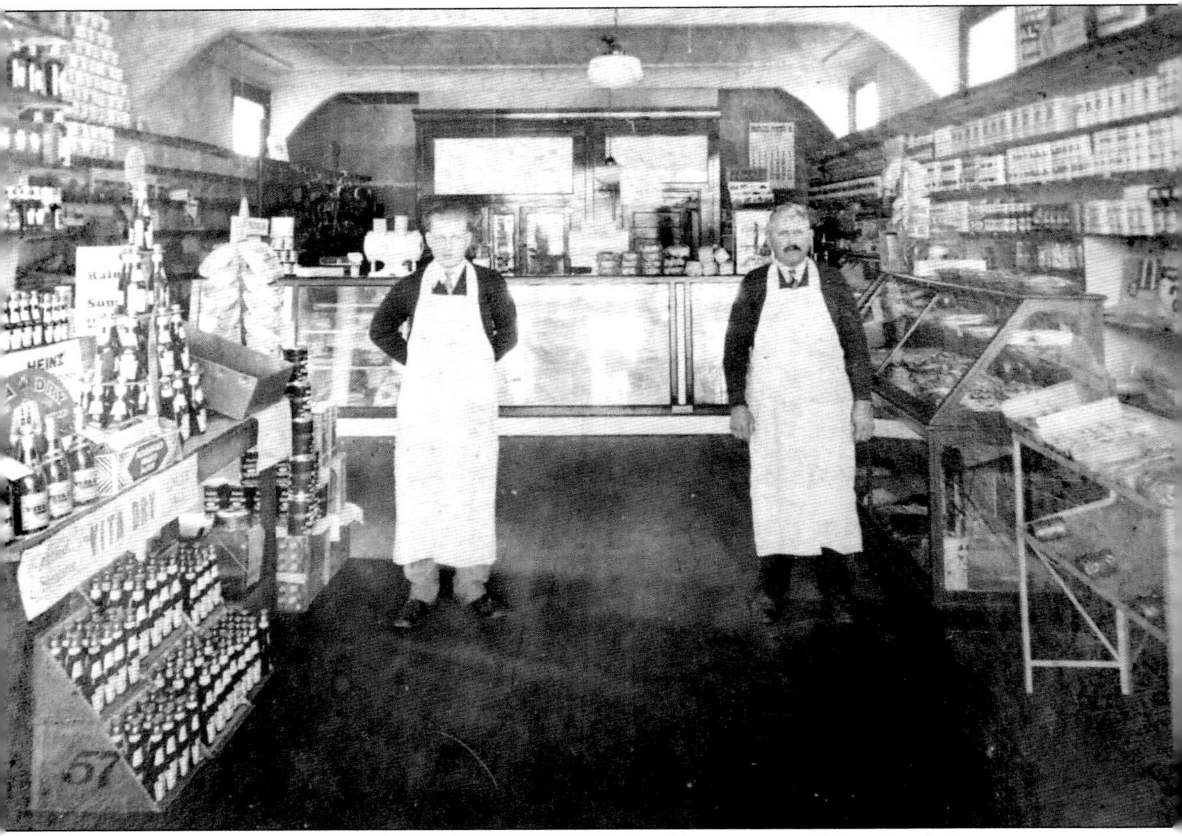

Hornung Meats, 541 Williams Avenue in Lindenwald, was one of Hamilton's longest operating butcher shops-grocery stores of the twentieth century. In this picture, founder Lewis Hornung stands in the store with his son, Vernon, in 1931. A meat peddler initially based in nearby Symmes Corner in Fairfield Township, Lewis traveled by wagon for years. When new health regulations hampered door-to-door meat sales, Hornung opened the store in Lindenwald's growing business district in 1921. The family worked in a rectangular room with the meat counter stretching across one end. Customers stood there and chatted about families, the weather, food, and nearly every topic. When their father died in the 1950s, Vernon and his brothers Mark and Waldo (Emerson) operated the store as a partnership, renamed Hornung Brothers Meats. Waldo, the youngest, sold the store name and retired in the 1980s. (Courtesy the authors.)

Six

INDUSTRY
"KNOWN IN WORLD MARKETS"

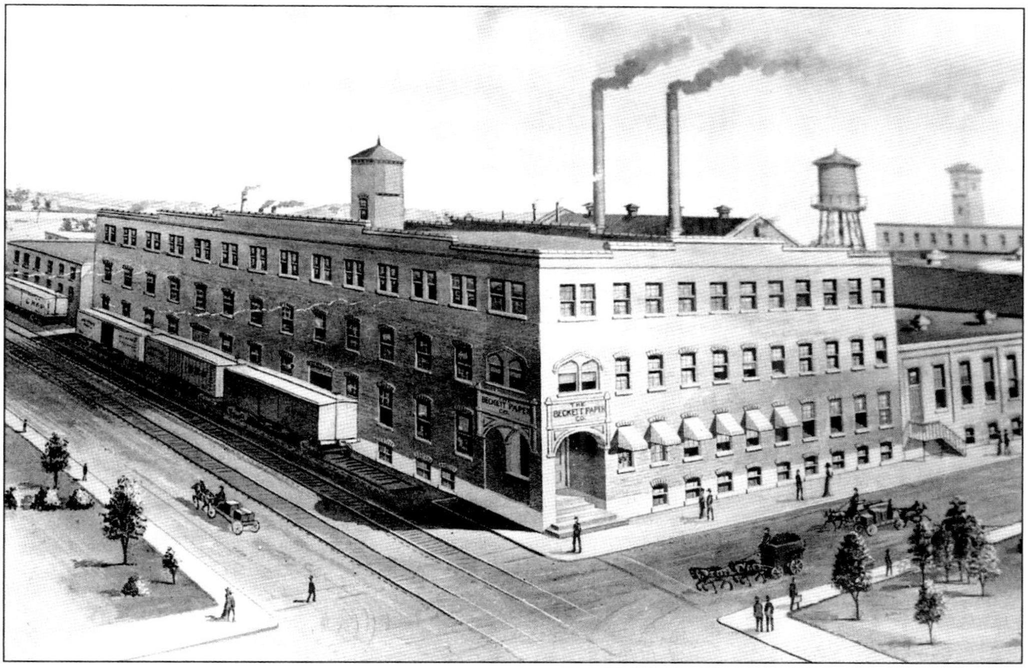

When International Paper Co. announced in December 2004 that it was selling its 156-year-old Beckett Paper Co. to Mohawk Paper Mills of New York, the story was big news in Hamilton. The factory, founded by William Beckett in 1848, has been a mainstay of Hamilton industry for years. The old brick plant is a link between Hamilton's industrial past and modern present. Beckett built his mill on Dayton Street, not far from downtown, where he could take advantage of the canals. By the end of the century, the factory had become a leading area paper manufacturer and employer. At the time of the sale, the Beckett plant employed 227 people involved in making fine writing papers. International bought the company in 1986. (Courtesy the BCHS.)

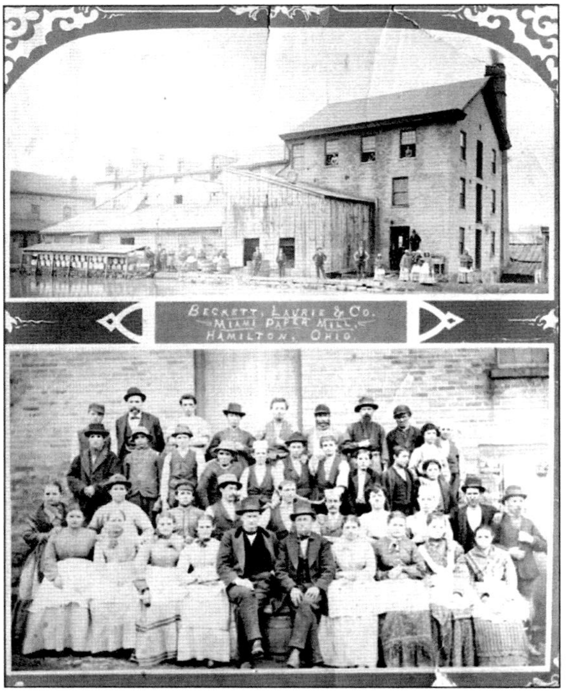

This is a photograph of the Beckett, Laurie & Co.'s Miami Paper Mill and its employees in the 1880s. After a partnership that lasted about 30 years, the Beckett family bought out their partners, the Laurie family, in 1885, and the firm became known simply as Beckett Paper. By 1913, Beckett produced one-fifth of all the paper used in automobile catalogues. (Courtesy the BCHS.)

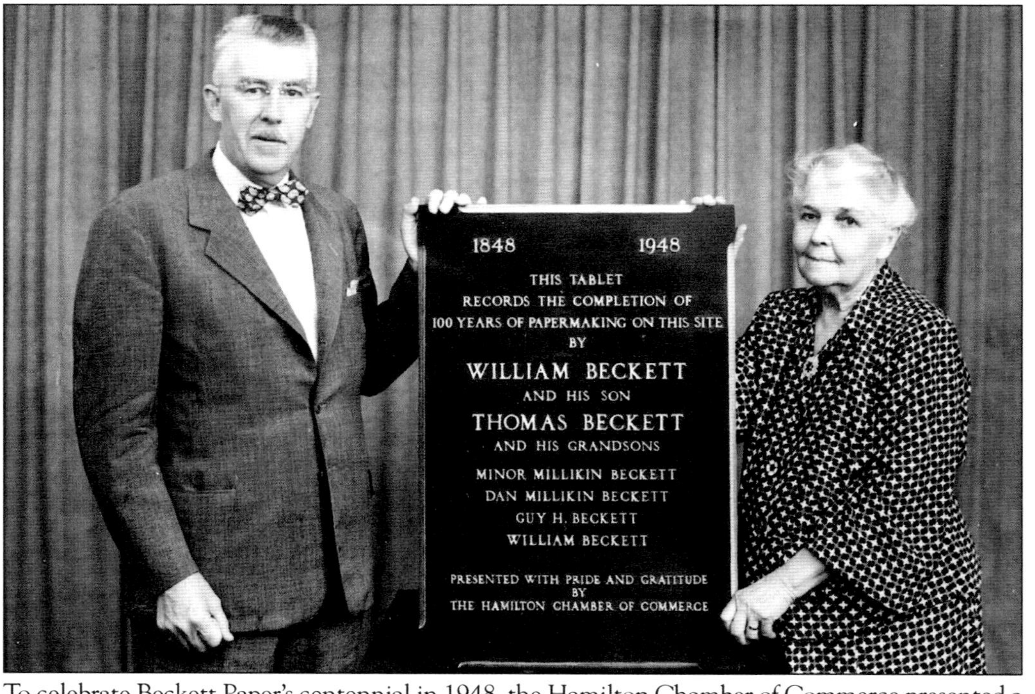

To celebrate Beckett Paper's centennial in 1948, the Hamilton Chamber of Commerce presented a commemorative tablet to the firm. Standing with it were Cy Fitton, who served on Beckett's board of directors, and Mrs. Mary Beckett, of the papermaking family. The company manufactured papers named Buckeye Cover, Buckeye Text, and Beckett Cover. (Courtesy the BCHS.)

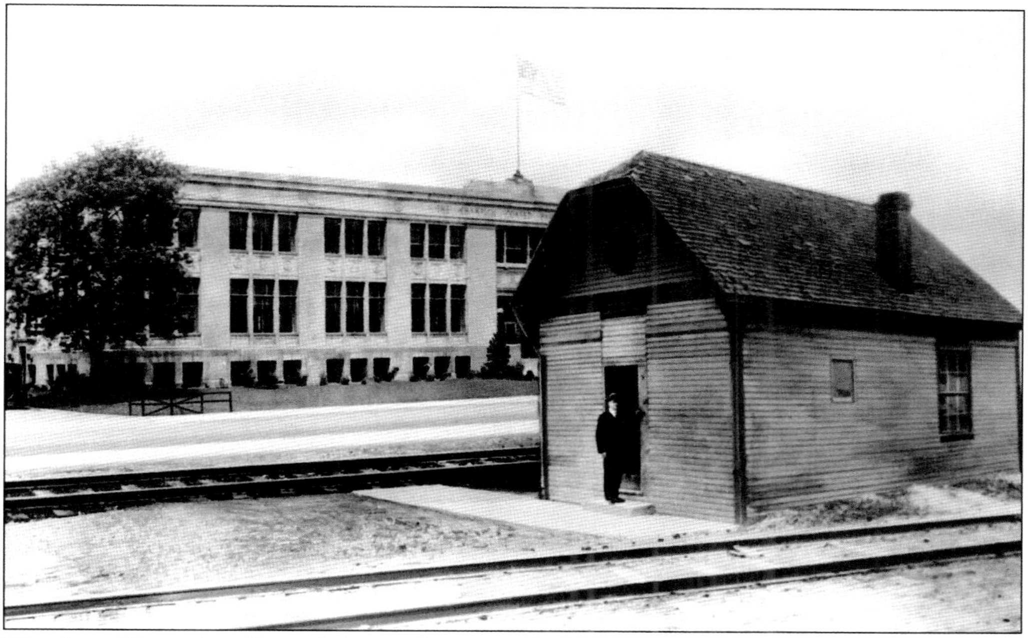

The first Champion Coated Paper Company building of the 1800s was a small wooden structure that later stood across from the company's office building on "B" Street. By 1910, Champion claimed its 27-acre plant was the world's largest manufacturer of coated papers. (Courtesy the BCHS.)

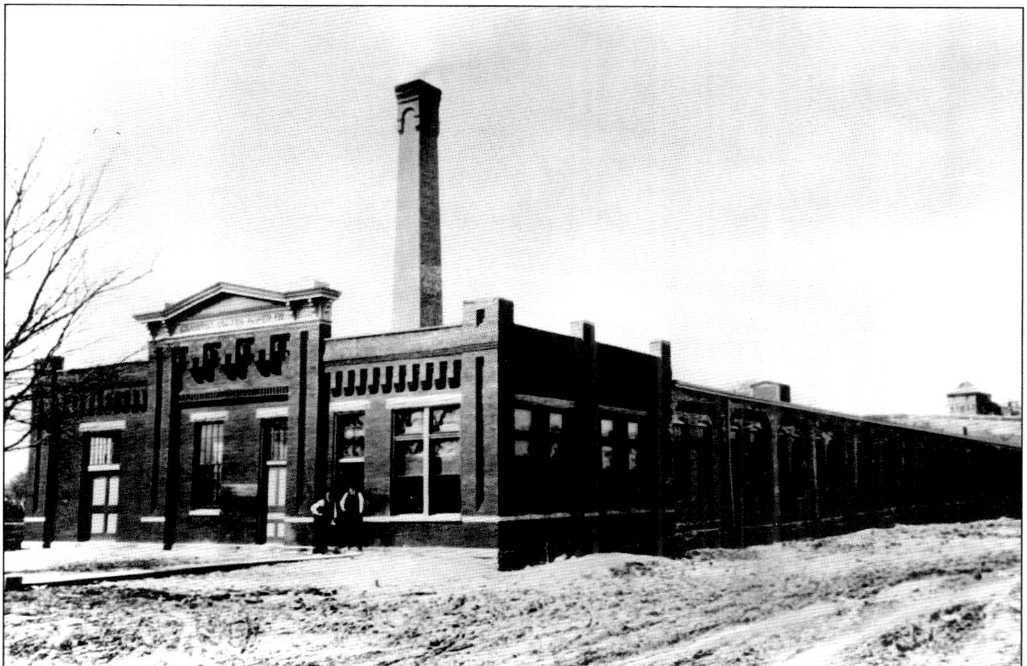

Two workers stand in front of the original Champion Coated Paper Company mill, built in 1894. The photograph is probably from the early 1900s. (Courtesy the BCHS.)

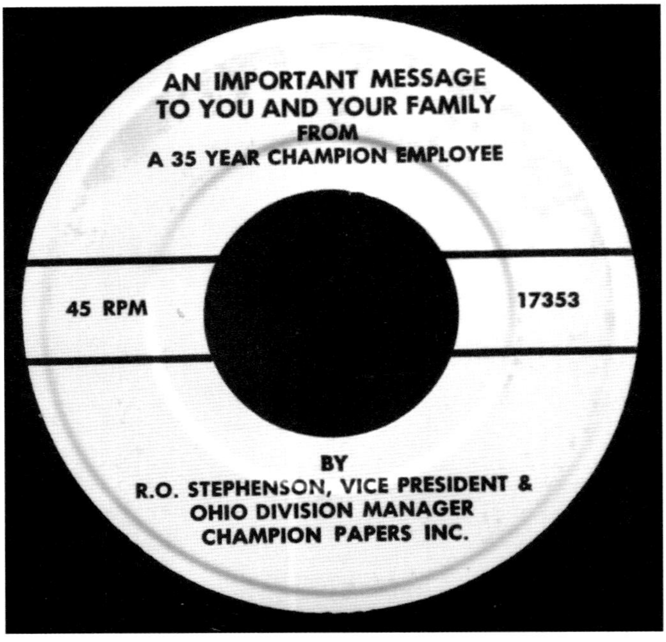

On August 27, 1966, R.O. Stephenson, a Champion vice president, issued a message to the company's employees on a 45-rpm disc. The company believed the phonograph record could be played in nearly every employee's home. (Courtesy the BCHS.)

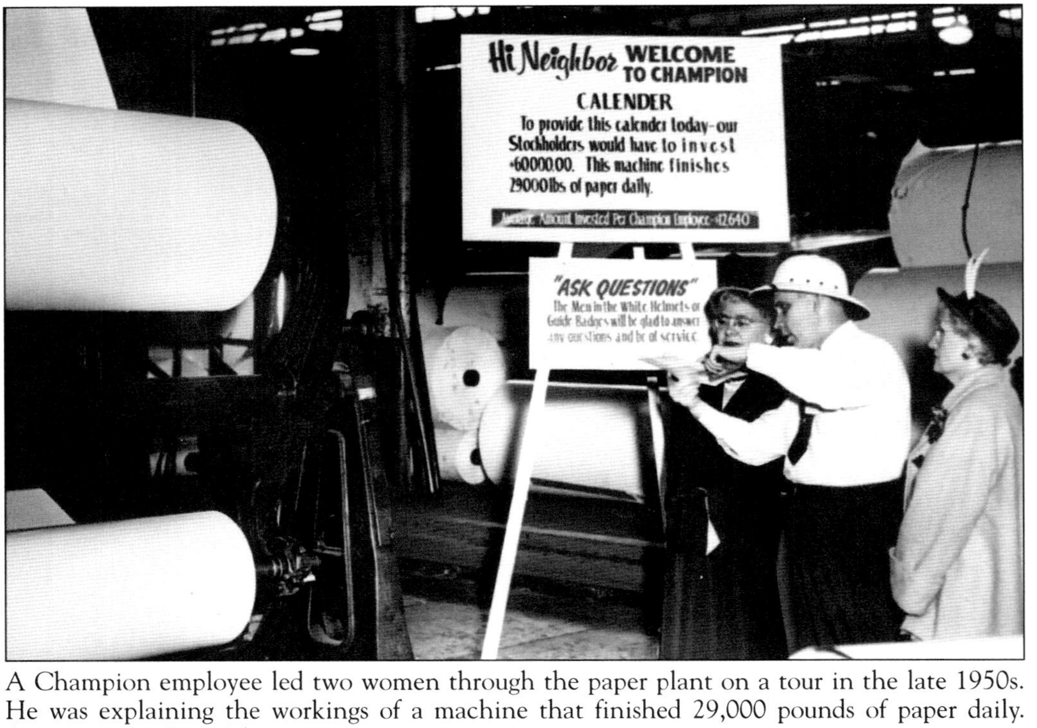

A Champion employee led two women through the paper plant on a tour in the late 1950s. He was explaining the workings of a machine that finished 29,000 pounds of paper daily. (Courtesy the BCHS.)

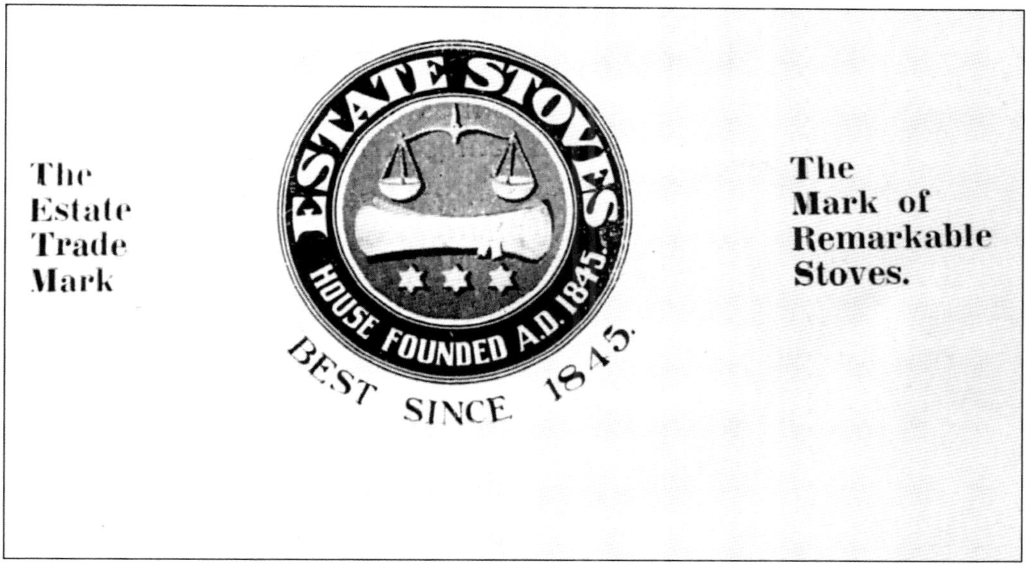

The logo of the Estate Stove Company was a familiar Hamilton industrial image for more than a century. The company opened its factory in 1845. The firm operated both as Estate and the F. & L. Kahn & Brothers Company. The factories boasted of having 10 acres of floor space to supply the demand for its stoves and ranges. Today, collectors seek the company's antique stoves. (Courtesy the BCHS.)

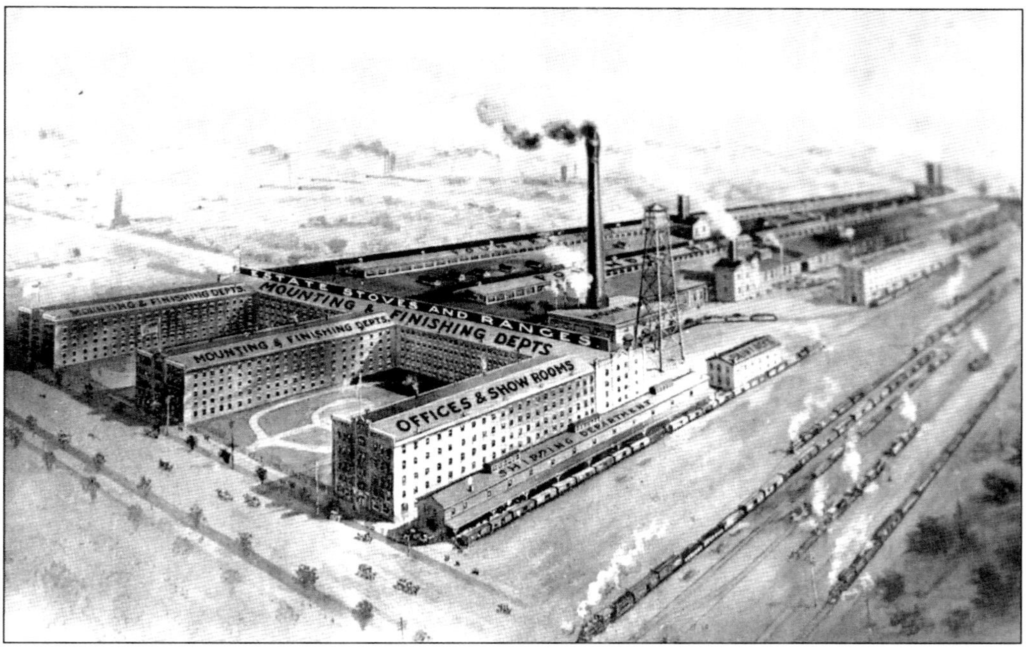

Estate Stove factory, on the east side of Hamilton, is pictured as it appeared in the early 1900s. The company manufactured appliances for coal, wood, gas, and electric. Estate's massive brick buildings, some five stories high, were razed *c.* 2000 when Hamilton sought to rid itself of unsightly Victorian factories. (Courtesy the BCHS.)

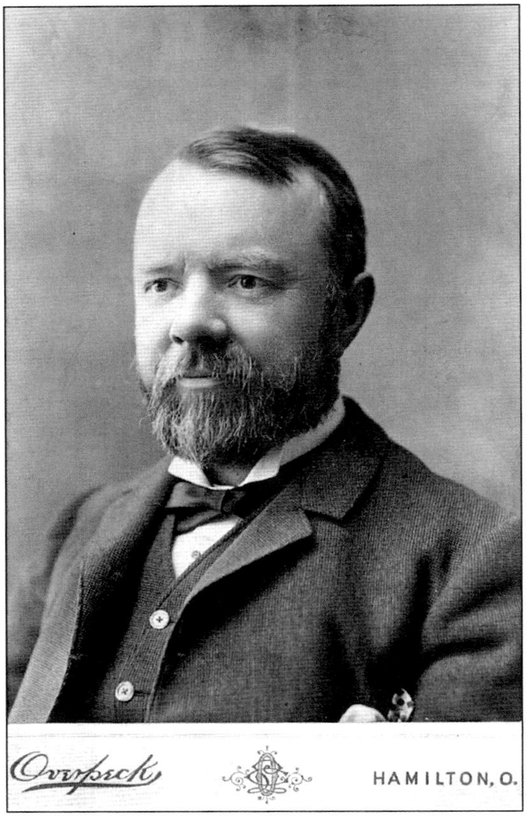

Hamilton's William Ritchie founded the Advance Manufacturing Company, which made gasoline engines. His son Oscar joined him in the business. This photograph, taken by a Hamilton photographer in the early 1900s, showed William dressed in a suit and ready to make a deal. (Courtesy the BCHS.)

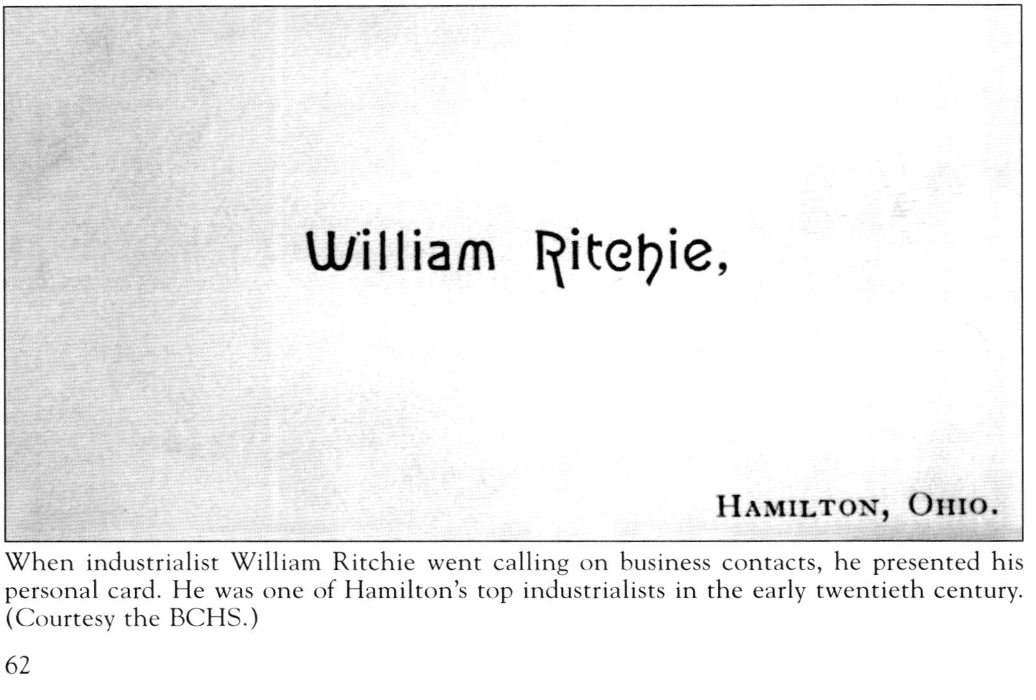
William Ritchie,

HAMILTON, OHIO.

When industrialist William Ritchie went calling on business contacts, he presented his personal card. He was one of Hamilton's top industrialists in the early twentieth century. (Courtesy the BCHS.)

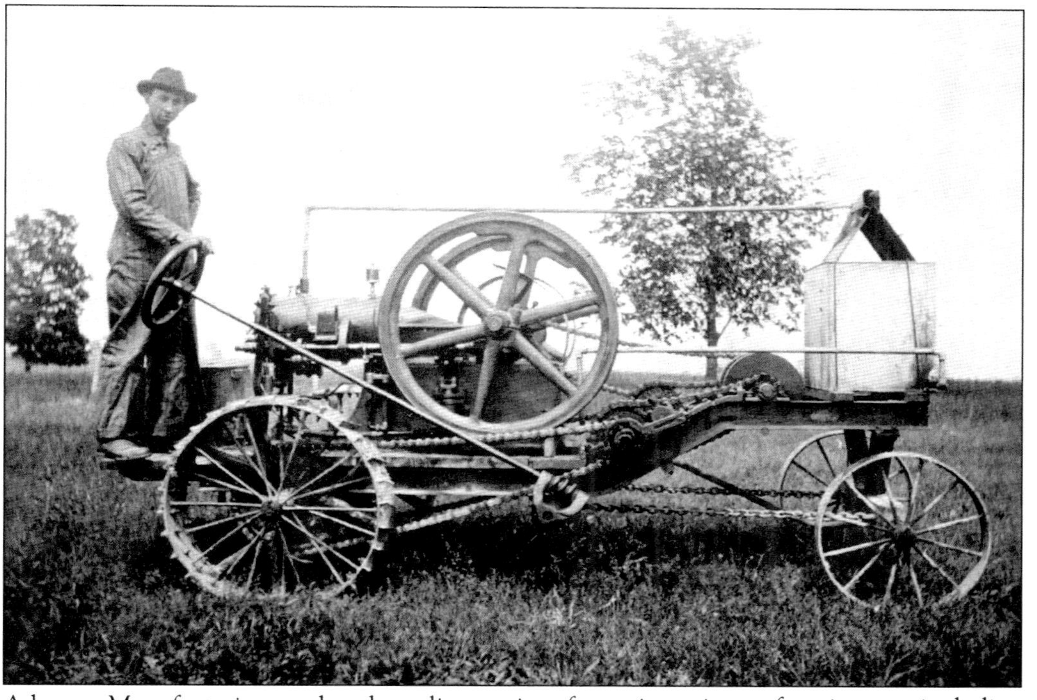

Advance Manufacturing produced gasoline engines for various pieces of equipment, including farm machinery and early road pavers. The man standing on the frame was Oscar Ritchie, the son of company founder William Ritchie. (Courtesy the BCHS.)

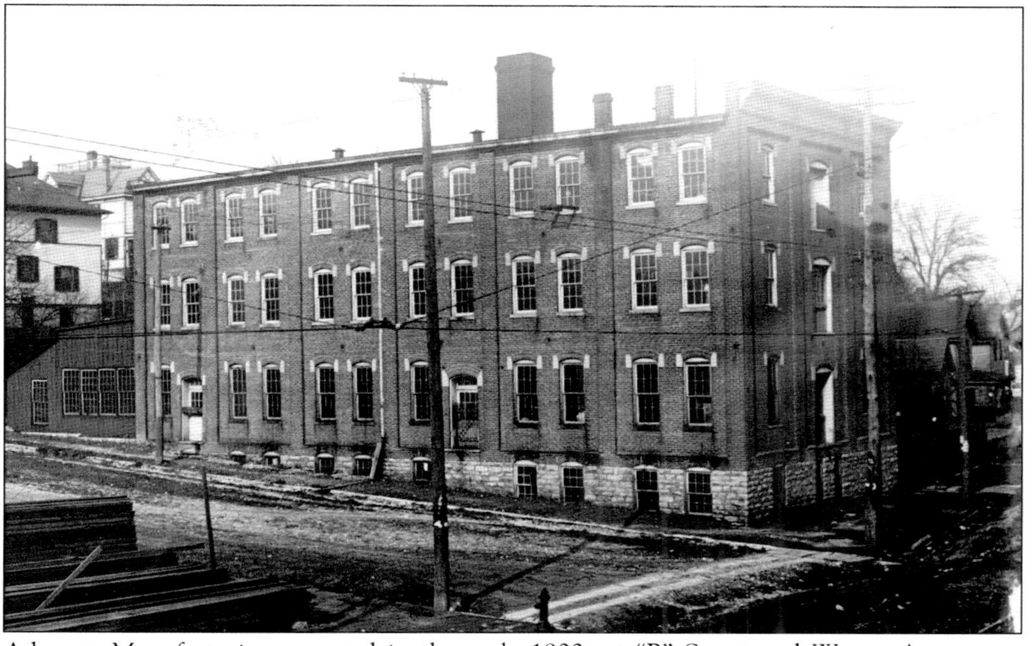

Advance Manufacturing operated in the early 1900s at "B" Street and Wayne Avenue on Hamilton's west side. The building still stands today. (Courtesy the BCHS.)

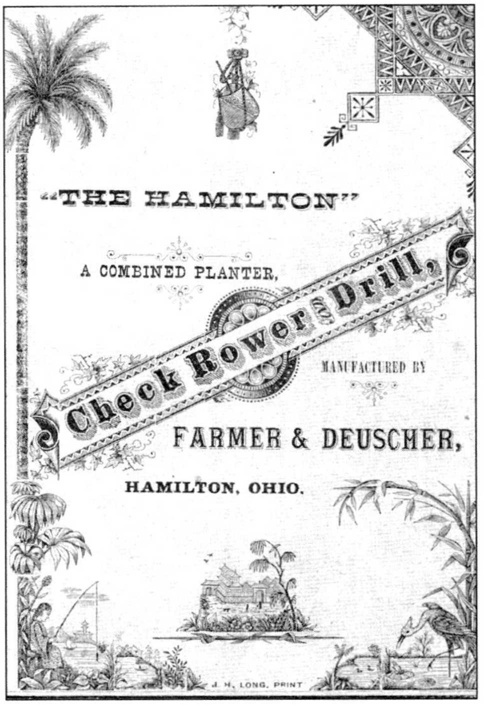

This advertising booklet, published in 1882, showed "The Hamilton," a combined corn planter manufactured by Farmer & Deuscher of Hamilton. The booklet featured testimonials from farmers and discussed a check rower and drill, for use on the farm. (Courtesy the authors.)

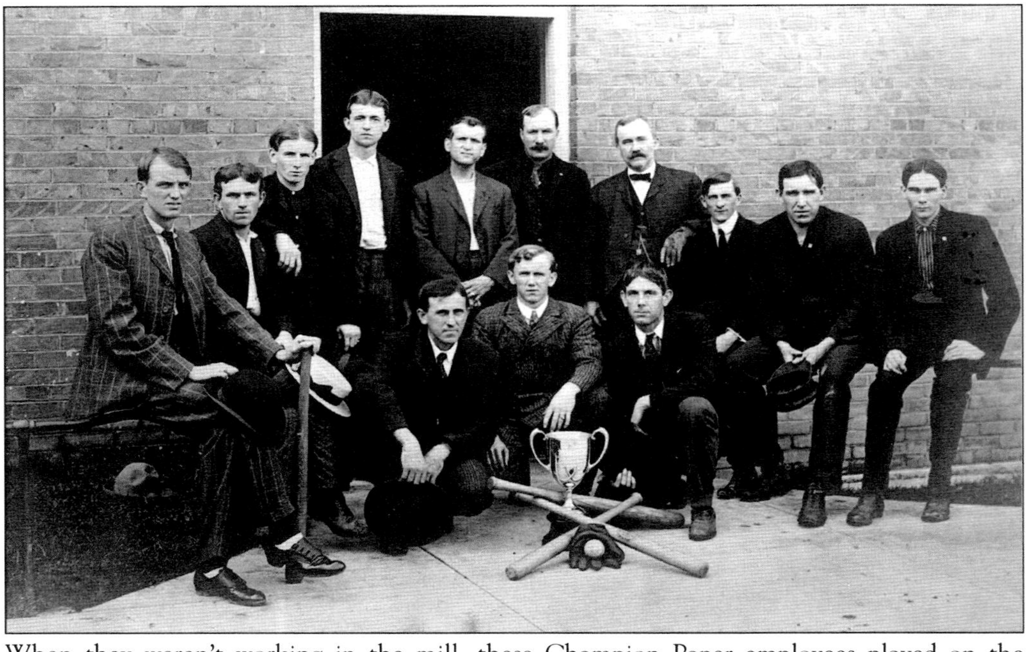

When they weren't working in the mill, these Champion Paper employees played on the company's winning baseball team. From left to right in front they were listed as John Hines, George Nenbrook, and Jack Quantz. In back, they are Walter McClintock, Andy Schuler, Harry Sutton, Harry Garver, William Shuler, Roxy David, James Harris, James Wilson, A.O. Rolfe, and Frank Beckett. (Courtesy the BCHS.)

H. P. DEUSCHER, HAMILTON, OHIO.

OUR

LOD CRUSHER

—IS—

E BEST—because it does better work in ss time than any other implement for the ırpose.

E CHEAPEST—because it is all iron ccepting the frame and will last for generaons.

MANUFACTURED BY

. P. DEUSCHER,

HAMILTON, OHIO.

7 H. P. DEUSCHER, HAMILTON, OHIO.

OUR CLOD CRUSHER

STRONG, SIMPLE and DURABLE.

The most complete Clod Crushing impleme invented. Next to the Reaper it is the mo labor-saving implement on the farm. Read a fe

TESTIMONIALS:

BOWLING GREEN, OHIO.

Every farmer that wants an increase in his cro should be the possessor of "Our Soil Pulverizer."

E. E. FARMER,
Superintendent Wood Co. Infirmary.

PAINESVILLE, OHIO.

The "Clod Crusher" purchased of you this spring h given excellent satisfaction. It is the best impleme for the purpose we have ever used.

STORRS & HARRISON NURSERY CO.

OXFORD, BUTLER COUNTY, OHIO.

I have tested the "Clod Crusher" on my farn Its advantage over a roller is that the flanges on th sections have cutting edges on both sides and are thu able to reduce the clods. I give it my heartiest indorsement.

WALDO F. BROWN.

ROME, OHIO.

It only has to be known to become popular with a intelligent farmers.

JOS. McFARLAND.

DAYTON, OHIO.

We are proud of "Our Clod Crusher" and are showin it to all of our customers.

THE HEIKES NURSERIES CO.

RISING SUN, IND.

The "Clod Crusher" does its work well.

J. C. TURNER.

The H.P. Deuscher Company served farmers throughout Ohio, Indiana, and the rest of the nation at the turn of the twentieth century. Testimonials came from farmers throughout the Midwest. The company said in this advertisement, "Our Clod Crusher is the cheapest because it is all iron excepting the frame and will last for generations." (Courtesy the authors.)

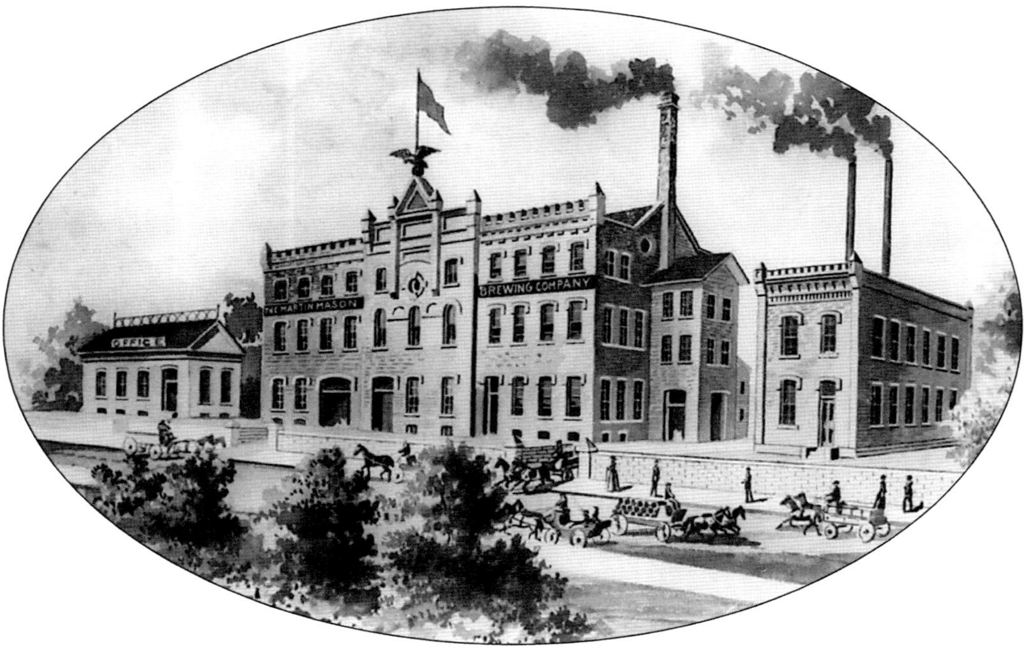

Daniel Beck and John Koeninger founded a brewery in 1852. The next year, fire destroyed their plant on South "C" Street in Rossville. In 1869, Henry Eger of White Oak in Hamilton County bought the firm. Martin Mason became a partner years later and incorporated the business under his name in 1896. At its peak, Martin Mason Brewing could produce 20,000 barrels of Mason's Beer annually. (Courtesy the authors.)

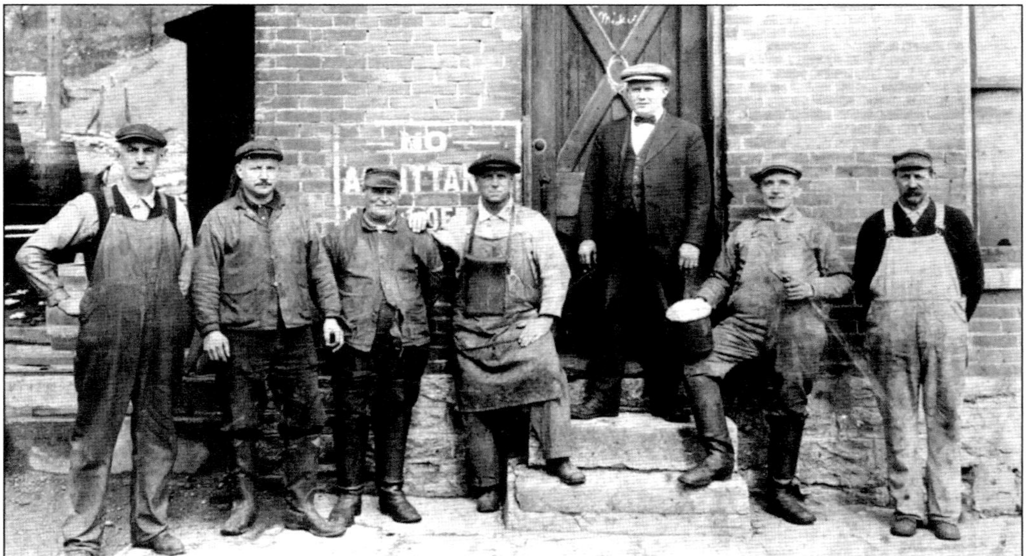

In the early 1920s, despite Prohibition, Martin Mason was still hanging on. This period photograph shows seven workers, including Carl Hally, second from the left; Wilbur Buehl, fourth from the left; and Karl Windgreiber, the seventh. The other men were unidentified. (Courtesy the BCHS.)

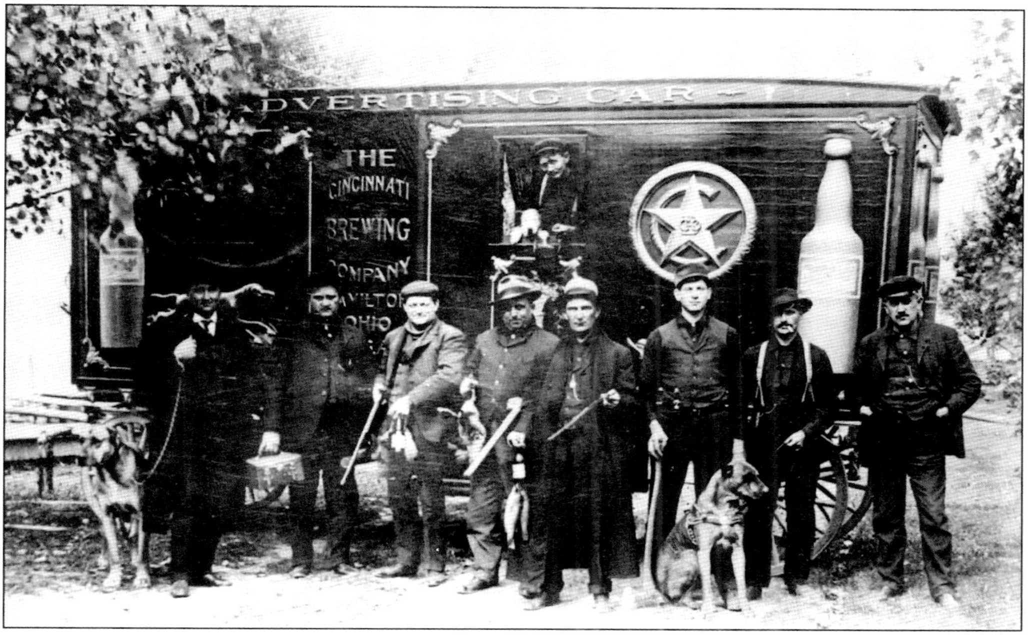

Another Hamilton brewery, the Cincinnati Brewing Company, used a wooden advertising car to promote its products. These unidentified sportsmen and company employees were shown with the car in the early 1900s. (Courtesy the BCHS.)

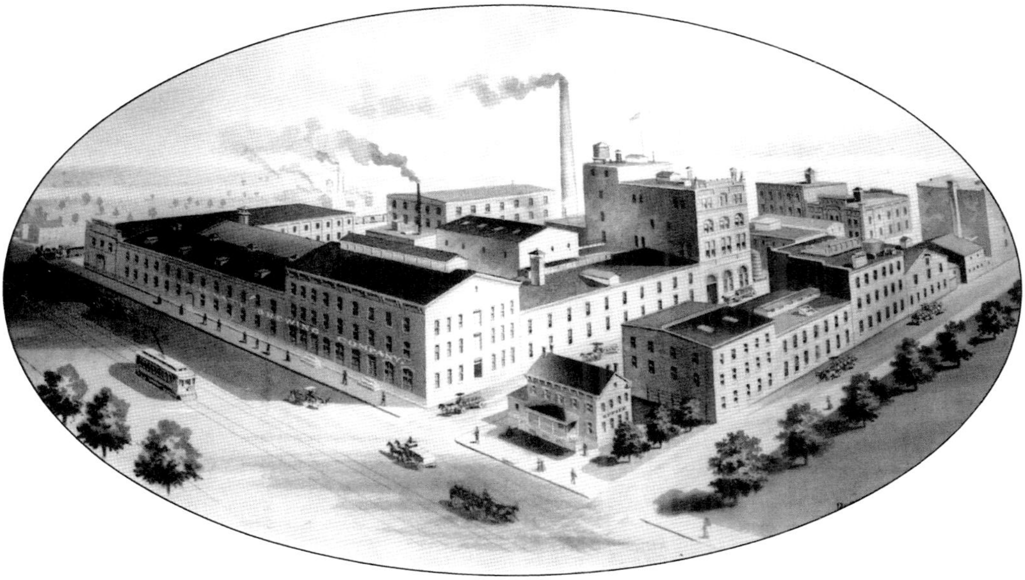

The Cincinnati Brewing Company stood on South Front Street, next to Cincinnati & Indianapolis Railroad tracks. Peter Schwab, a native of Bavaria, founded the company in 1879. He sold beer called Just Plain Old Uncle Peter's. Hamilton's first artificial ice plant opened at the company in 1890. Schwab used the ice in the brewery and also sold ice to the public. This picture dates to c. 1914. (Courtesy the authors.)

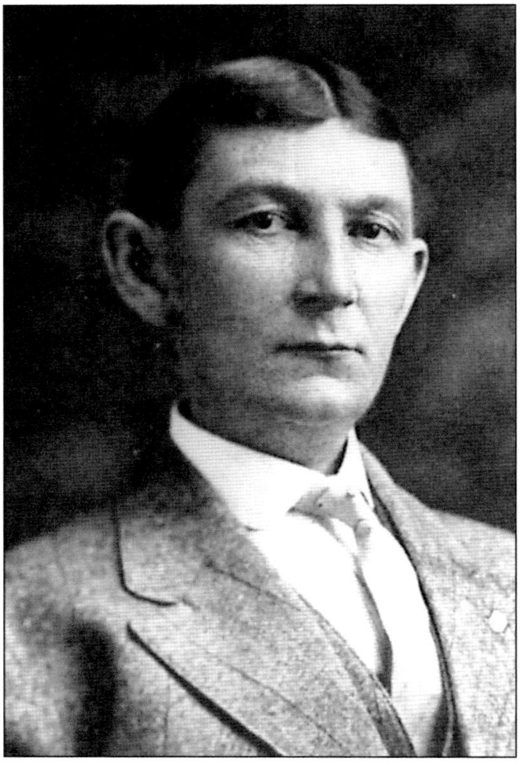

Peter E. Schwab, the son of the German-American entrepreneur Peter Schwab, followed his father as president of the Cincinnati Brewing Company. This photograph was taken in 1914. (Courtesy the authors.)

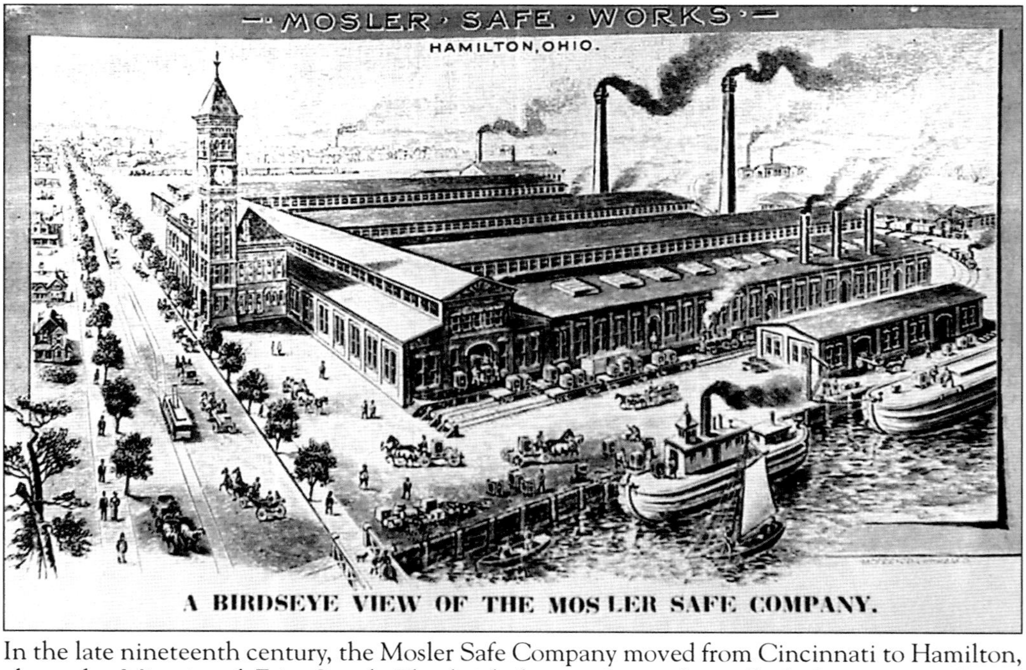

In the late nineteenth century, the Mosler Safe Company moved from Cincinnati to Hamilton, along the Miami and Erie Canal. The brick factory featured a tall clock tower on Grand Boulevard. (Courtesy the authors.)

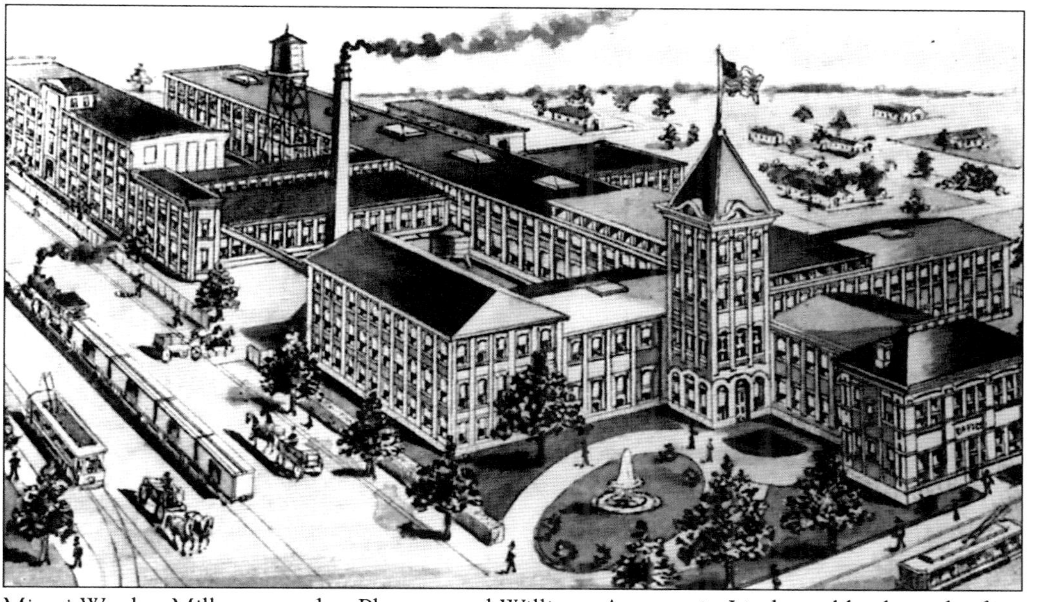

Miami Woolen Mills operated at Pleasant and Williams Avenues in Lindenwald, where the firm was a major employer. In the 1860s, the Asa Shuler and J.W. Benninghofen factory used Ohio wool to make items for Hamilton's papermaking machines. By the early 1900s, the company was making blankets and Indian shawls. Generations of neighborhood residents worked there. Although the mill closed decades ago, the building is still used. (Courtesy the BCHS.)

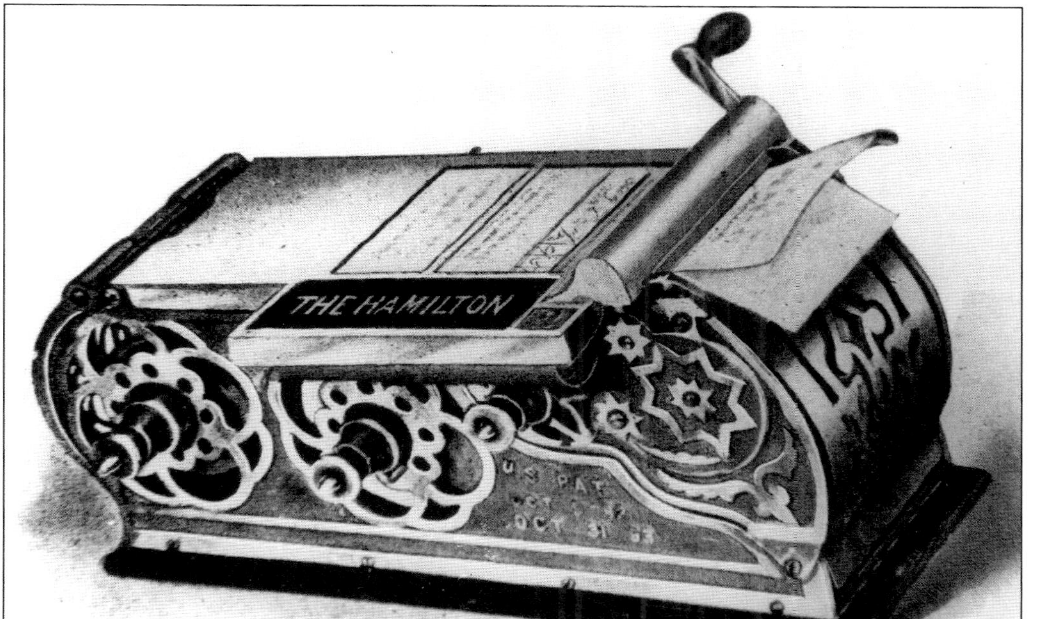

The Hamilton Autographic Register Company in Lindenwald built "The Hamilton," a machine that made up customers' bills for stores—a major achievement in the early 1900s. This rendering is from 1914. The old brick Autographic building still stands. (Courtesy the authors.)

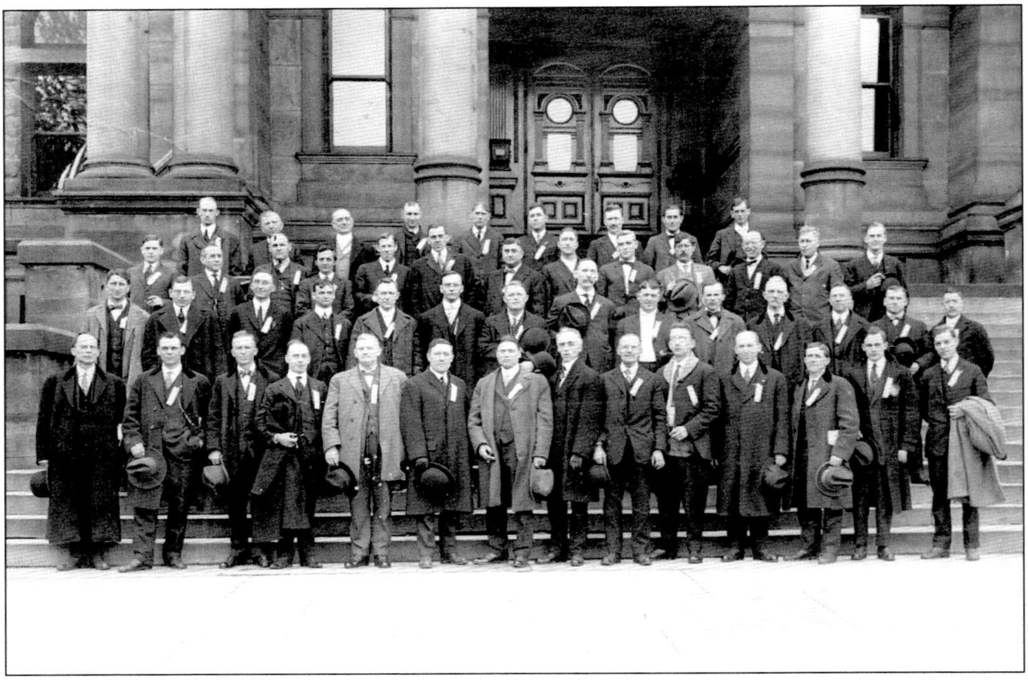

On May 6, 1917, the Ohio State Metal Trades Council met in Hamilton and posed in front of the Butler County Courthouse. Hamilton, a major industrial center in the region, was a logical choice for the meeting site. (Courtesy the BCHS.)

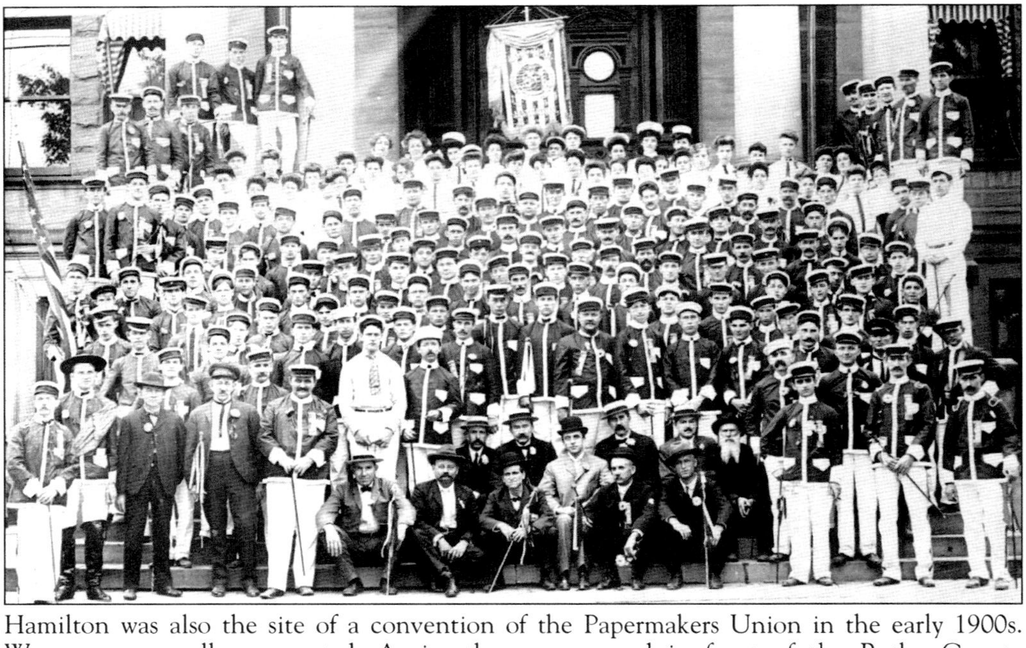

Hamilton was also the site of a convention of the Papermakers Union in the early 1900s. Women were well represented. Again, the group posed in front of the Butler County Courthouse. (Courtesy the BCHS.)

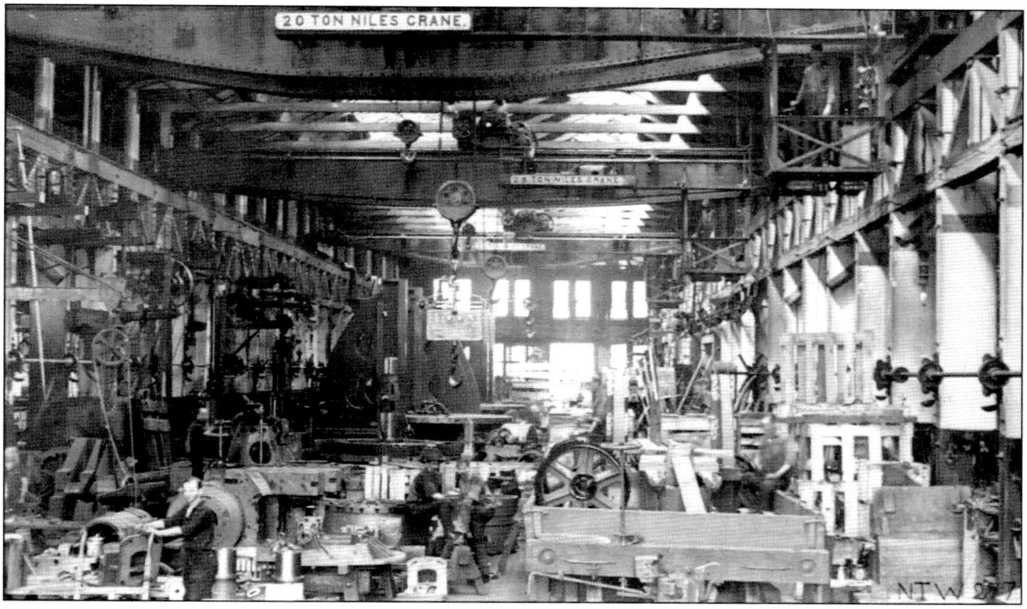

This photograph from the early 1900s showed the Niles Tool Works' "20 Ton Niles Crane," which ran across the top of the company's massive brick factory in north Hamilton. The building, with the faded words "Niles Tool," still stands. The firm manufactured machine tools. (Courtesy the BCHS.)

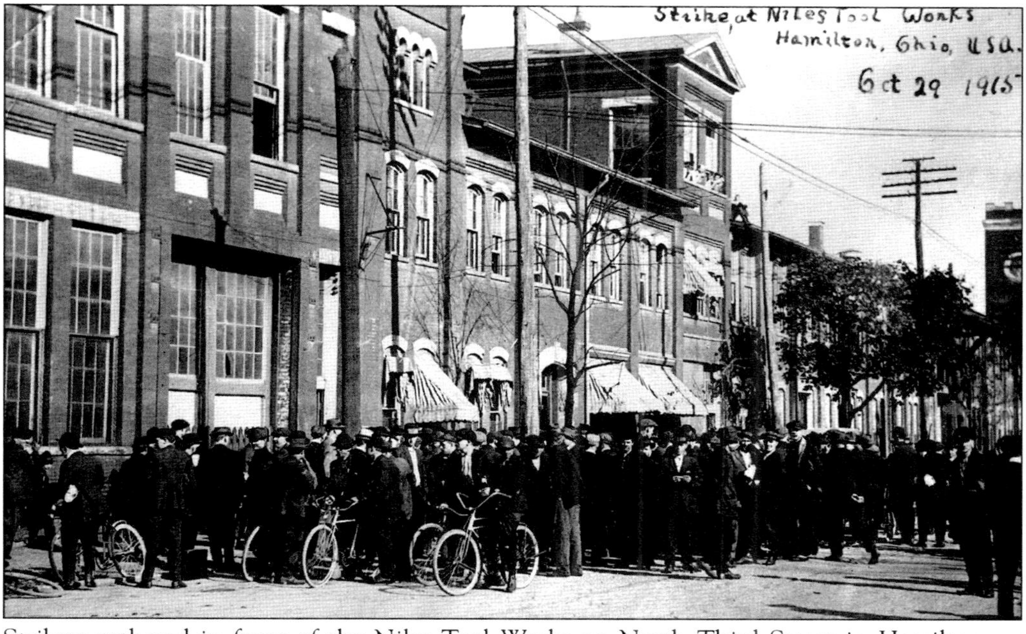

Strikers gathered in front of the Niles Tool Works on North Third Street in Hamilton on October 29, 1915. Niles was a major Hamilton industry and Hamilton a microcosm of growing American industrial might. With the proliferation of labor unions and an increased demand for manufactured goods in the twentieth century, workers began to demand better treatment, working conditions, and pay. (Courtesy the BCHS.)

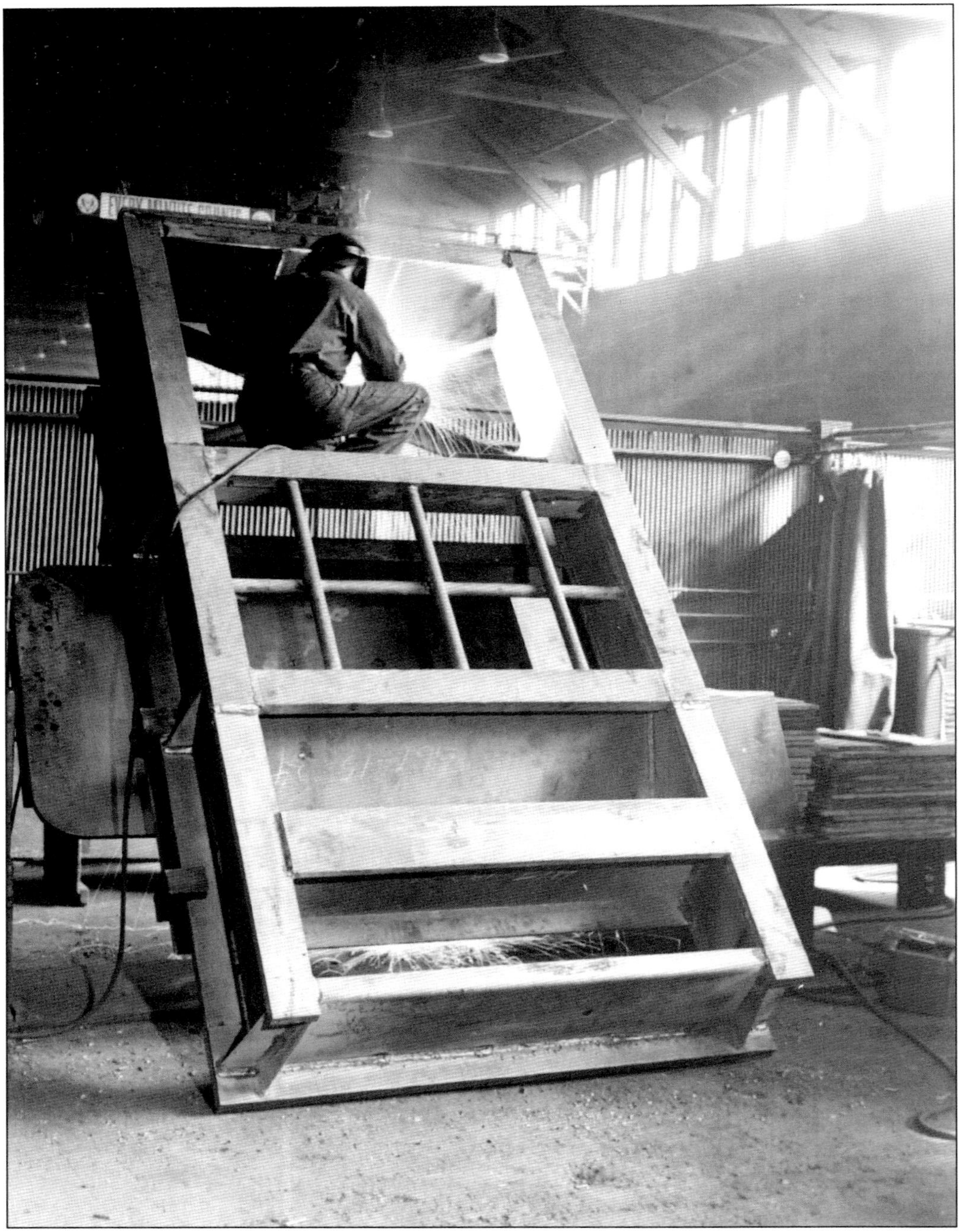

In this photograph taken during World War II, a Mosler Safe Company worker welded a piece that would be used on a military escort ship. Switching from safe and vault door manufacturing to military manufacturing, Mosler became a key industry for Hamilton during the war. The old brick Mosler factory was torn down in 2004 to make room for development on State Route 4 and Grand Boulevard. (Courtesy the BCHS.)

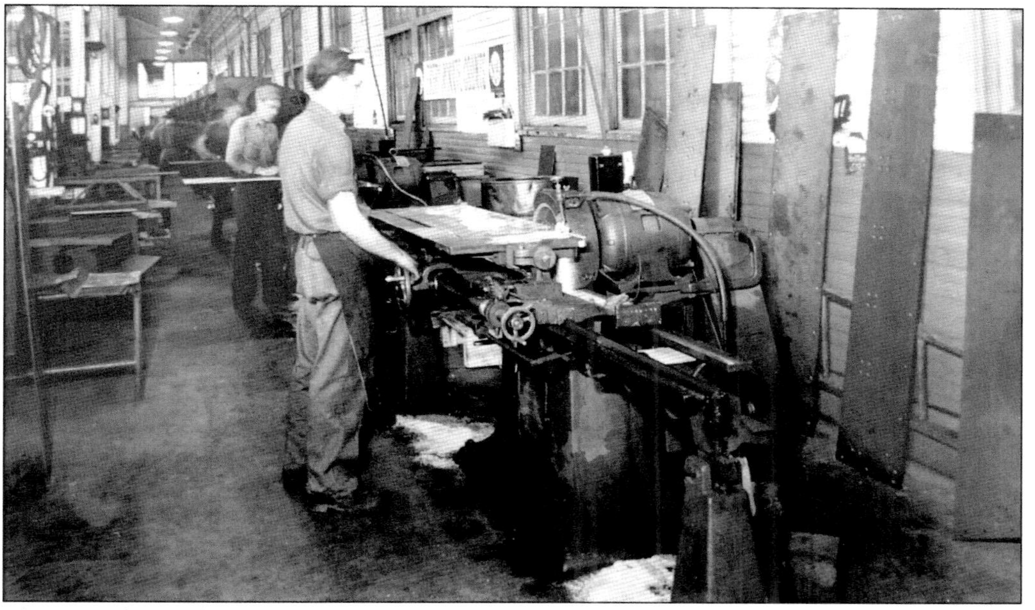

Three Mosler workers worked on a knife grinder for armor plating during World War II. The sign on the wall read, "Every minute counts." A poster, partially covered by a piece of metal, showed a soldier and the caption, "He's a fighting fool," meaning that U.S. soldiers wouldn't stop until the job was done. (Courtesy the BCHS.)

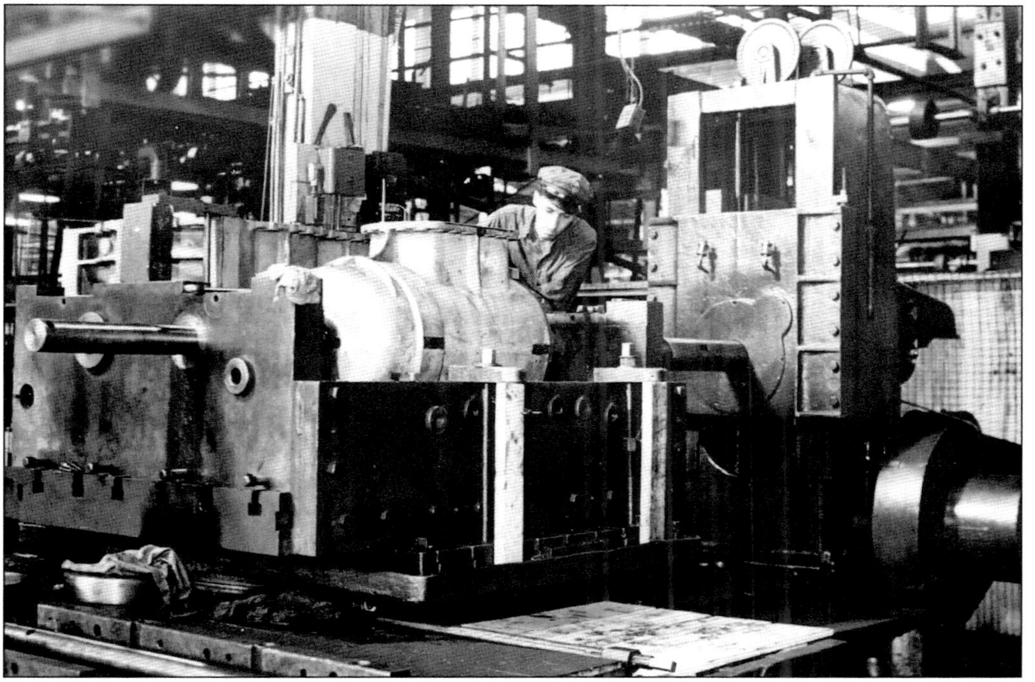

As scores of young men left Hamilton for military duty in World War II, patriotism ran high in the home and in the workplace. Mosler made submarine diesel engine parts as well as mounts for 37mm guns for various military vehicles. (Courtesy the BCHS.)

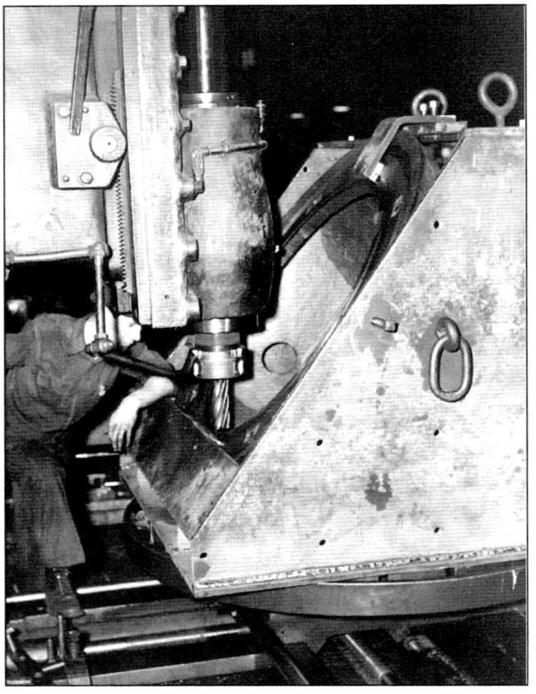

A Mosler worker drilled holes for a gun emplacement during World War II. In those days, the factory that once produced safes and vault doors was retooled for war production. Public and private energies were all focused on winning the war. (Courtesy the BCHS.)

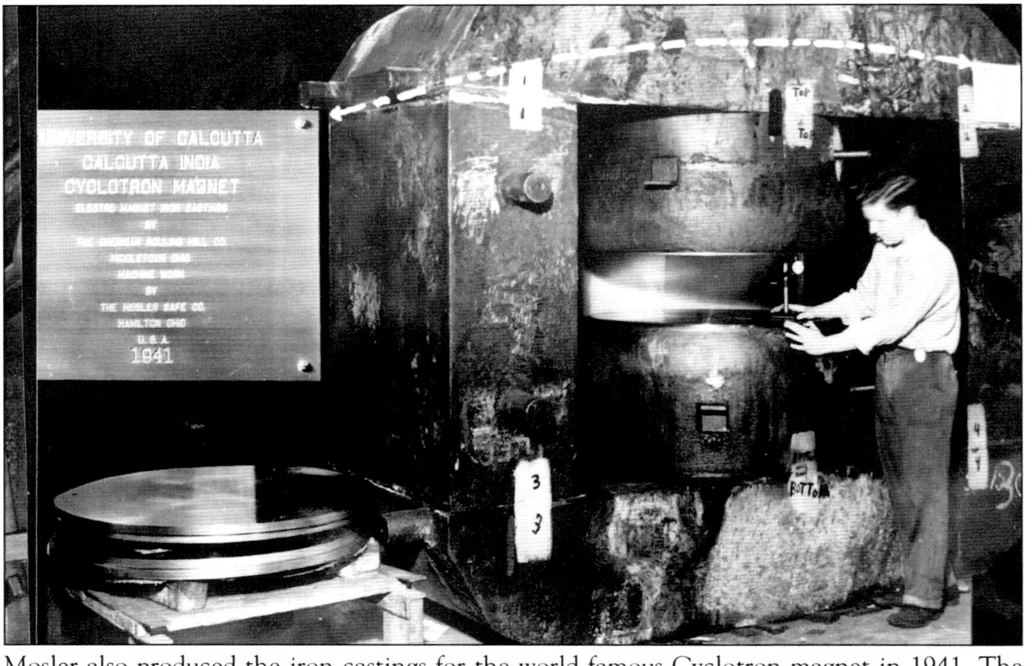

Mosler also produced the iron castings for the world-famous Cyclotron magnet in 1941. The magnet was used in scientific experiments at the University of Calcutta and later displayed at the Massachusetts Institute of Technology, the University of Minnesota, Ohio State University, and the Carnegie Institute. (Courtesy the BCHS.)

Seven

FLOODS

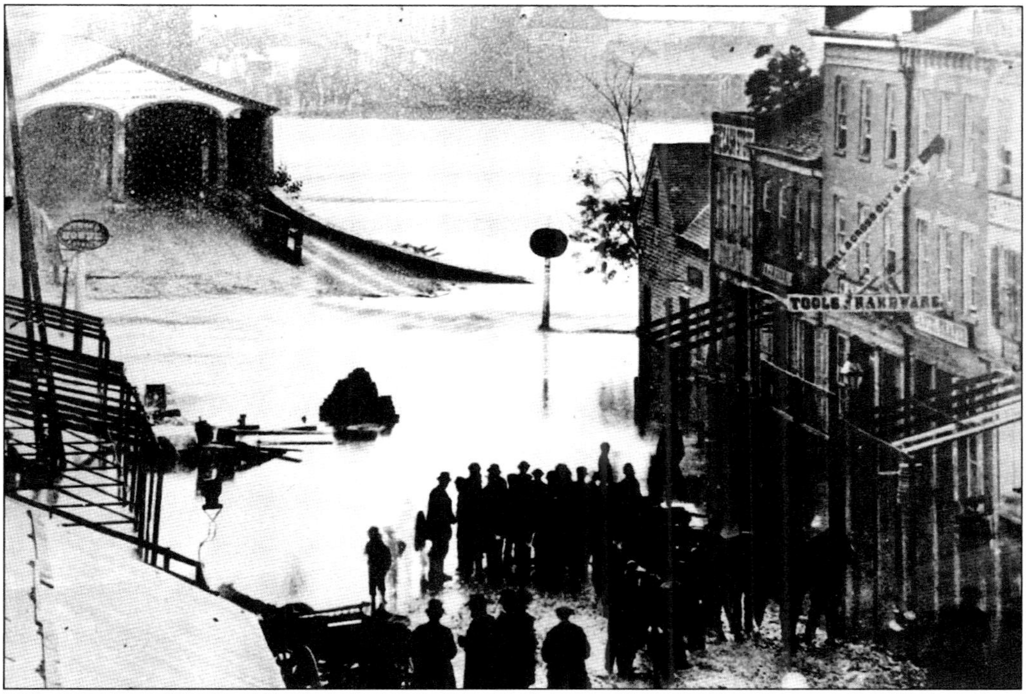

Hamilton's first bridge, at High and Main Streets, is ready to wash away in September of 1866. This bridge, with 17 windows and Venetian blinds, was replaced by a suspension bridge in 1867. It was succeeded by a steel truss bridge *c.* 1895. The Flood of 1913 washed it away. Since then, Hamilton has suffered no major flooding. (Courtesy the BCHS.)

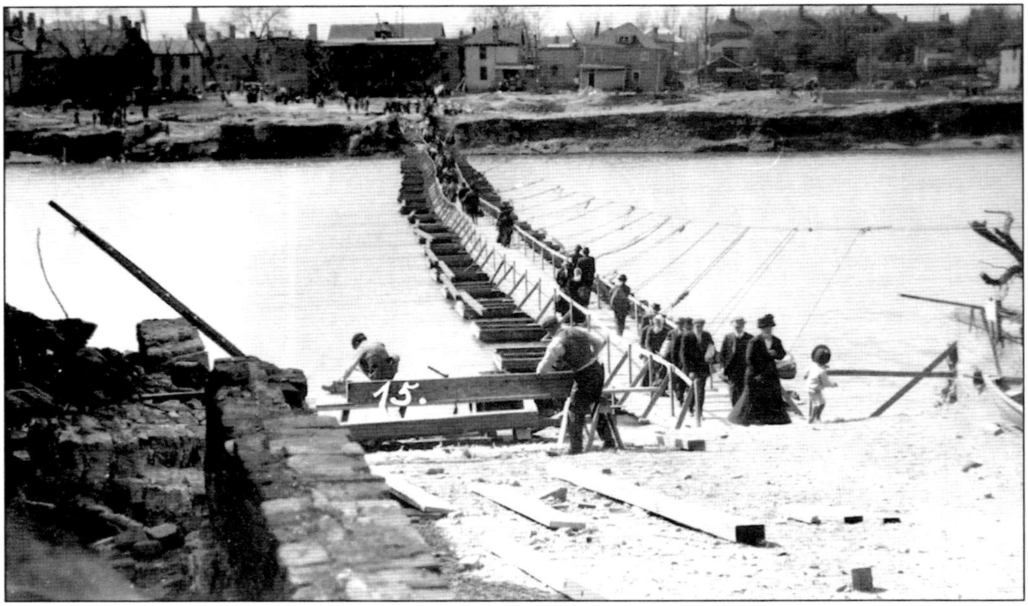

Notations on the back of this photograph date it to a flood in 1898, although it could be 1913 or earlier. People cross a pontoon bridge that links the east and west sides of the river. When such events occurred, the city was forced to operate while being cut in half. It strained city services as well as employers. The walk must have been difficult. (Courtesy the BCHS.)

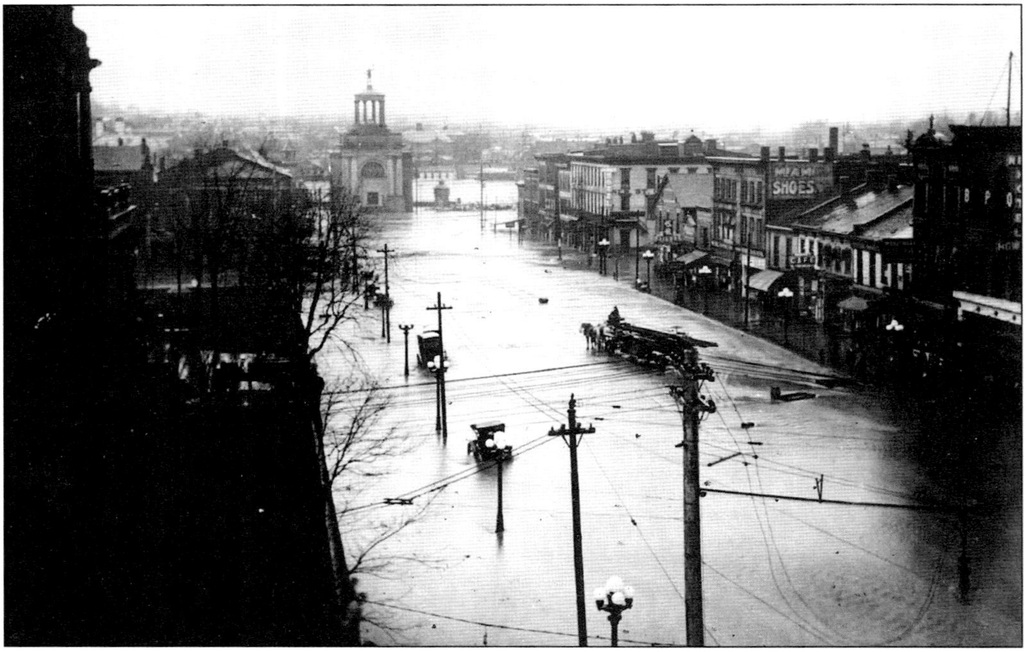

No one who lived through Hamilton's Flood of March 1913 ever forgot it. Here, a photographer aimed at a gloomy sight—the Butler County Courthouse, looking west toward the Memorial Building and a flooded High Street. By then, the river had crested, and its waters had receded to more manageable levels. Horses could finally pull a wagon down High. (Courtesy the BCHS.)

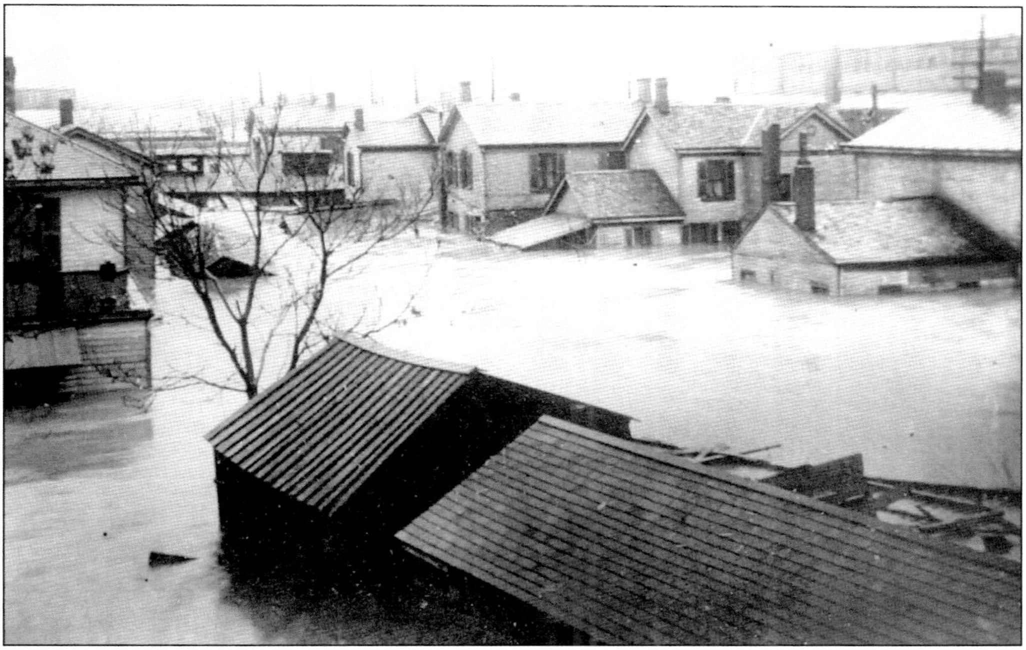

The rains came on Tuesday morning, March 25, 1913, and continued for days. Lindenwald and East Hamilton were not seriously affected. In this picture, rising water forced residents to the second floors, probably on the north side of town. (Courtesy the BCHS.)

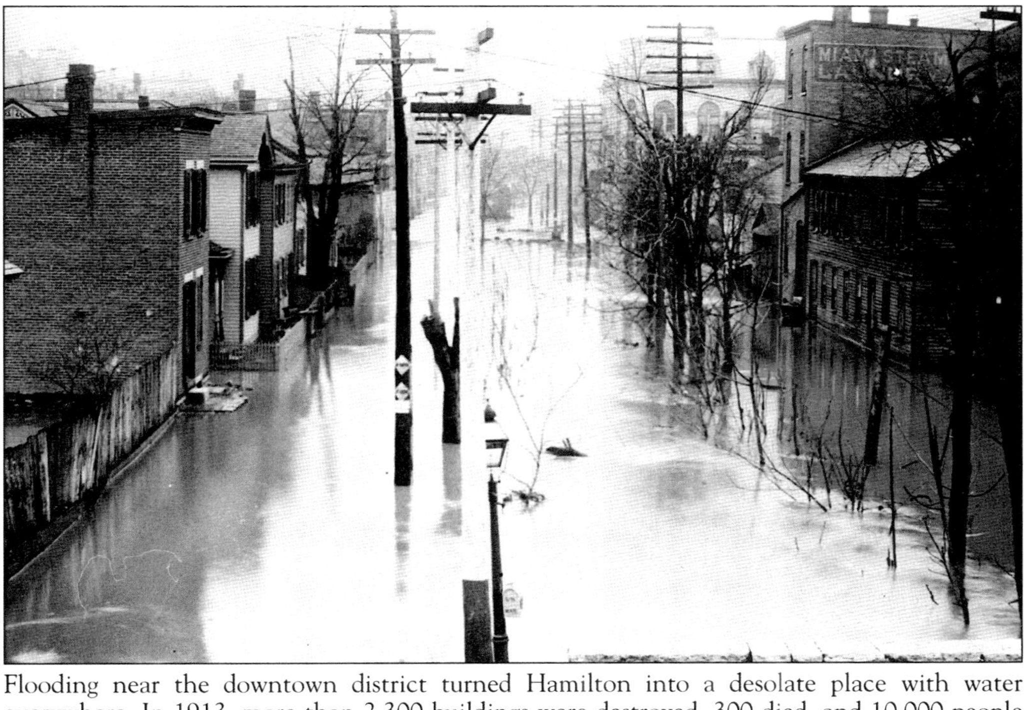

Flooding near the downtown district turned Hamilton into a desolate place with water everywhere. In 1913, more than 2,300 buildings were destroyed, 300 died, and 10,000 people were forced out of their homes. (Courtesy the BCHS.)

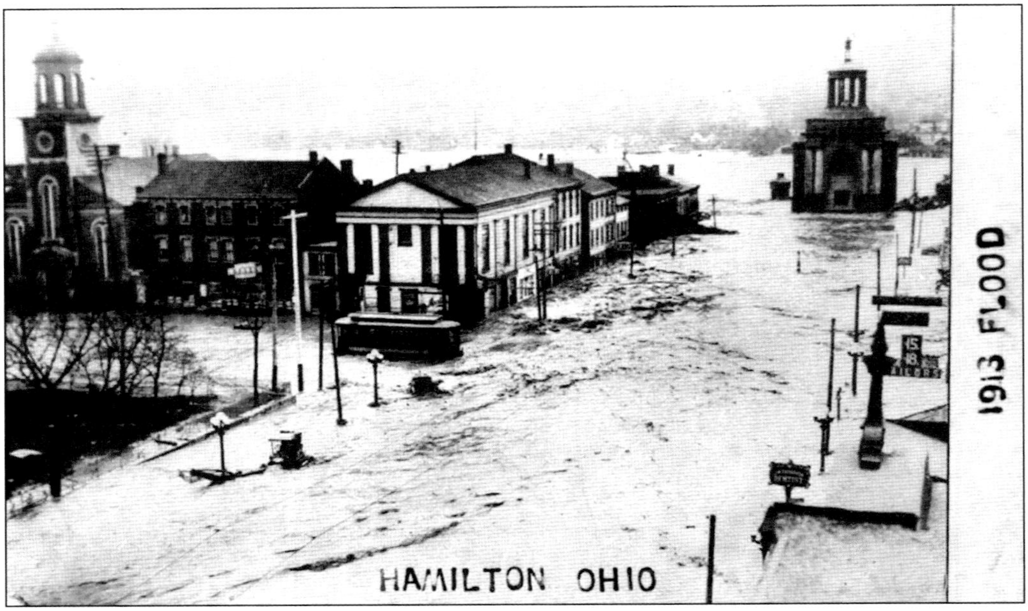

Beyond the Memorial Building on the far right of this picture, the angry Great Miami rose so high that it couldn't be distinguished from the water flowing through High and Front Streets in downtown Hamilton during the height of the 1913 Flood. (Courtesy the BCHS.)

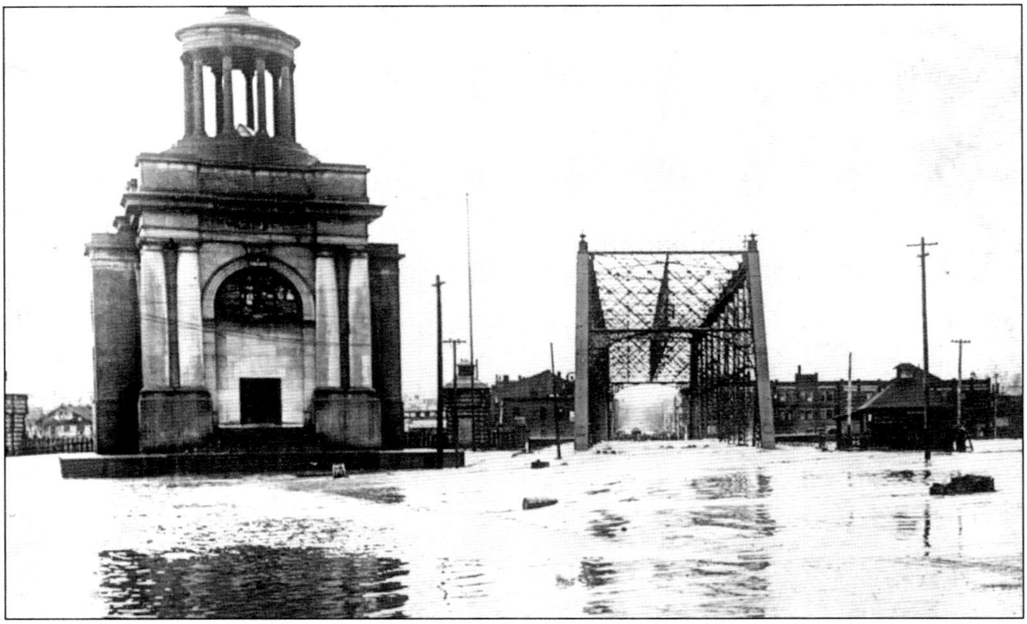

River water rose over the deck of the iron High and Main Street Bridge, which linked downtown Hamilton with the Rossville neighborhood. (Courtesy the authors.)

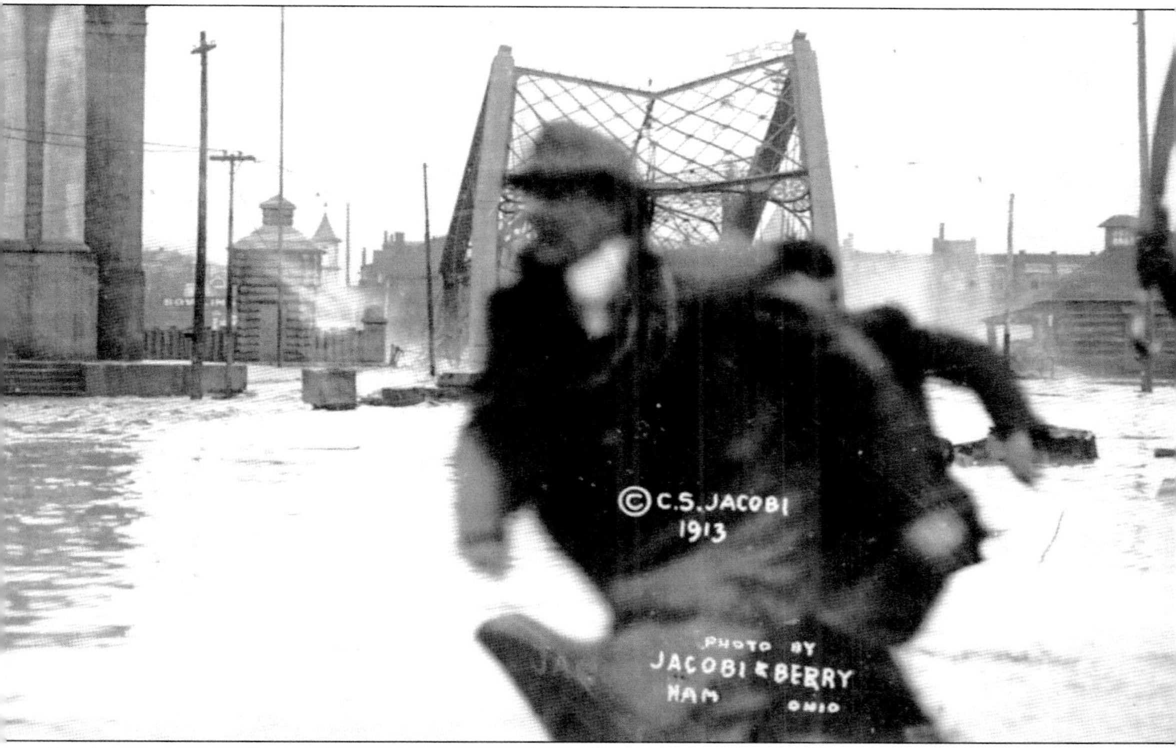

In this image, as the High-Main Street Bridge collapsed, two men ran to avoid being sucked into the swirling waters. Photographer C.S. Jacobi and other photographers roamed the bleak city all week looking for news shots. Meanwhile, the river claimed the Black Street Bridge to the north and the Columbia and the CH&I Railroad Bridge to the south. Bridge losses alone totaled $500,000. (Courtesy the authors.)

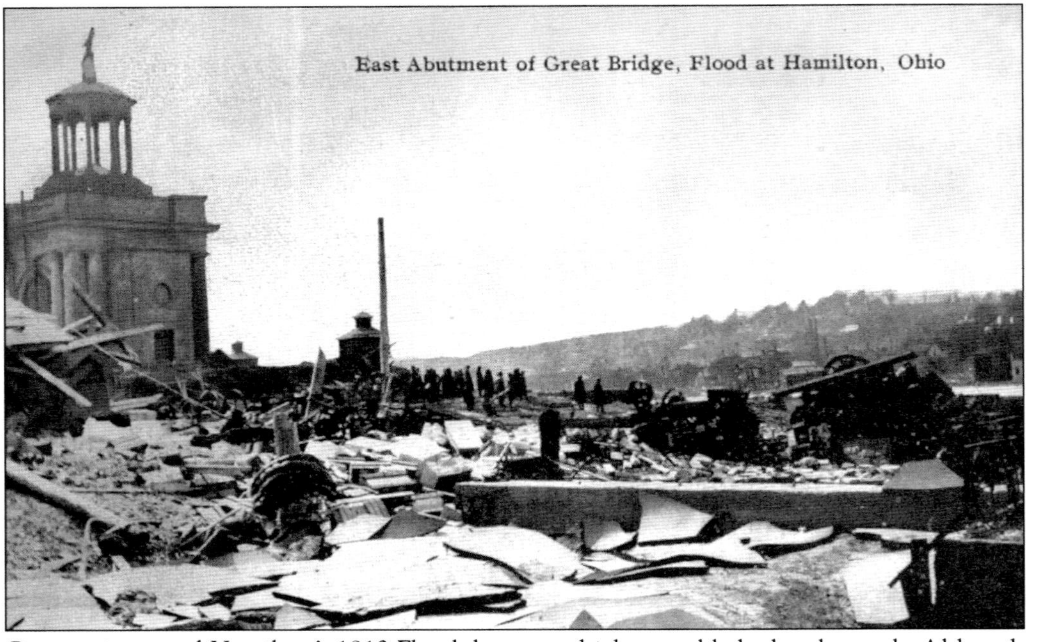

Citizens inspected Hamilton's 1913 Flood damage, which resembled a bomb attack. Although located at the flood's ground zero, the Soldiers, Sailors and Pioneers Monument and its sandstone blockhouses were spared from destruction. Some people in the city called it a miracle. The Flood of March 1913 was the largest disaster to ever strike the city. Heavy rainfall created what has been described as "two raging rivers" rushing through the downtown area. Streets resembled canals. (Courtesy the authors.)

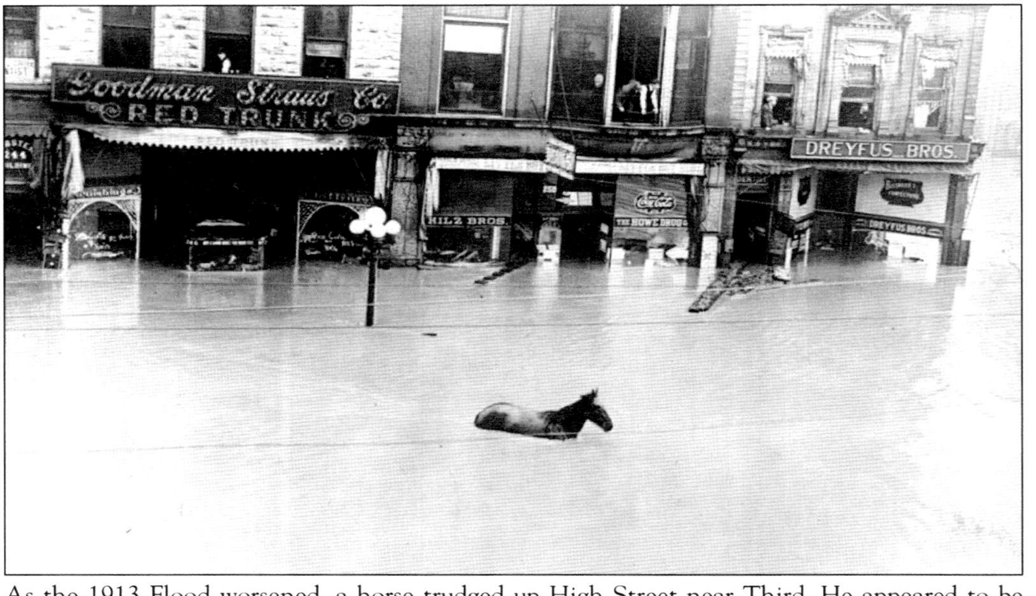

As the 1913 Flood worsened, a horse trudged up High Street near Third. He appeared to be swimming. People watched him from second-floor apartments. This part of downtown received between seven and 12 feet of water, and dozens of horses drowned. At a few places closer to the river, the water stood at nearly 24 feet. (Courtesy the authors.)

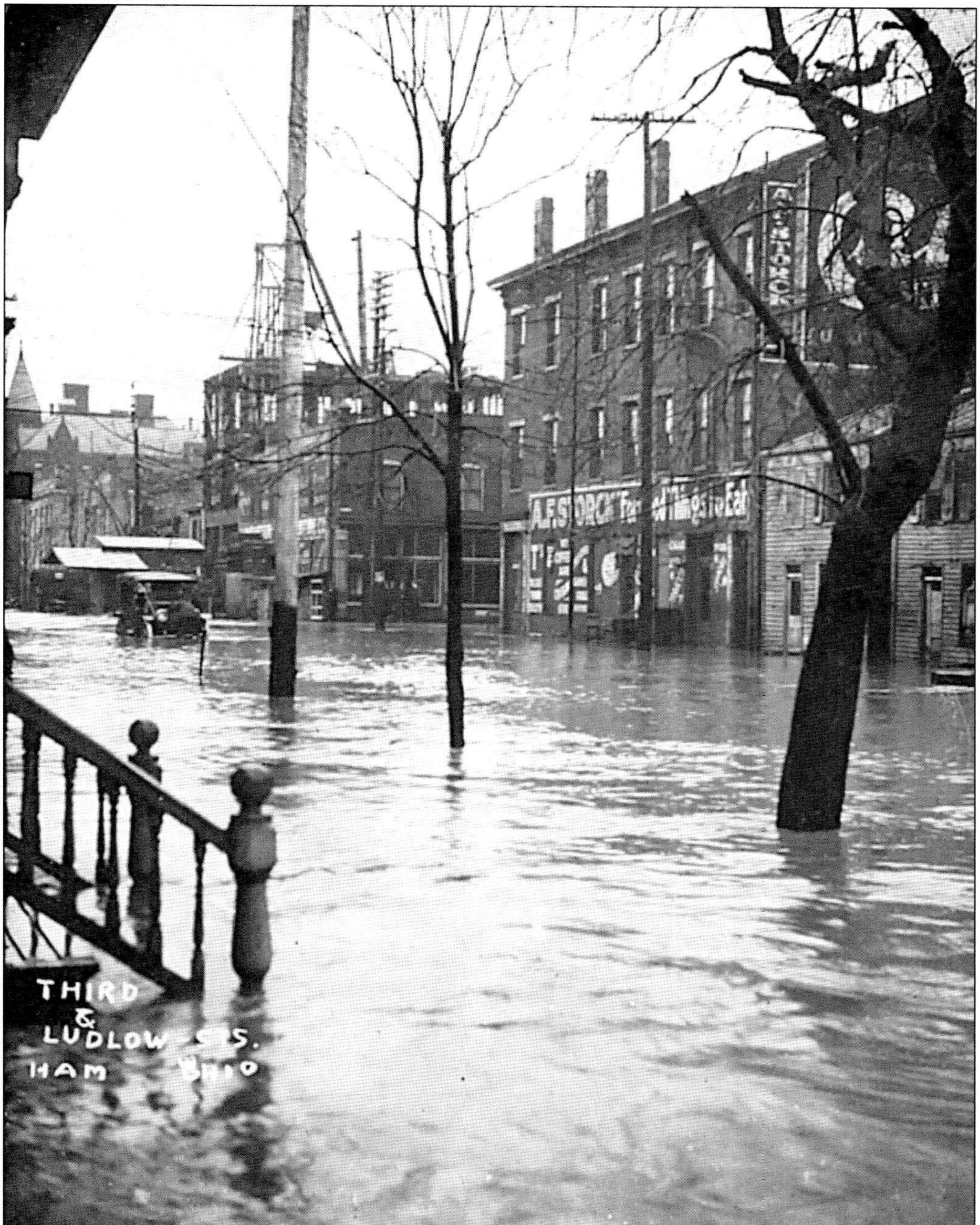

As waters rose during the 1913 Flood, the flood waters entered businesses at Third and Ludlow Streets. To the left, an automobile tried to navigate through the intersection. A few days after this photograph was taken, driving was impossible downtown. (Courtesy the BCHS.)

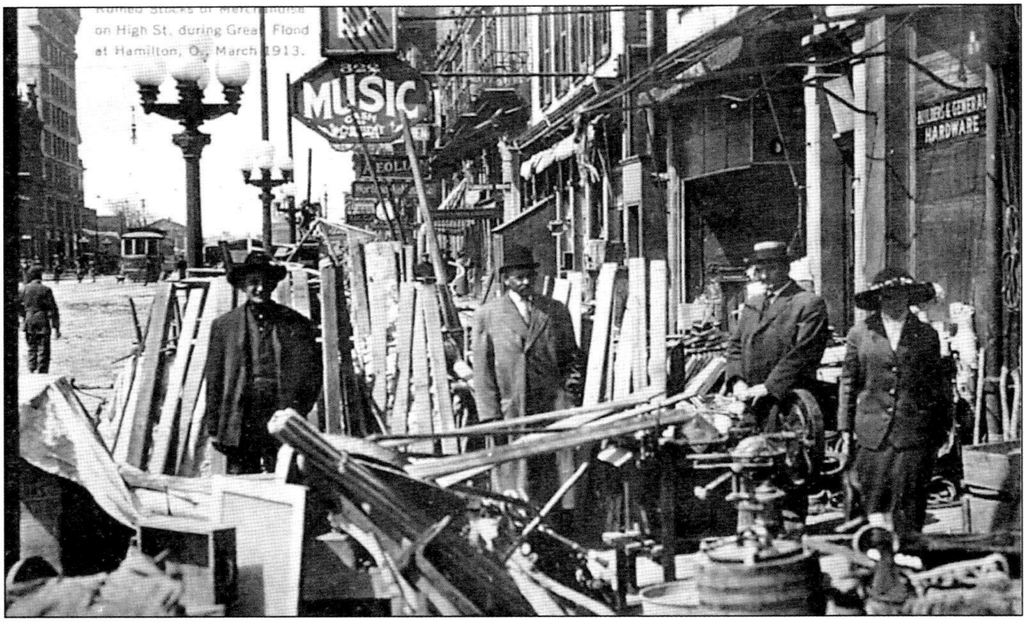

Citizens stood near ruined merchandise on High Street's 300 block, after the Flood of March 1913. A short time earlier, the street was covered with high water. Over three days, between 9 and 11 inches of rain fell in the area. In only 48 hours, the Great Miami rose from 4.8 feet to a record 34.6 feet. (Courtesy the authors.)

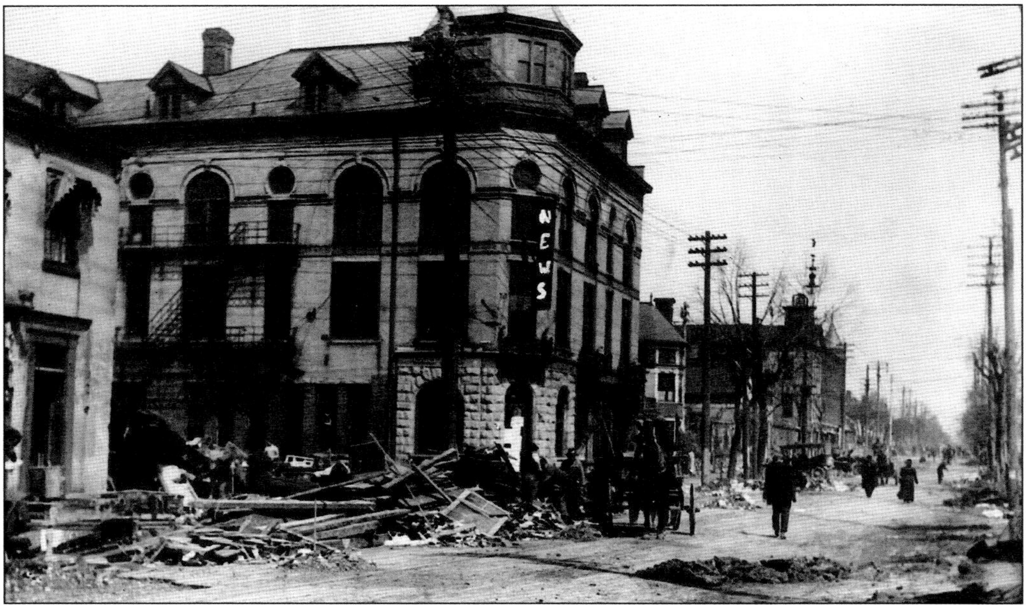

The cleanup continued around the *Daily Republican News* offices on the northwest corner of Third and Market Streets in downtown Hamilton. Except for one edition on March 26, the newspaper managed to publish an edition every day after the March 25 flood. Stranded printers worked on a manual press on the second floor. Water came within a foot of them. (Courtesy the BCHS.)

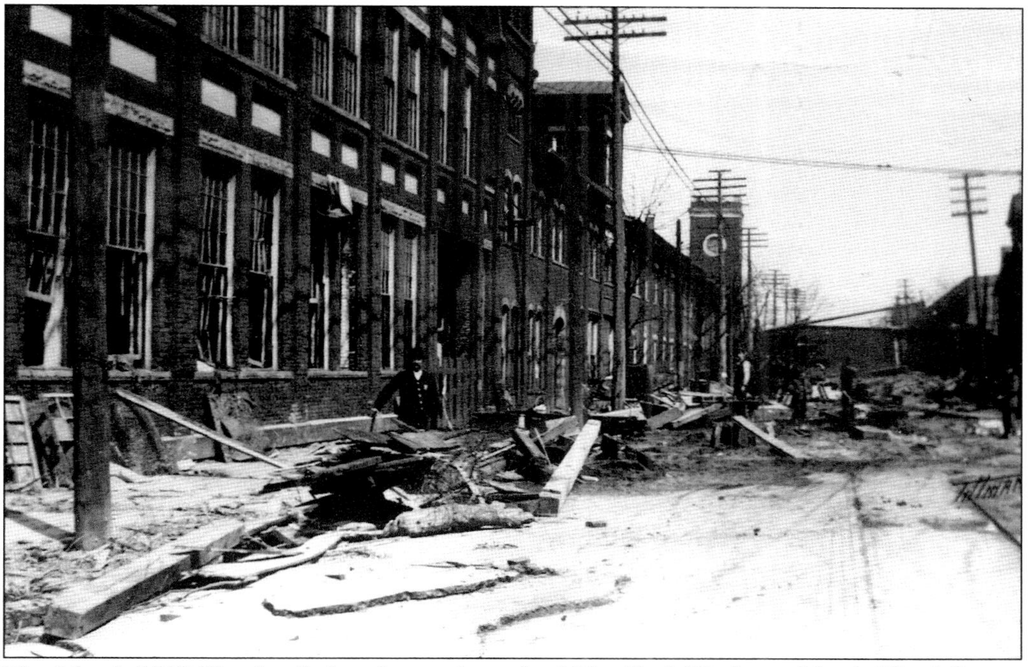

The March 1913 Flood rolled as far north as the Niles Tool Works on North Third Street, damaging the factory. This photograph was taken during the cleanup. (Courtesy the BCHS.)

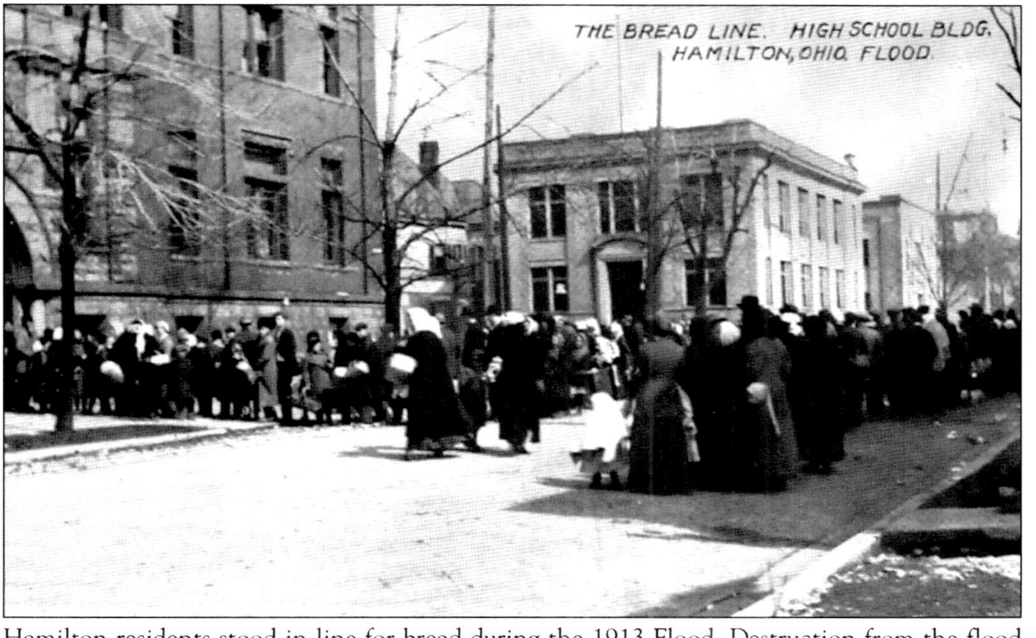

Hamilton residents stood in line for bread during the 1913 Flood. Destruction from the flood left thousands of people without food and water for days. It took months for the city to return to normal. Some people were so emotionally and financially devastated by the flood that they never fully recovered. Some businesses closed permanently. It remains the largest disaster to ever strike Hamilton. (Courtesy the authors.)

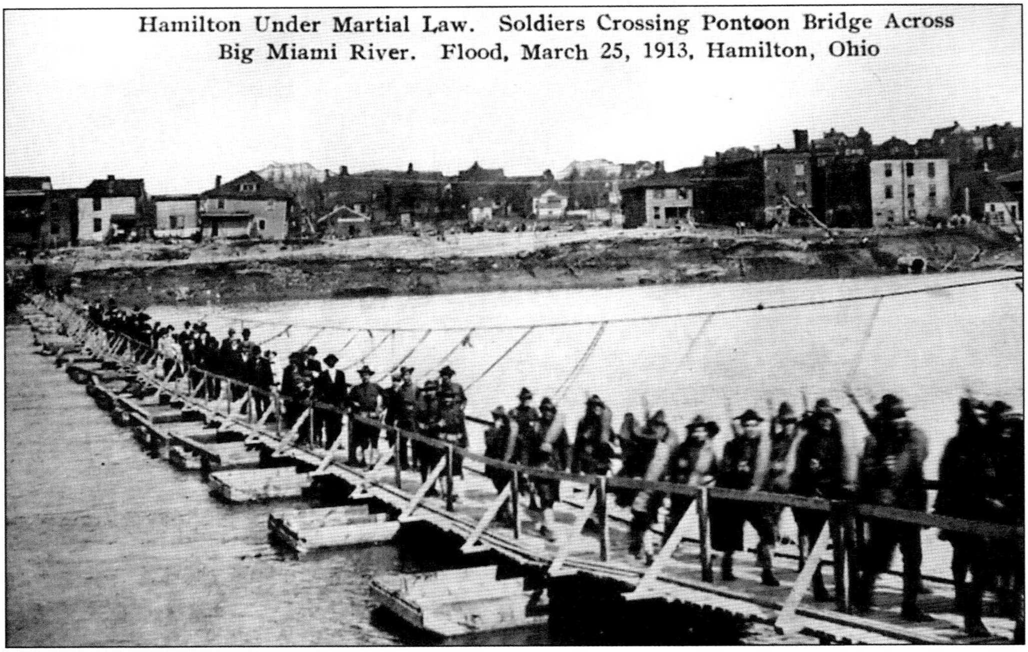

Authorities built a pontoon bridge to connect downtown Hamilton with its Rossville neighborhood on the west side. Supplies had to be carried across the river by hand. Under martial law, the city depended on soldiers to help victims, protect property, clean up, and assist in any way needed. (Courtesy the authors.)

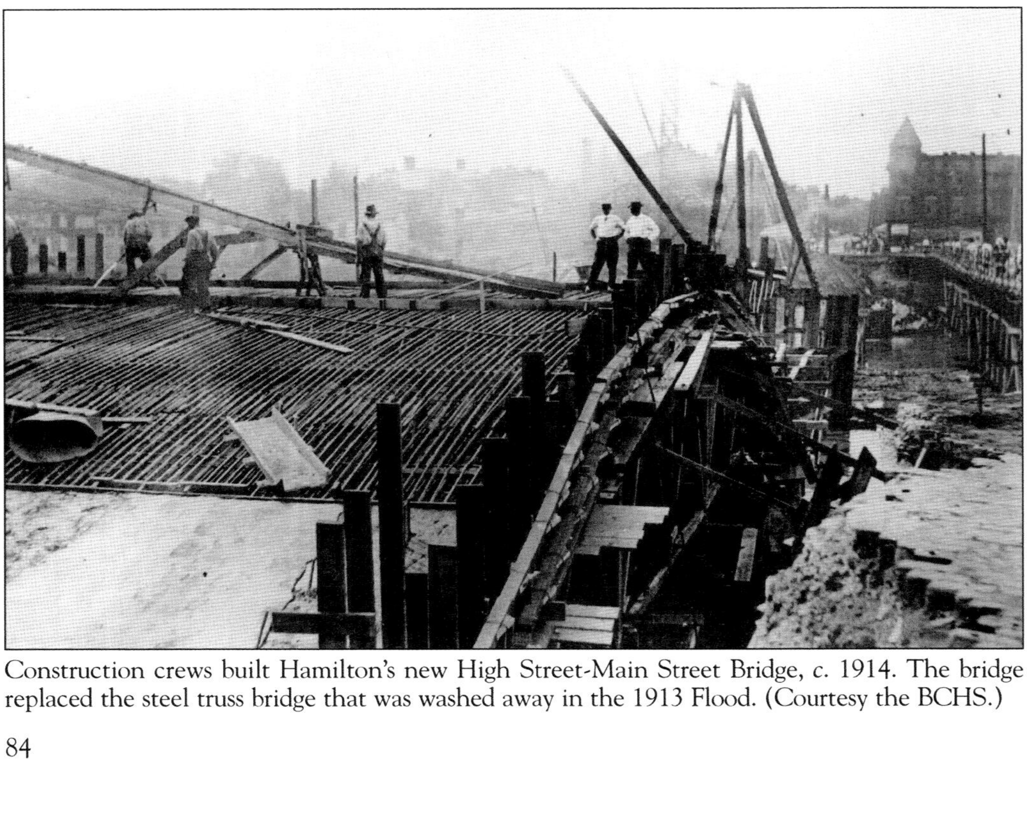

Construction crews built Hamilton's new High Street-Main Street Bridge, *c.* 1914. The bridge replaced the steel truss bridge that was washed away in the 1913 Flood. (Courtesy the BCHS.)

Eight

LEISURE

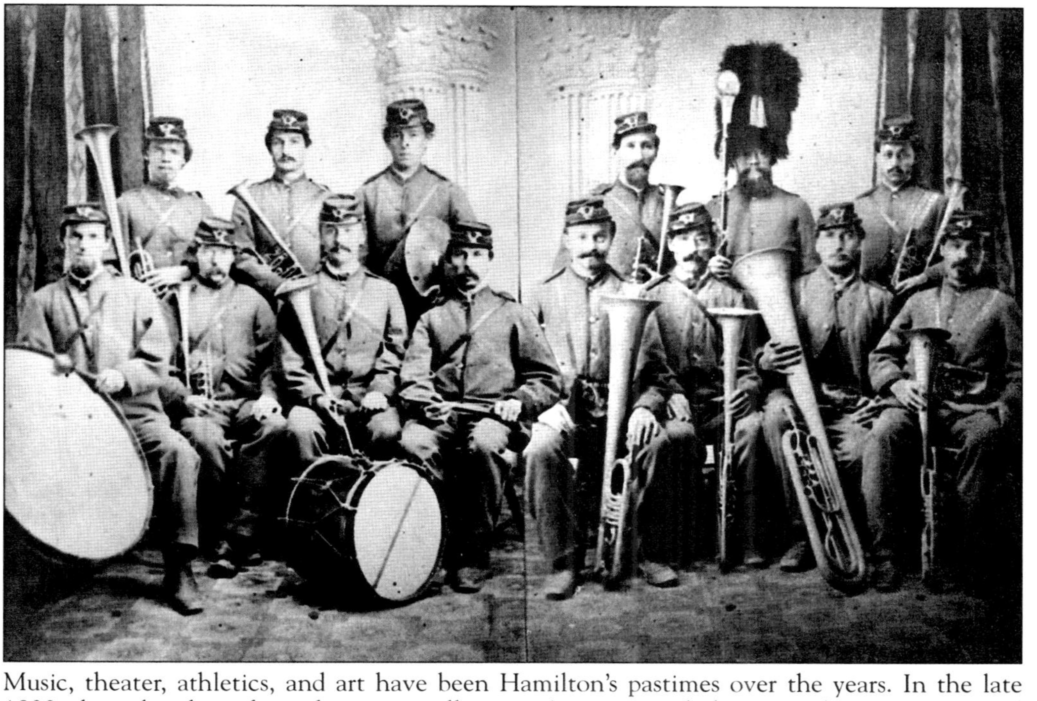

Music, theater, athletics, and art have been Hamilton's pastimes over the years. In the late 1800s, brass bands performed in towns all across America, including Hamilton. Sousa's Band was a top recording act of the era. Local bands were also popular, playing at fairs, weddings, and public events. Hamilton had its share of brass bands, too. This photograph of Finzel's Band was from the late 1890s. The musicians were not identified. (Courtesy the BCHS.)

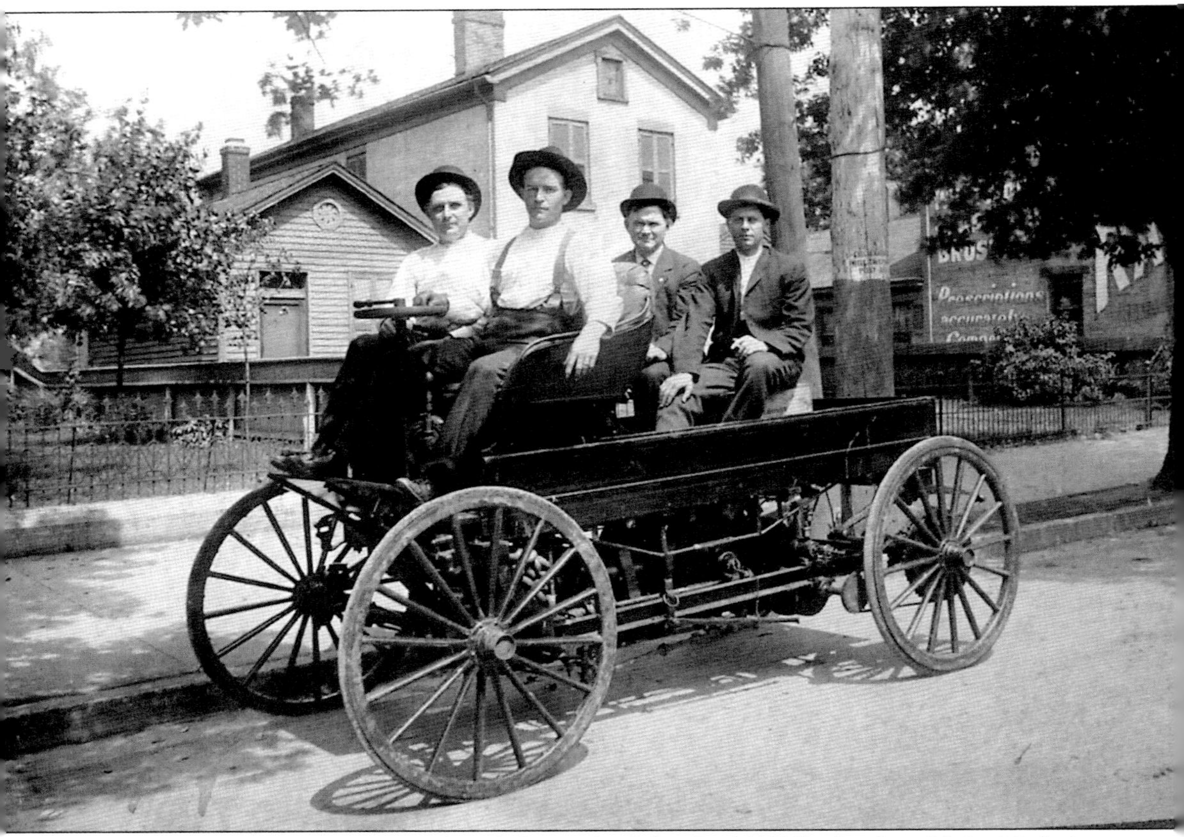

In 1898, four Hamilton men—from left to right, John (Jack) Willenbrick and John Nicholas in the front seat and Teddy Tillman and Otto Zollers in the rear—left for a fishing camp on Riley's Island near Hamilton. They hauled provisions in their truck, which was built by the city's own Ritchie family of Advance Manufacturing. (Courtesy the BCHS.)

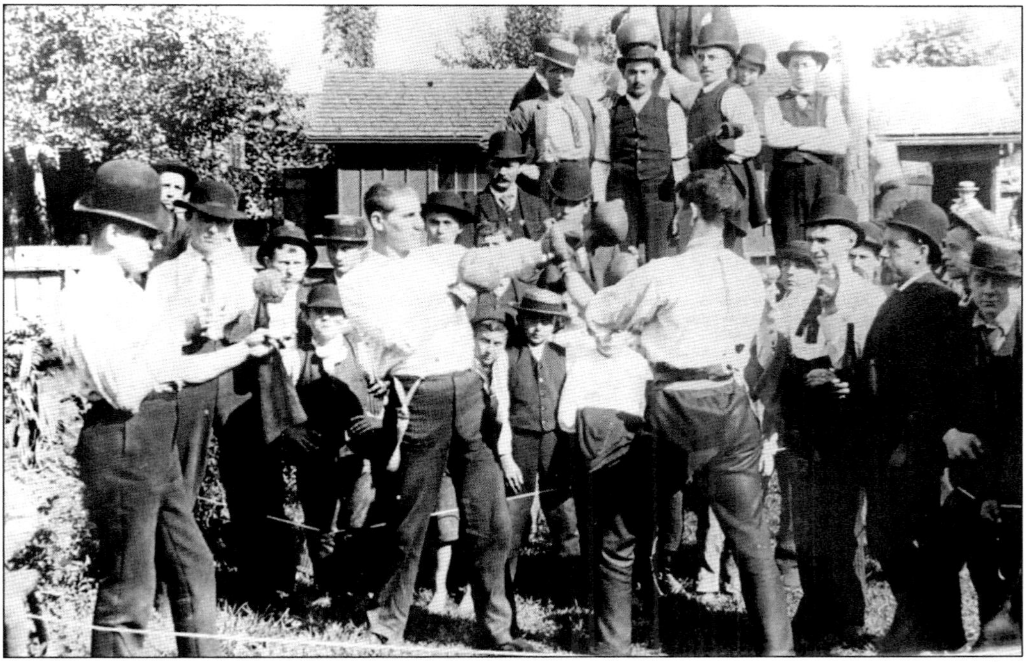

In Hamilton and throughout America in the early 1900s, boxing was a rough sport. At this match, two unidentified boxers prepared to fight in front of plenty of spectators. At least the fighters had enough sense to wear boxing gloves, although they went without head protection. (Courtesy the BCHS.)

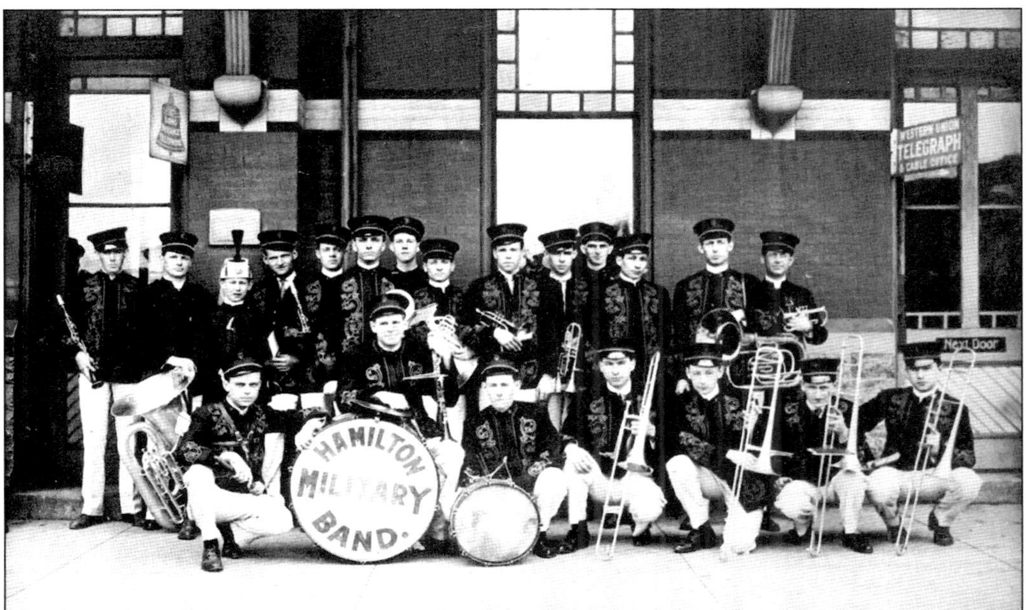

Looking formal and dignified, the Hamilton Military Band arrived in front of the Western Union Telegraph and Cable Office at Second and Market Streets in the early part of the twentieth century. (Courtesy the BCHS.)

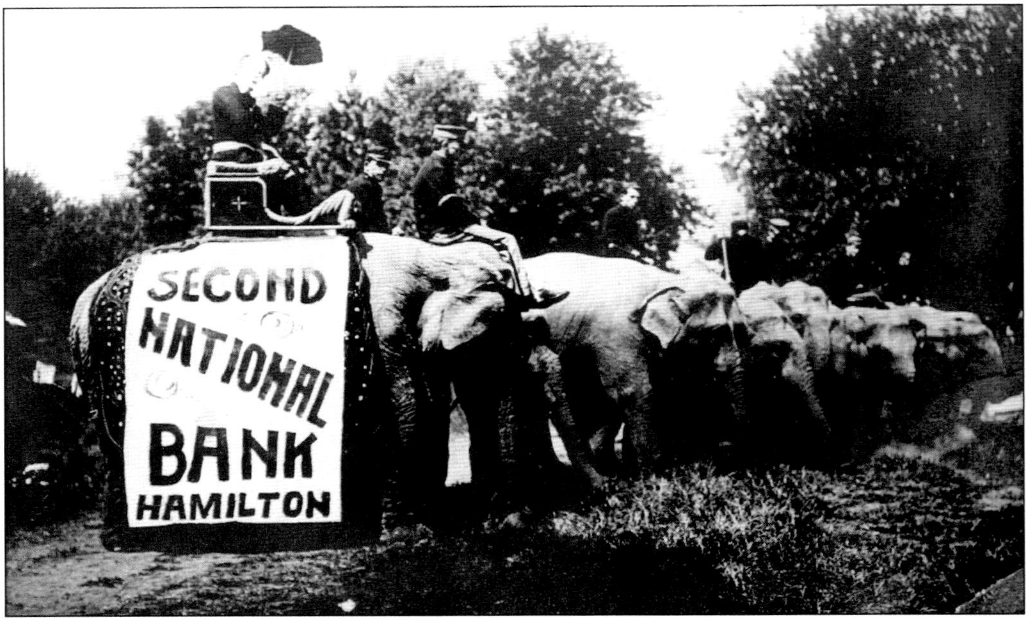

At the turn of the twentieth century, Hamilton's Second National Bank decided to be first in jumbo promotions by draping an advertising sign across a circus elephant. It ranks as one of the city's largest campaigns. (Courtesy the BCHS.)

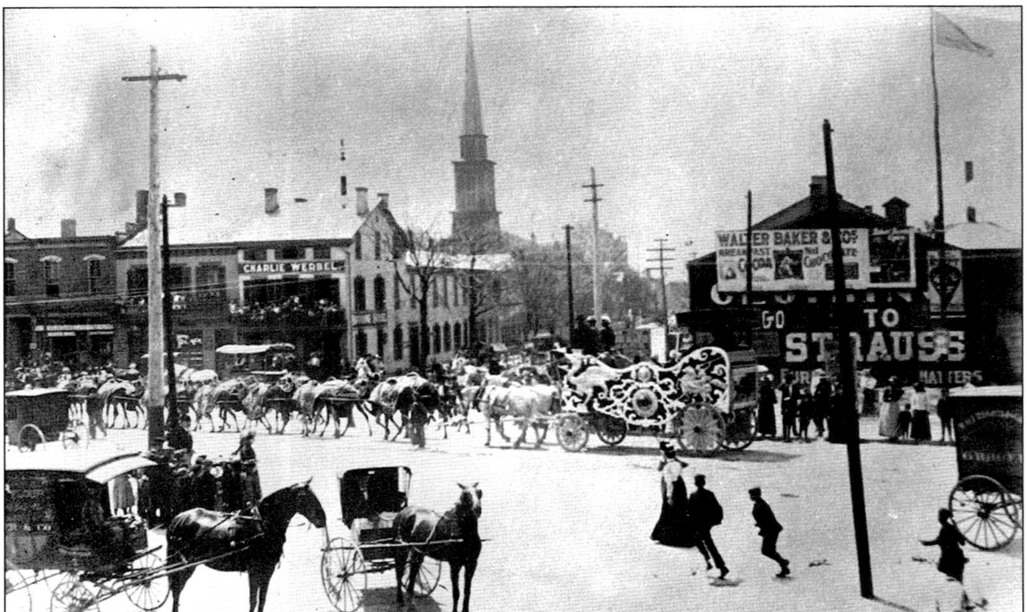

A circus rolled across downtown Hamilton in 1904. Boys ran to watch the fancy wagons. A circus in town was as good as a vacation to children in the early 1900s. This photograph was taken at the east end of High Street. (Courtesy the BCHS.)

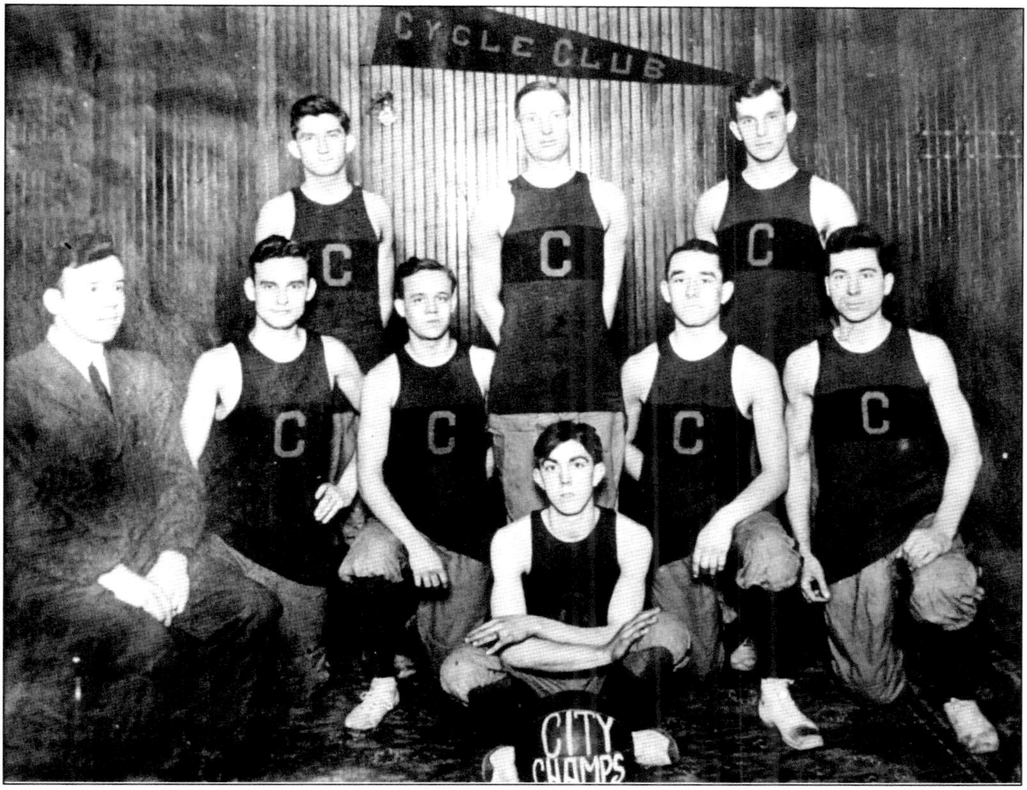

The Tour de France might be the gold standard for cyclists today, but in the early 1900s, local races were followed just as eagerly. These trim but unidentified Hamilton men—members of the local Cycle Club—became the city champions in 1907. (Courtesy the BCHS.)

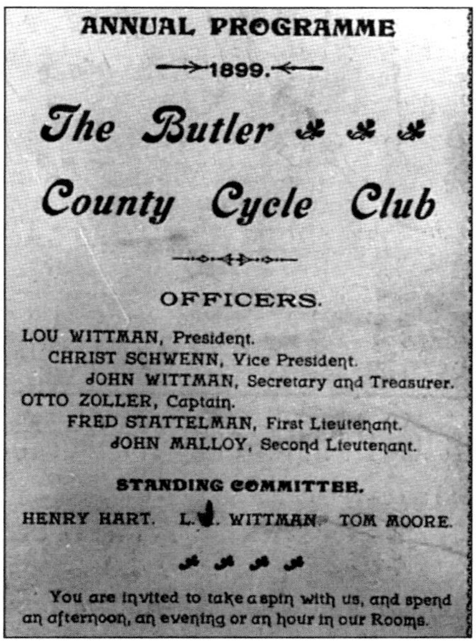

ANNUAL PROGRAMME

→1899.←

The Butler

County Cycle Club

OFFICERS.

LOU WITTMAN, President.
CHRIST SCHWENN, Vice President.
JOHN WITTMAN, Secretary and Treasurer.
OTTO ZOLLER, Captain.
FRED STATTELMAN, First Lieutenant.
JOHN MALLOY, Second Lieutenant.

STANDING COMMITTEE.

HENRY HART. L. [illegible]. WITTMAN. TOM MOORE.

You are invited to take a spin with us, and spend an afternoon, an evening or an hour in our Rooms.

Bicycling, a major national craze in the 1890s, came to Hamilton in the form of the Butler County Cycle Club, with offices at 33 High Street. (Courtesy the BCHS.)

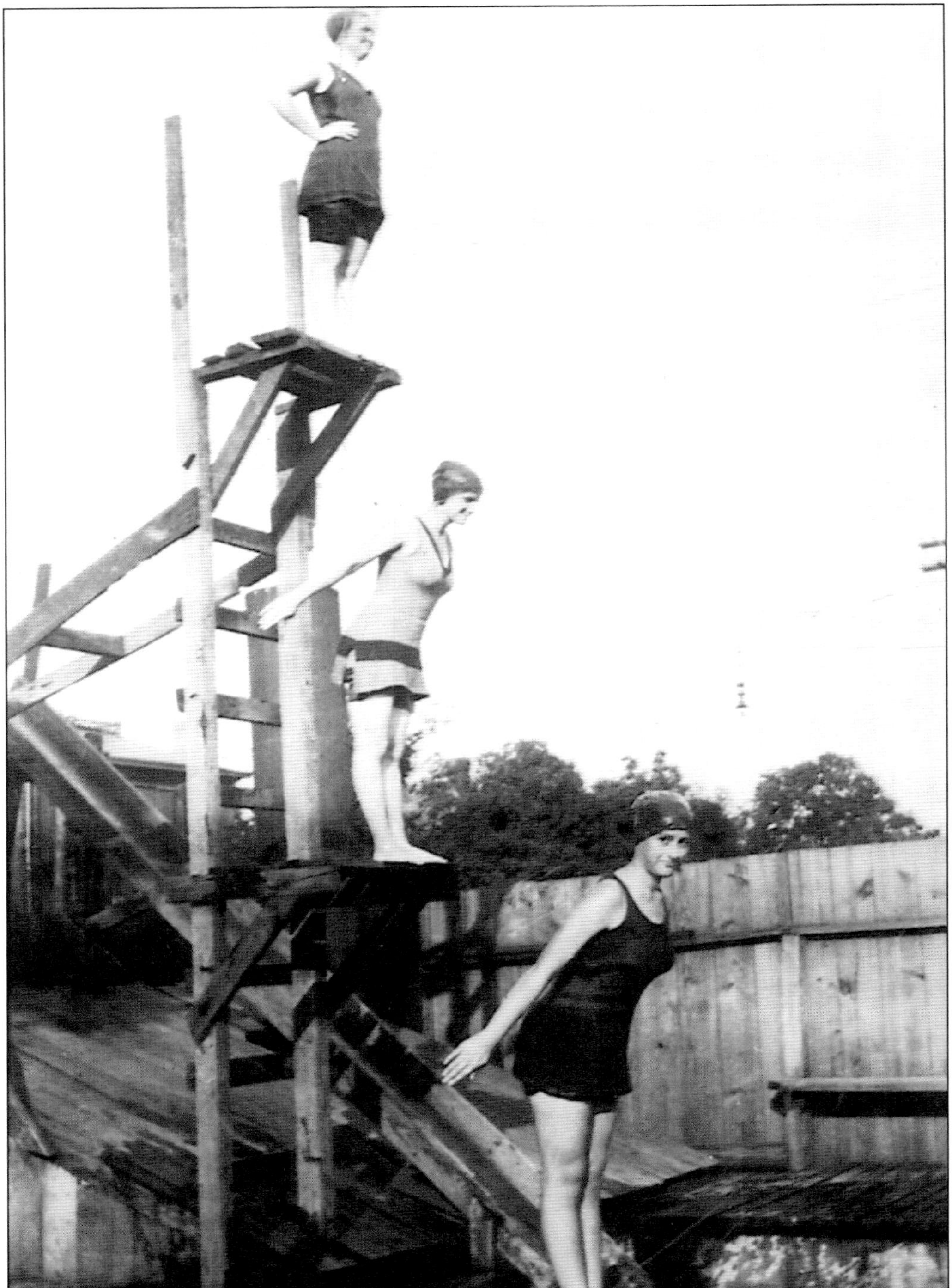

Swimsuit styles change, but nothing can beat a cool dive on a hot summer day. In this photograph, c. 1920, three women paused for the camera before diving into a pool. The location was not identified, but it could have been the old city pool on Dayton Street. (Courtesy the BCHS.)

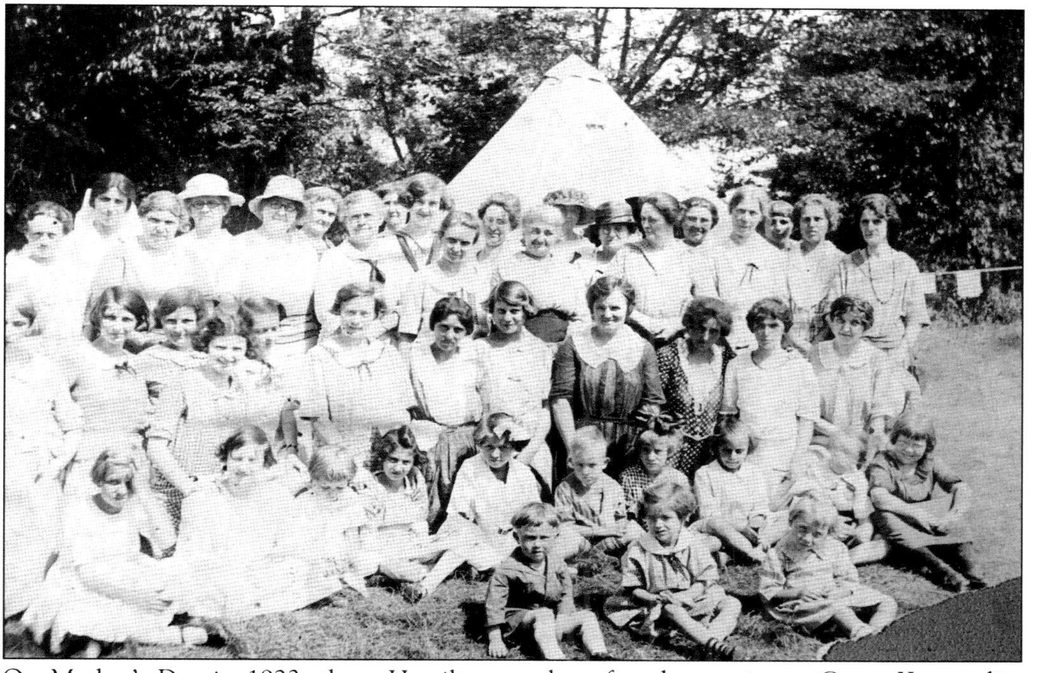

On Mother's Day in 1923, these Hamilton mothers found a respite at Camp Keewaydin, sponsored by the Hamilton YWCA. The children came along, too. (Courtesy the BCHS.)

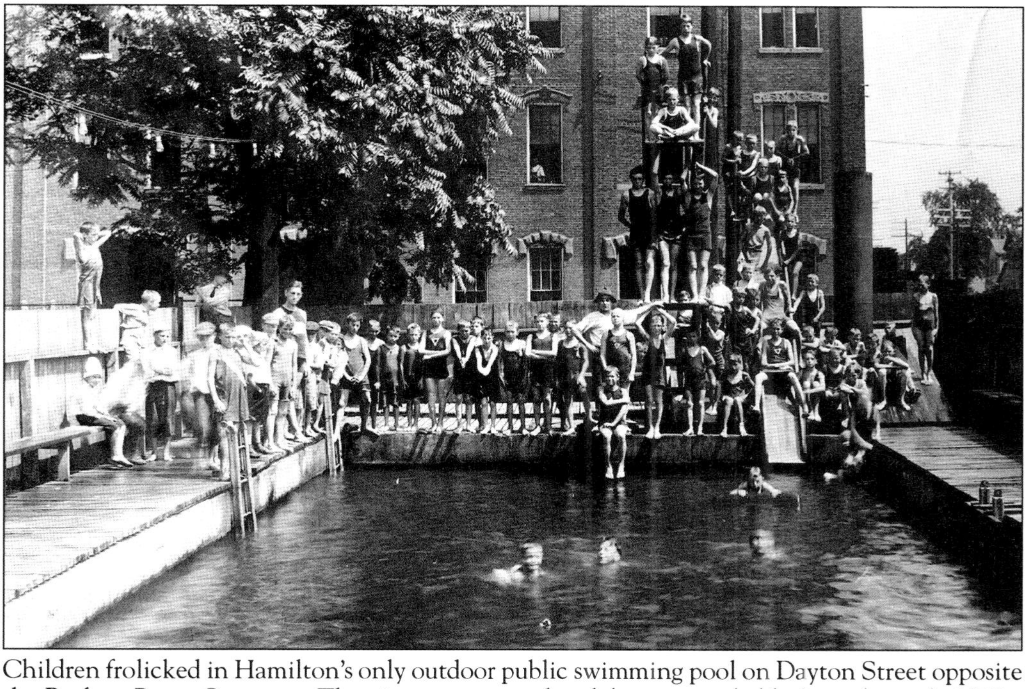

Children frolicked in Hamilton's only outdoor public swimming pool on Dayton Street opposite the Beckett Paper Company. The picture was not dated, but was probably from the early 1920s. (Courtesy the BCHS.)

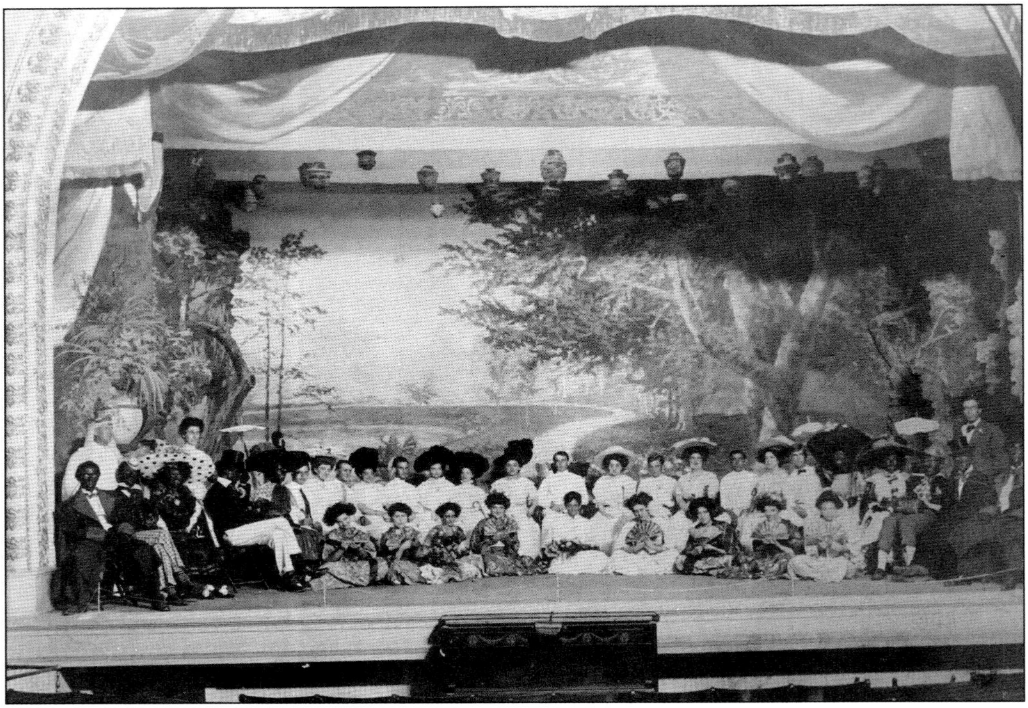

Musical theater has the ability to take audiences to different times and places. The *Minstrels in Japan* show was performed in Hamilton on July 10, 1908. The theater was not listed. (Courtesy the BCHS.)

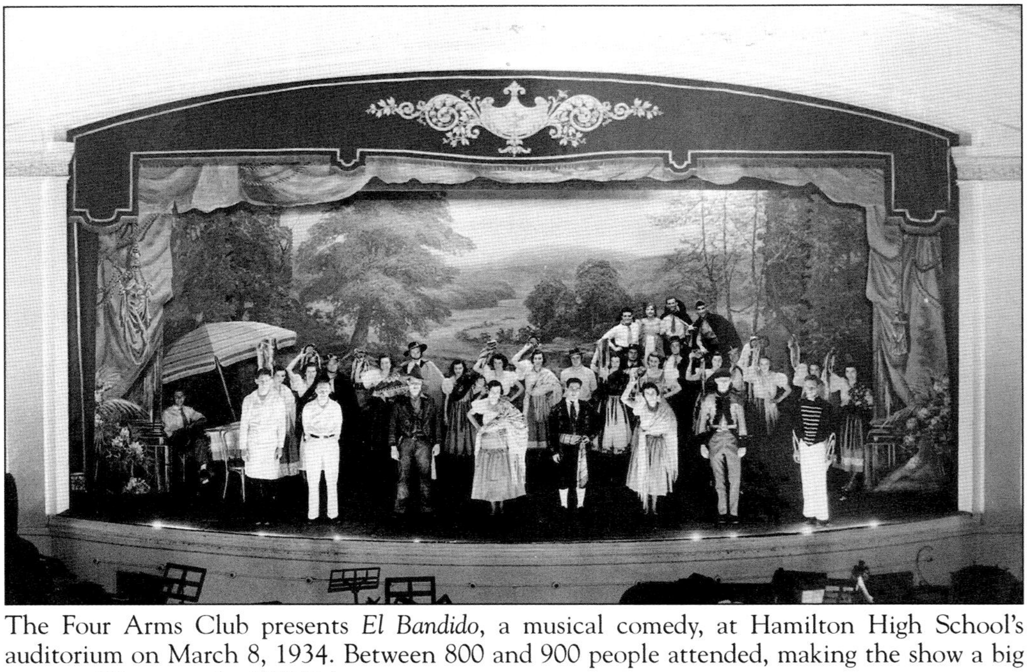

The Four Arms Club presents *El Bandido*, a musical comedy, at Hamilton High School's auditorium on March 8, 1934. Between 800 and 900 people attended, making the show a big success. (Courtesy the BCHS.)

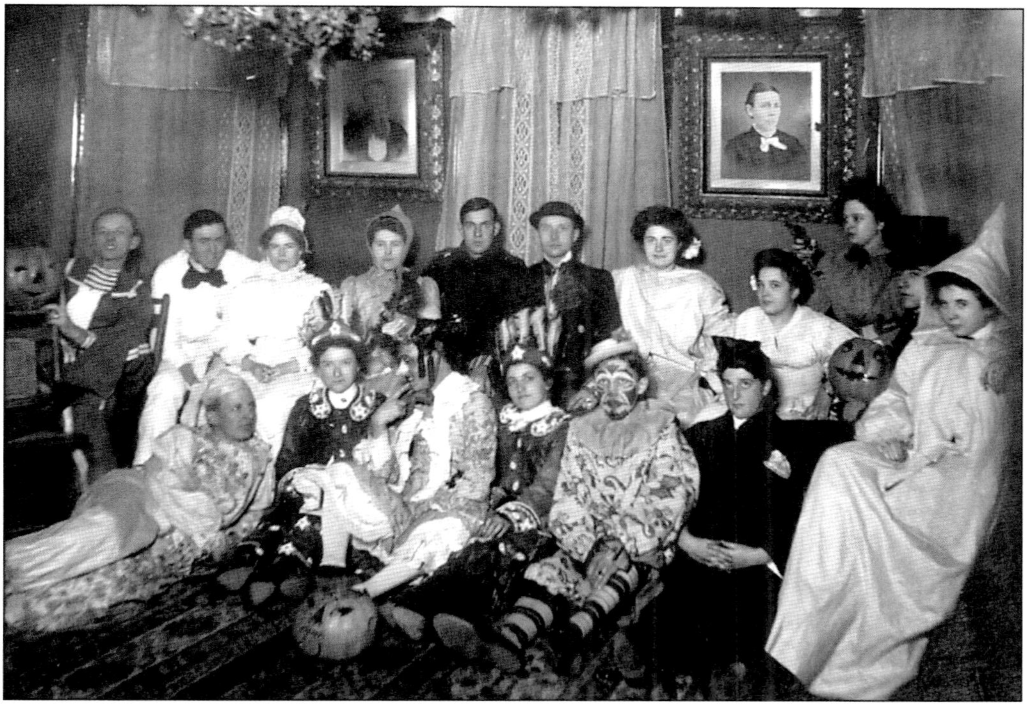

In this 1914 photograph, friends gathered for a Halloween party. The place and the people were not identified, but they all seemed to have had a great time. (Courtesy the BCHS.)

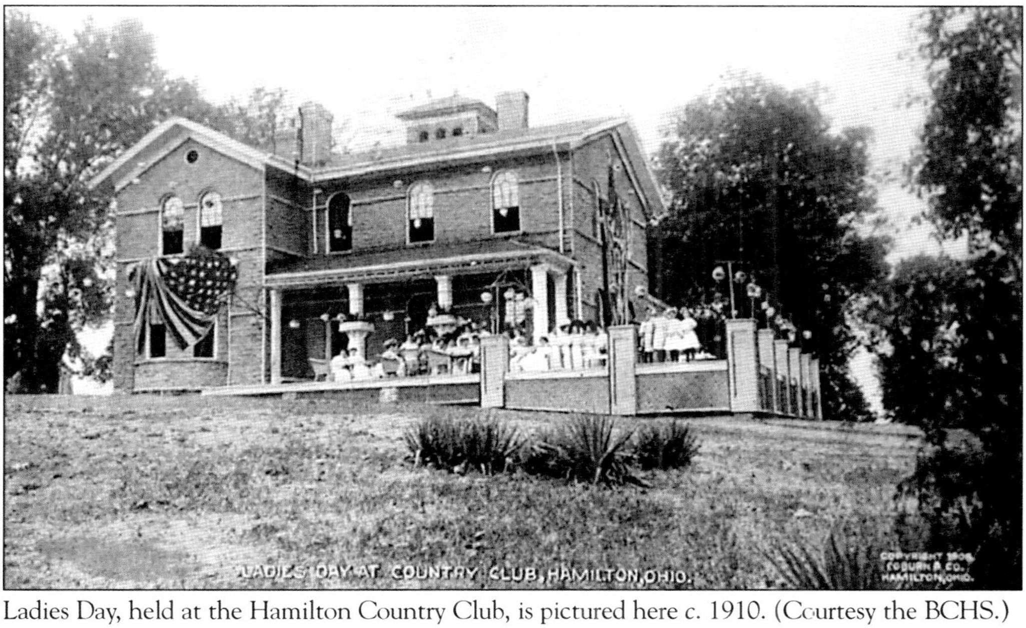

Ladies Day, held at the Hamilton Country Club, is pictured here *c.* 1910. (Courtesy the BCHS.)

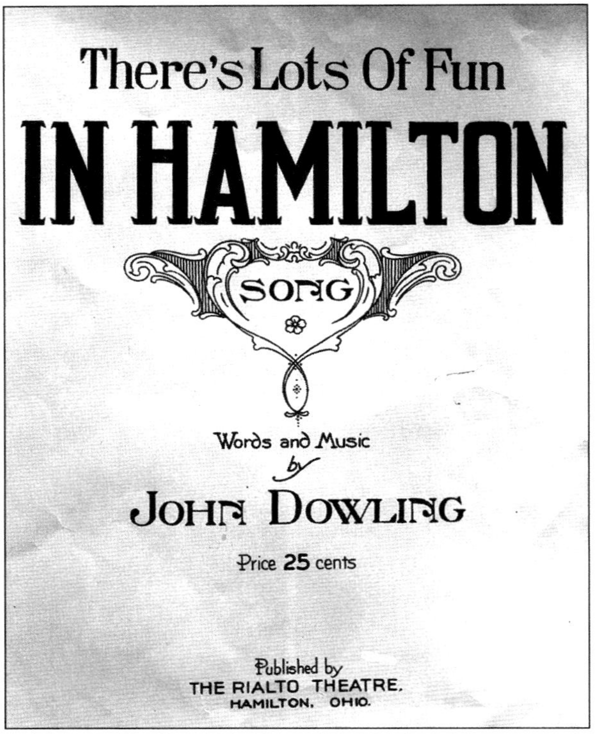

Owners of the Rialto Theatre published "There's Lots of Fun in Hamilton," a song written by John Dowling in 1924. The sheet music cost 25¢. The song went: "Not so far from the wicked city / Not so small and it's very pretty / Come and see then you'll agree / That it's just the place to raise a family." (Courtesy the BCHS.)

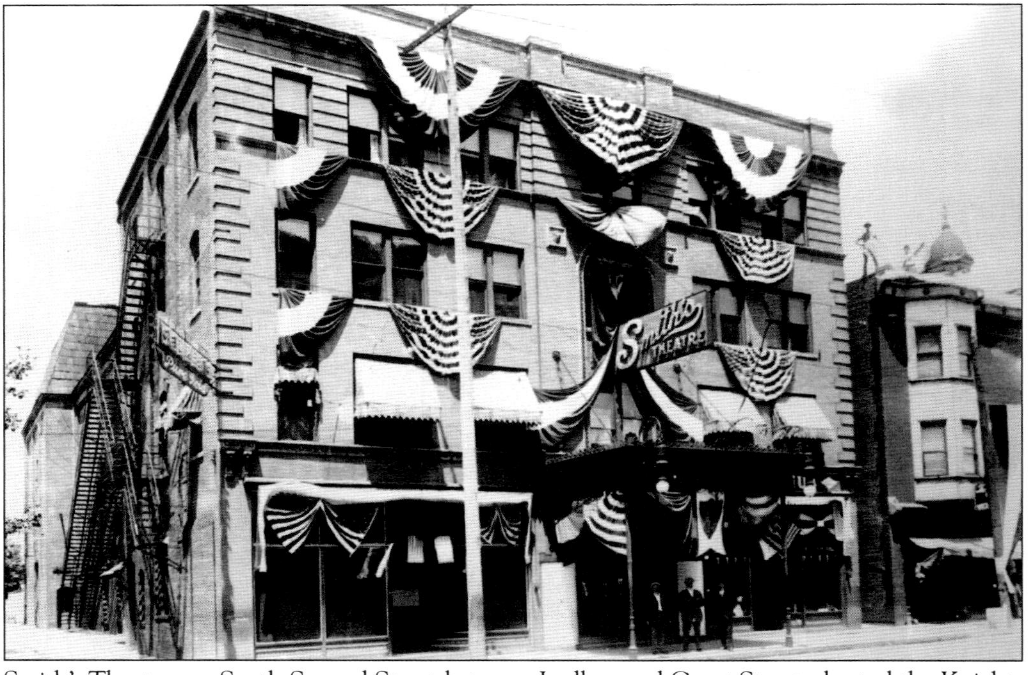

Smith's Theatre, on South Second Street between Ludlow and Court Streets, hosted the Knights of the Pythias Convention in 1911. The building was a popular destination in Hamilton in those days. It even featured a number of overnight guest rooms. (Courtesy the BCHS.)

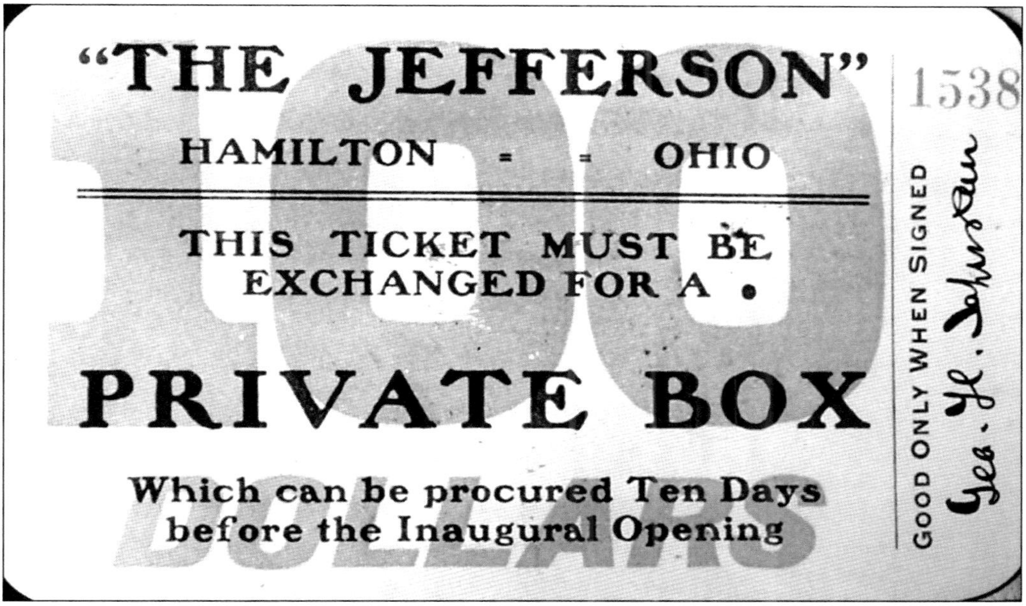

"THE JEFFERSON"

HAMILTON = = OHIO

THIS TICKET MUST BE
EXCHANGED FOR A

PRIVATE BOX

Which can be procured Ten Days
before the Inaugural Opening

100 DOLLARS

1538

GOOD ONLY WHEN SIGNED

The Jefferson, a vaudeville and live theater, opened in March of 1903. It featured everything from comedy to opera. (Courtesy the BCHS.)

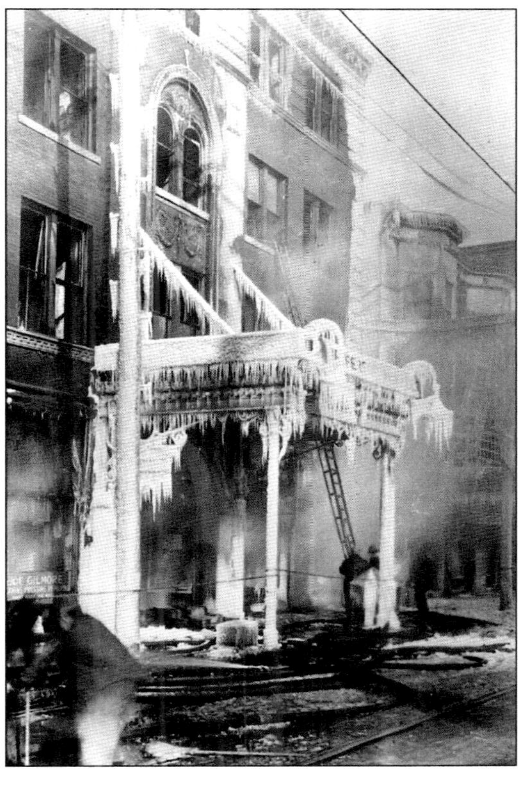

On January 4, 1928, the Jefferson burned. Water from firefighters' hoses froze on the marquee, giving the theater the appearance of a large icicle. (Courtesy the BCHS.)

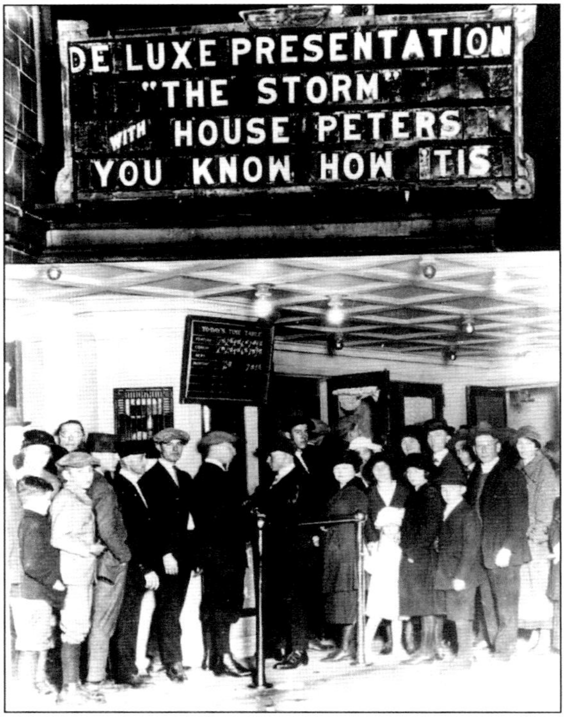

The Palace Theatre, 213 South Third Street, welcomed movie fans to a showing of *The Storm* with House Peters, *c.* 1925. By 1960, the Palace was relegated to a B-movie house. (Courtesy the BCHS.)

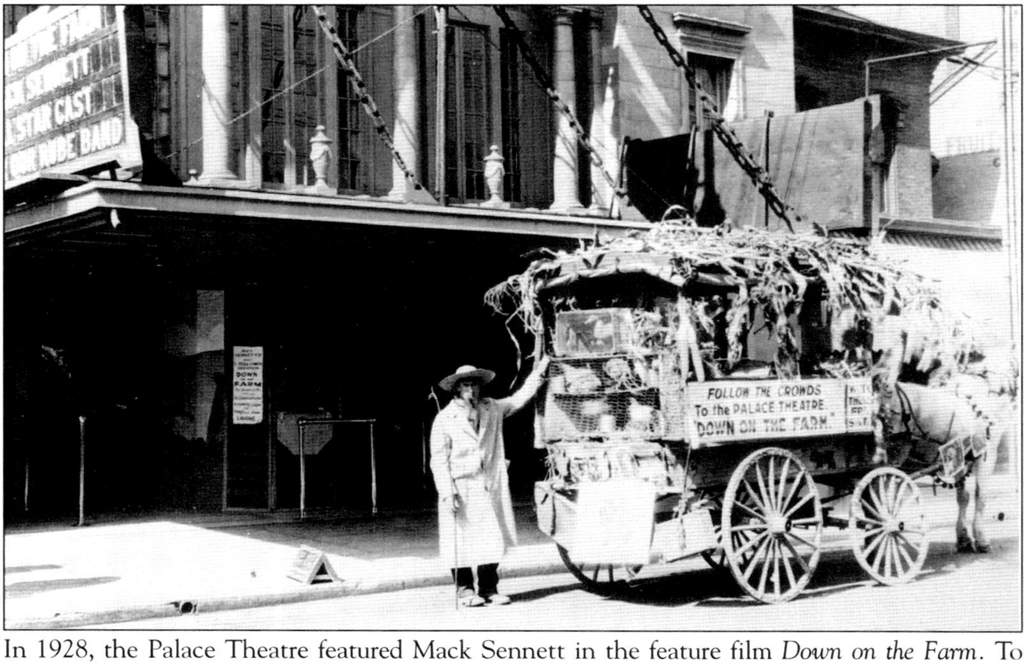

In 1928, the Palace Theatre featured Mack Sennett in the feature film *Down on the Farm*. To promote the movie, theater owners hired a rube band and man with a huckster wagon. His sign read, "Follow the crowds to the Palace Theatre. Down on the Farm." In 2005, the old Palace was being renovated as the home of the Greater Hamilton Civic Theater. (Courtesy the BCHS.)

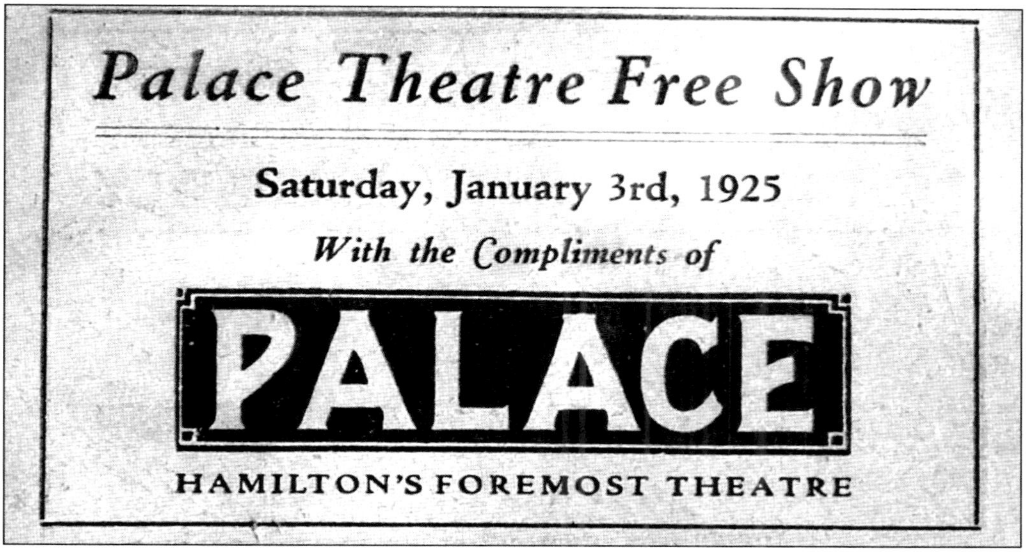

The Palace offered a free pass for its Saturday, January 3, 1925, performance. By that time, the Palace called itself "Hamilton's foremost theatre." By the late 1950s, it was just another declining movie house in an urban downtown. (Courtesy the BCHS.)

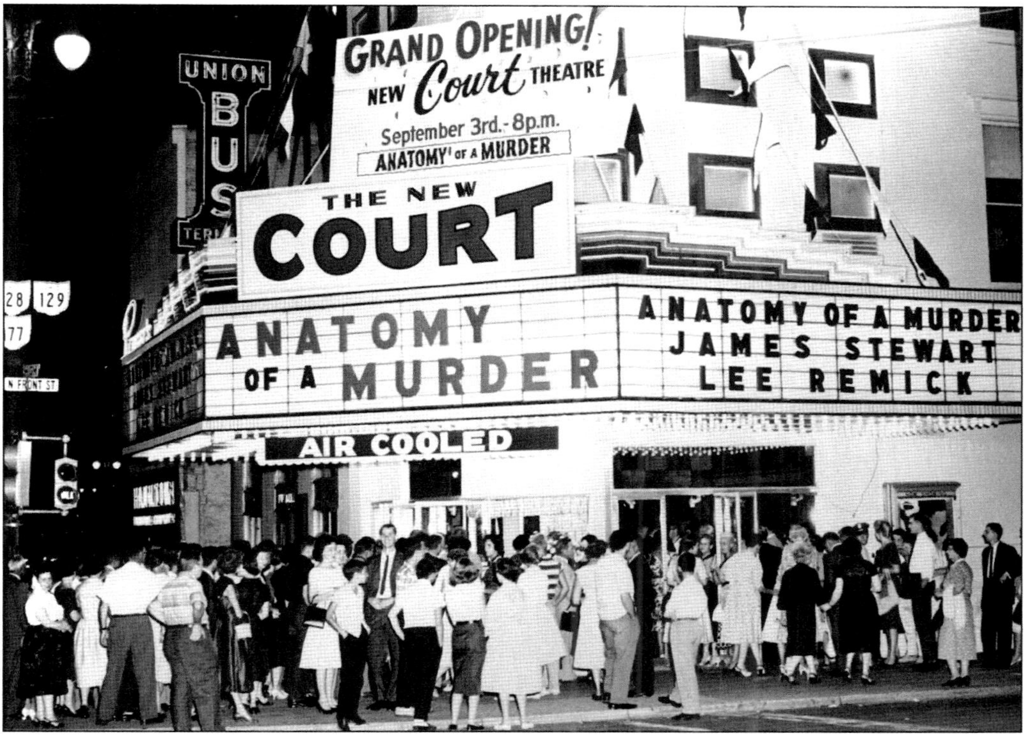

The old Rialto Theatre at Court and High Streets transformed itself into the Court Theatre in grand style—with a showing of James Stewart's *Anatomy of a Murder* in the early 1960s. Downtown Hamilton was still busy in those days. The old Union Bus Terminal is next door. The area where the Court once stood is now a city park. (Courtesy the BCHS.)

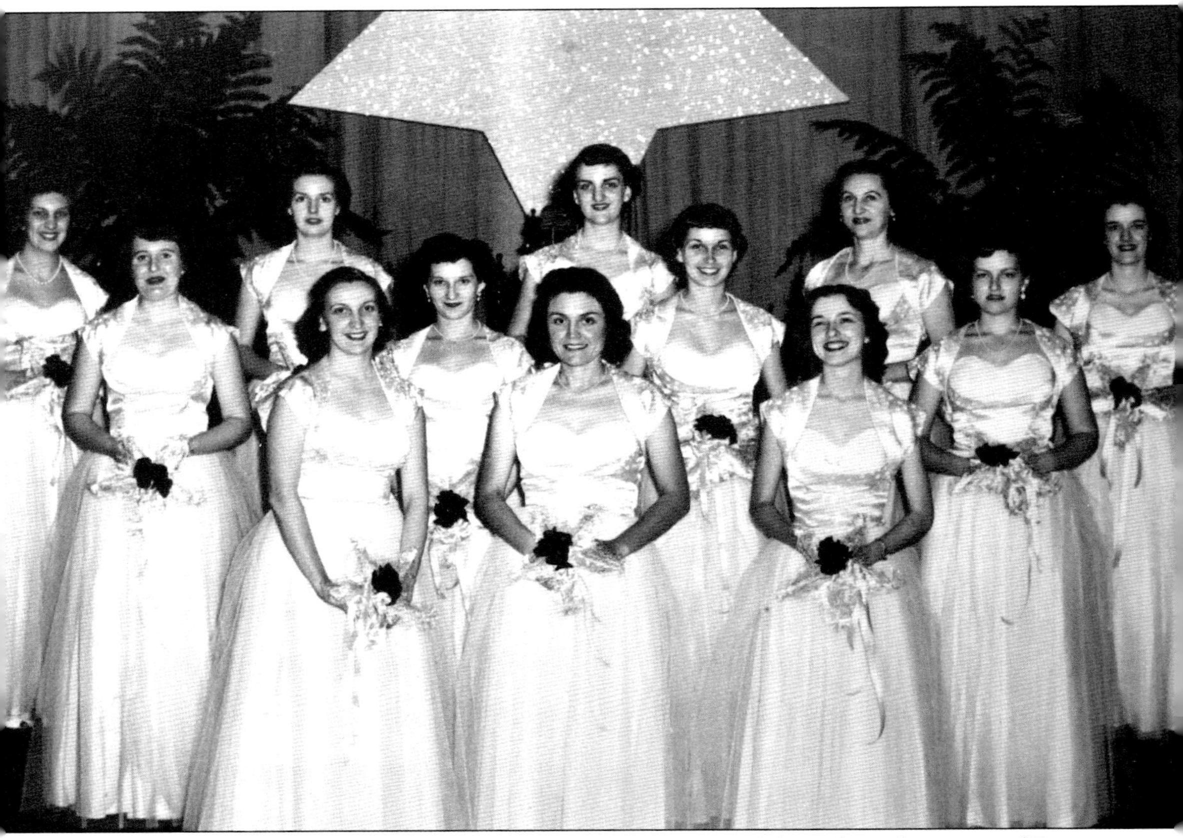

The ladies of Hamilton's Eastern Star, *c.* 1950, are attired for a formal portrait. (Courtesy the BCHS.)

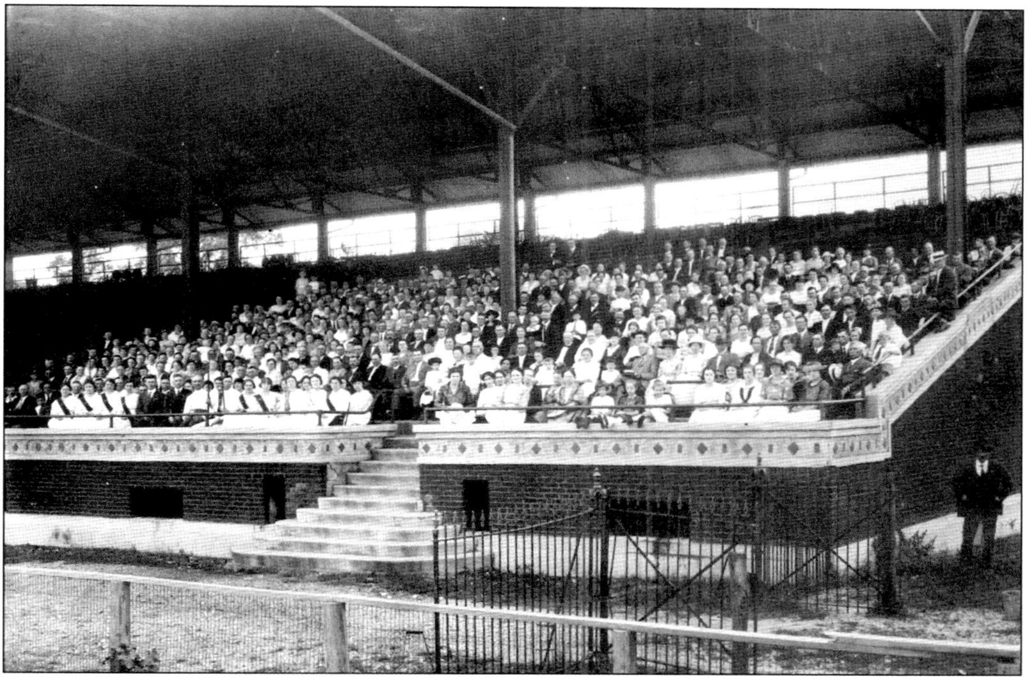

In this image from the early 1900s, racing fans watched the horses at the Butler County Fairgrounds in Hamilton. Harness racing continues to be a popular attraction at fairs across Ohio. (Courtesy the BCHS.)

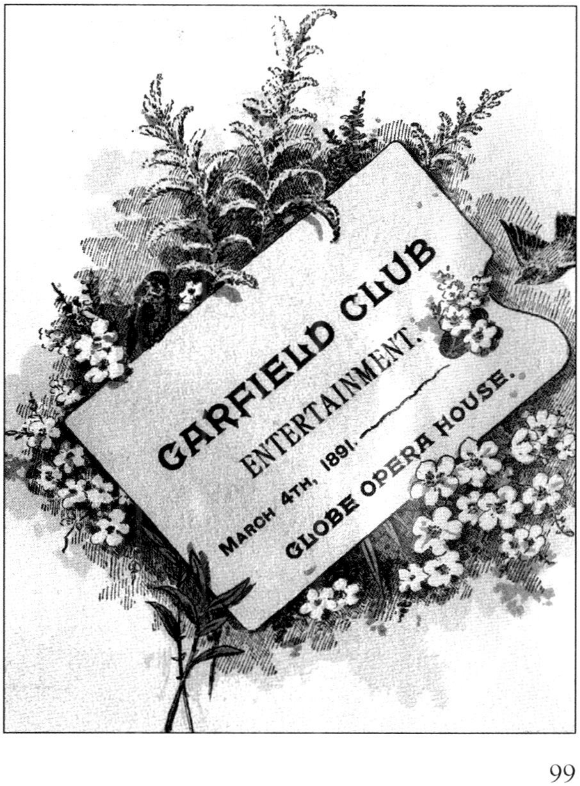

The Garfield Club offered entertainment in the Globe Opera House at High Street and Journal Square. The building was erected in 1866 and used for performances. Plays were held on the second floor. Meyer's Drug Store and a saloon operated on the first. In 1899, owner Walter Dixon sold the Globe to William C. Frechtling for $60,000. Robinson-Schwenn Department Store took over much of the building in 1913 and went on to operate there for a large part of the twentieth century. (Courtesy the BCHS.)

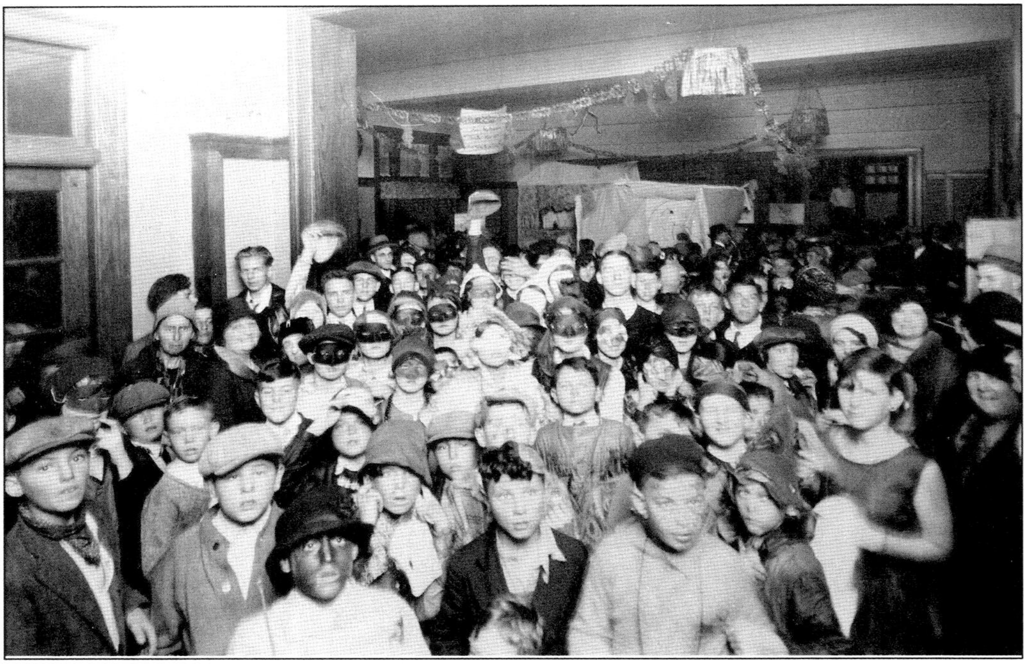

They knew how to celebrate Halloween in Hamilton in 1929. These boys gathered in the Boys Department of the YMCA downtown. Through the 1970s, Halloween was a major event in the lives of children in the city. They crowded the residential streets for treats and often went trick or treating a week early. (Courtesy the BCHS.)

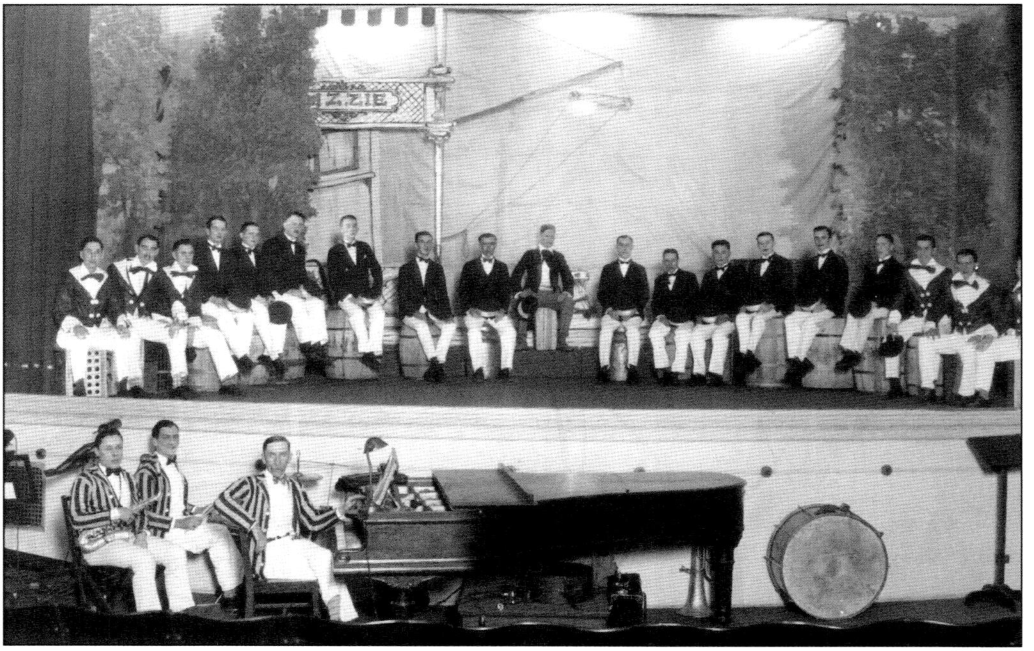

The cast of a minstrel show practiced at Hamilton High School's auditorium, c. 1920s. The auditorium was a gathering place for people who appreciated community arts. (Courtesy the BCHS.)

Nine

NEIGHBORS

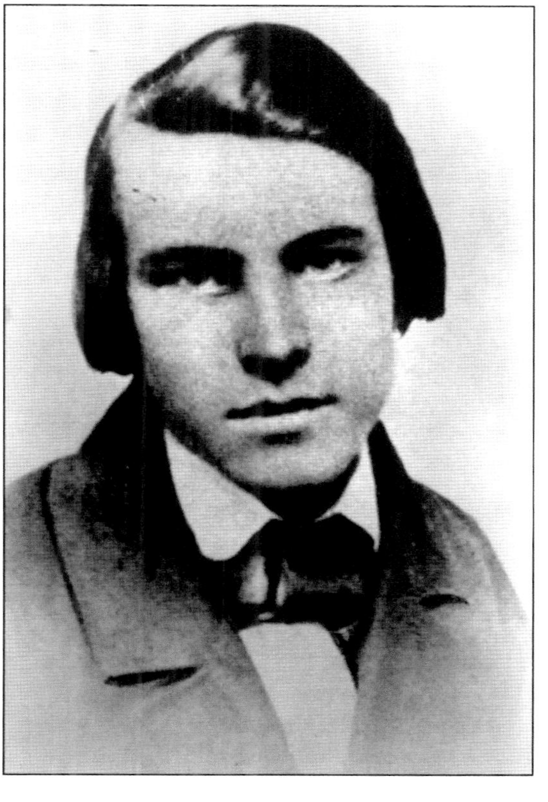

William Dean Howells (1837–1920), renowned American author, is pictured at age 18. He spent his boyhood in Hamilton, from 1840 to 1848, and wrote about it in *A Boy's Town*. He always broke in new pens by writing, "W.D. Howells, Hamilton, Butler County, Ohio." His father edited the *Hamilton Intelligencer*, a Whig newspaper. An Ohio historical marker downtown commemorates Howells, and the city offers a tour of sites he once visited. (Courtesy the BCHS.)

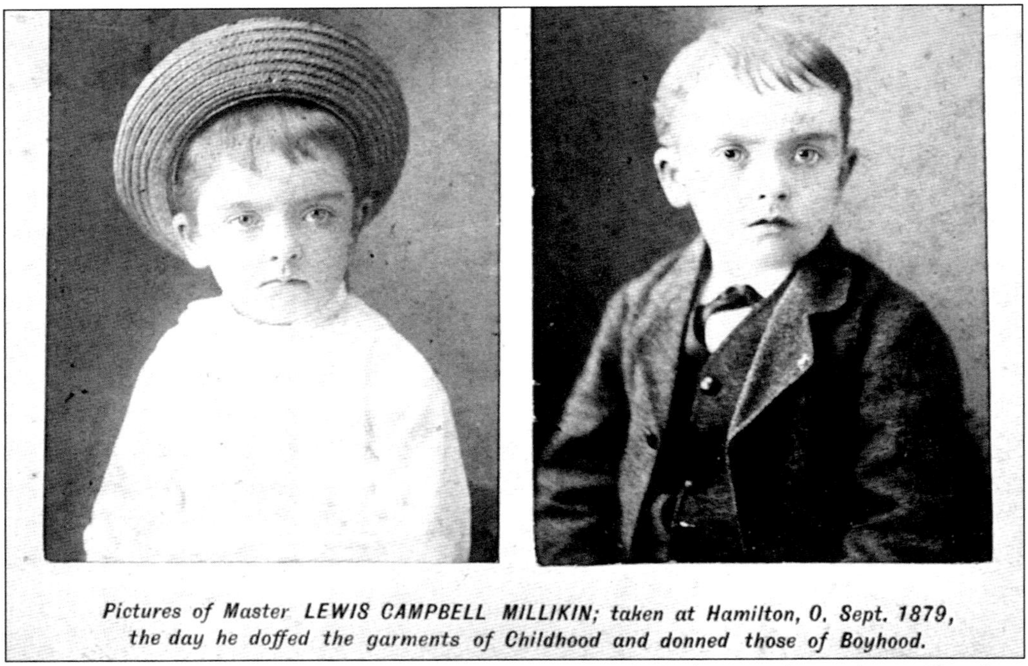

As photography advanced after the Civil War, the Tattershall photography studio in Hamilton chronicled local residents. In this picture, a young Lewis Campbell Millikin, of the prominent Millikin family, was shown coming "of age" by wearing an adult-style suit. (Courtesy the BCHS.)

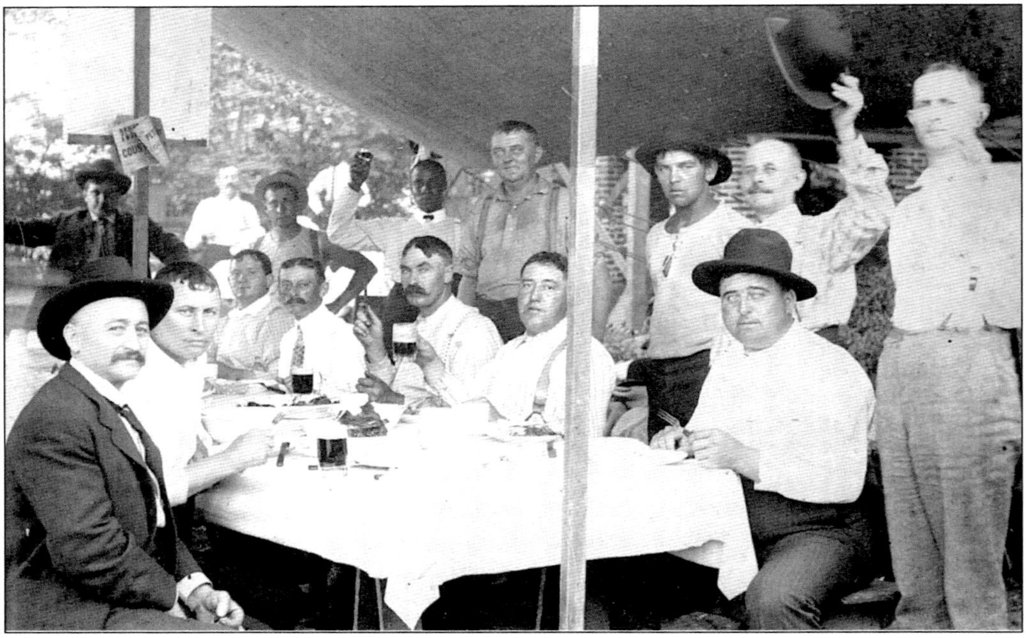

In this image taken at the Butler County Fairgrounds *c.* 1900, Democrats held a rally to elect Peter Schwab to the county board of commissioners. Max Herman waved a hat. Peter Schwab was identified as the man standing on the right. (Courtesy the BCHS.)

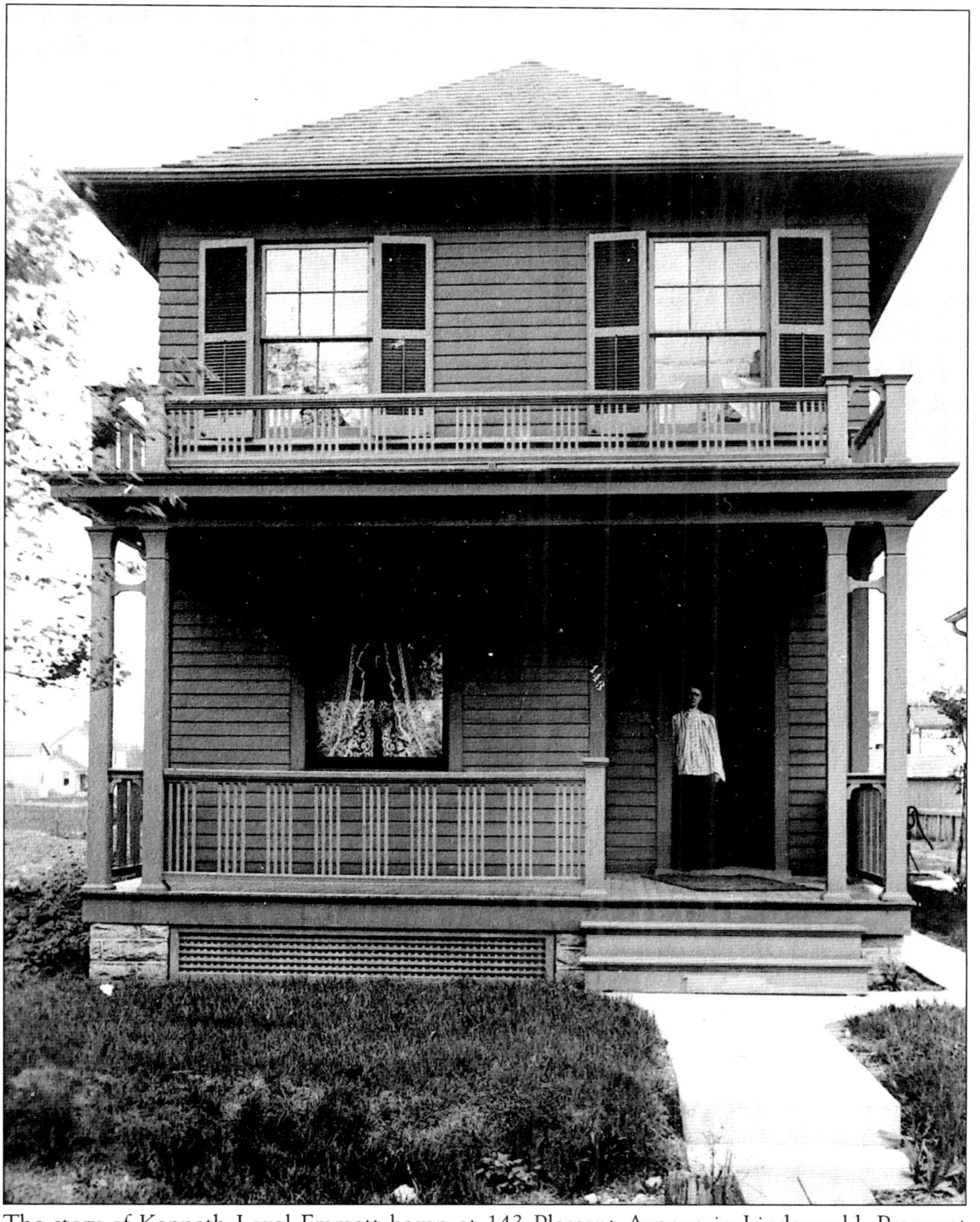

The story of Kenneth Loyal Emmett began at 143 Pleasant Avenue in Lindenwald. Pregnant in 1905, his mother stood at the front door. She kept a black scrapbook containing professional photographs of her son and handwritten notes dating from his birth to the time he left grade school. As the family disappeared over the decades, however, the scrapbook ended up at a tag sale in Maine in the early 2000s. A woman bought it for about $2. She called the Butler County Historical Society to inquire if any of his family members remain. Staff member Betty Maham could find none, but she loved the book so much that she agreed to take care of it. It chronicles not only Kenneth Emmett but also all Hamiltonians of the early 1900s. (Courtesy the BCHS.)

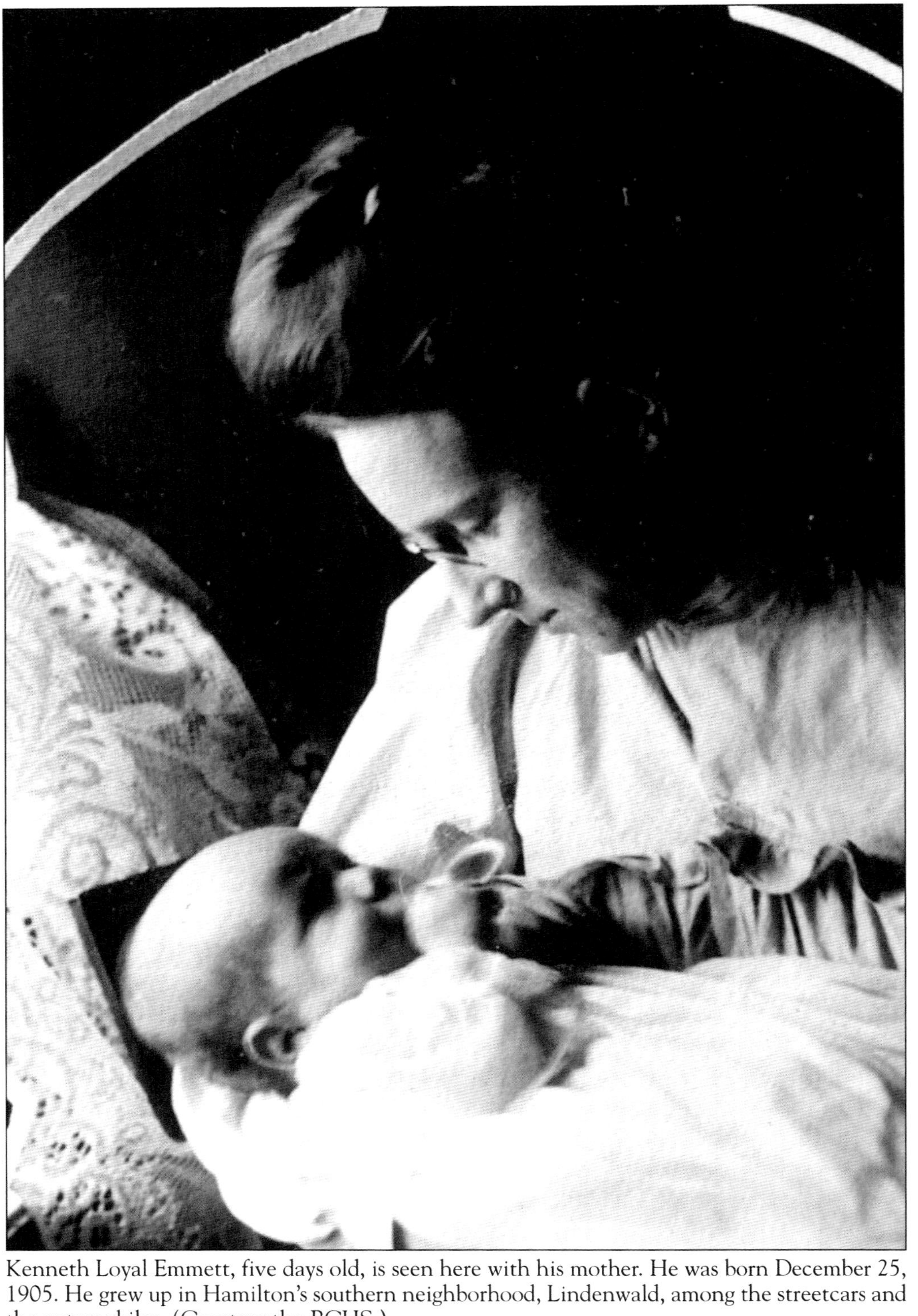

Kenneth Loyal Emmett, five days old, is seen here with his mother. He was born December 25, 1905. He grew up in Hamilton's southern neighborhood, Lindenwald, among the streetcars and the automobiles. (Courtesy the BCHS.)

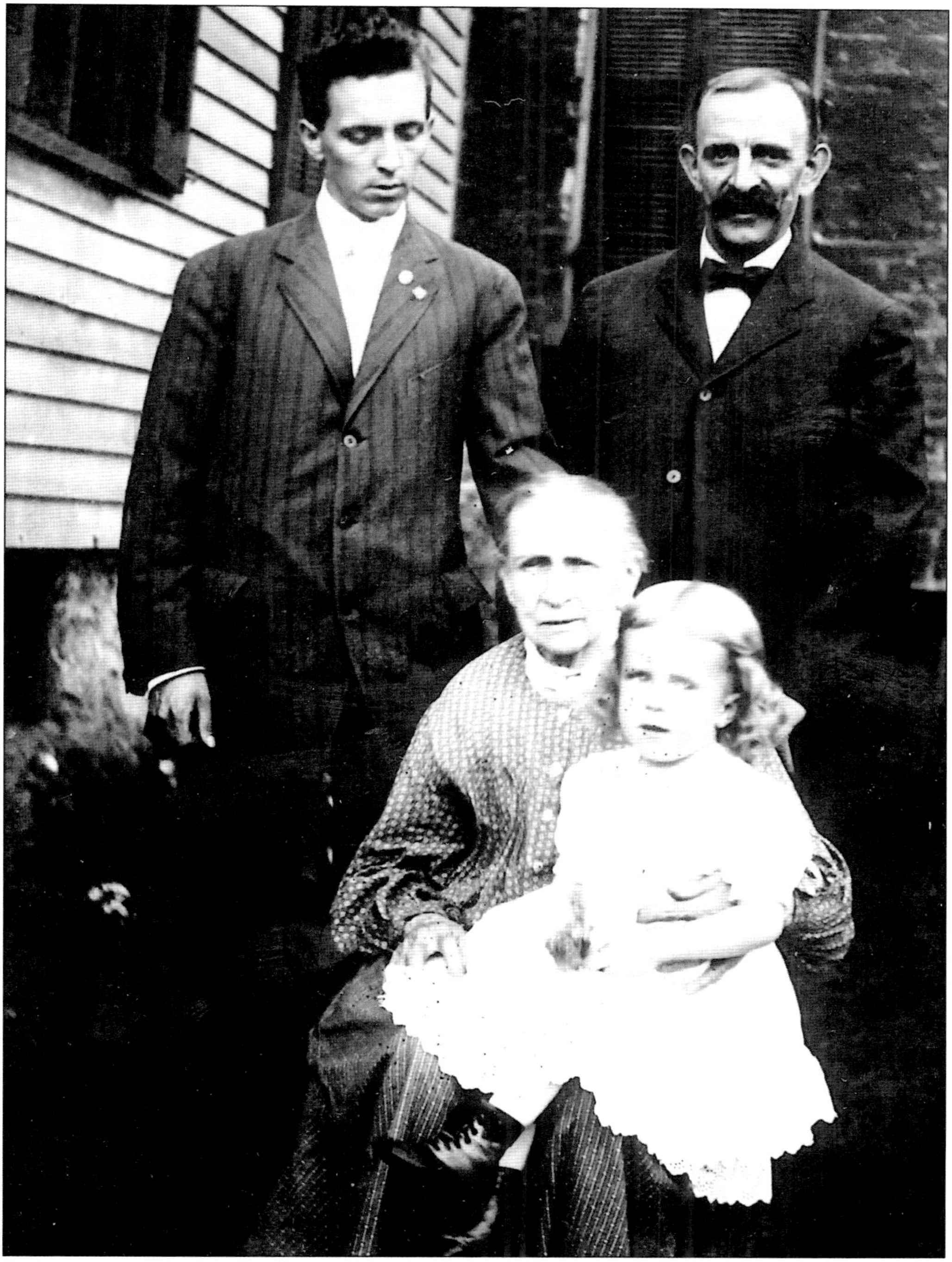

Sometimes Kenneth's family visited relatives in other parts of Hamilton. In this picture, 21-month-old Kenneth was a part of four generations. He is pictured here with his proud father, grandmother, and grandfather at their home at 121 North Fourth Street, in central Hamilton. The inner-city trip could be made on a streetcar that ran from Lindenwald to other parts of Hamilton. (Courtesy the BCHS.)

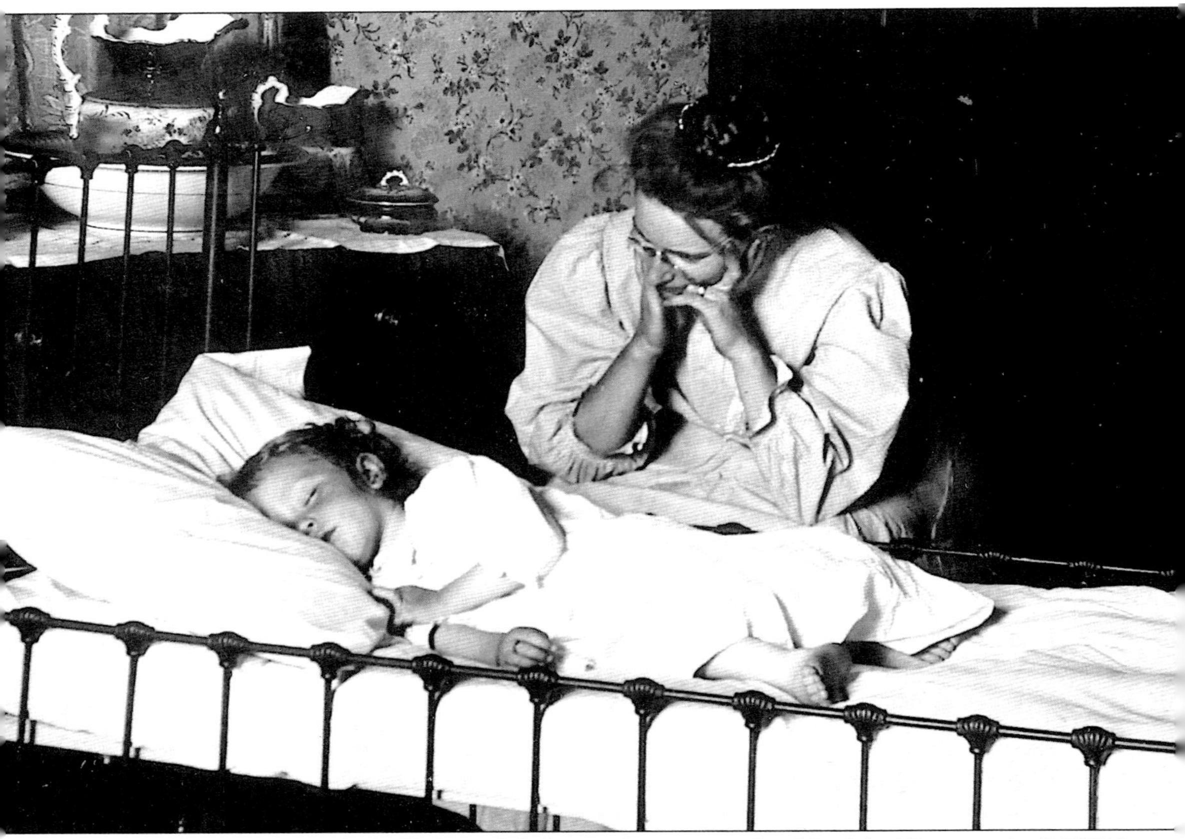

Kenneth, now two-and-a-half, slept while his mother contemplated his life. (Courtesy the BCHS.)

Kenneth, three-and-a-half years old, picked flowers in a field as the photographer captured the moment. (Courtesy the BCHS.)

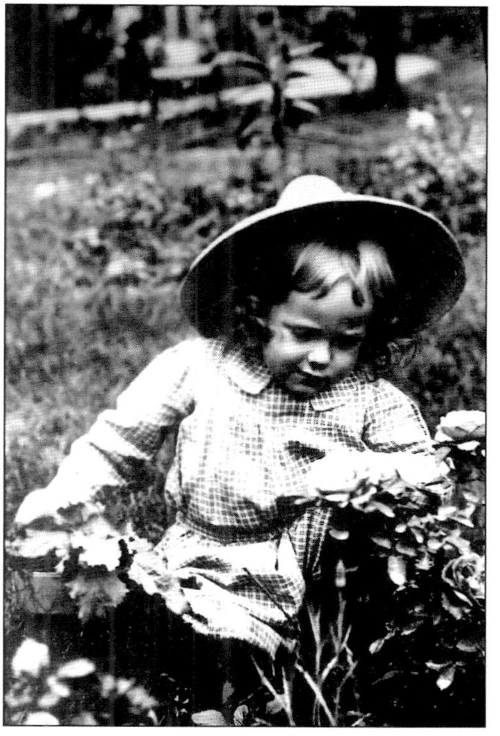

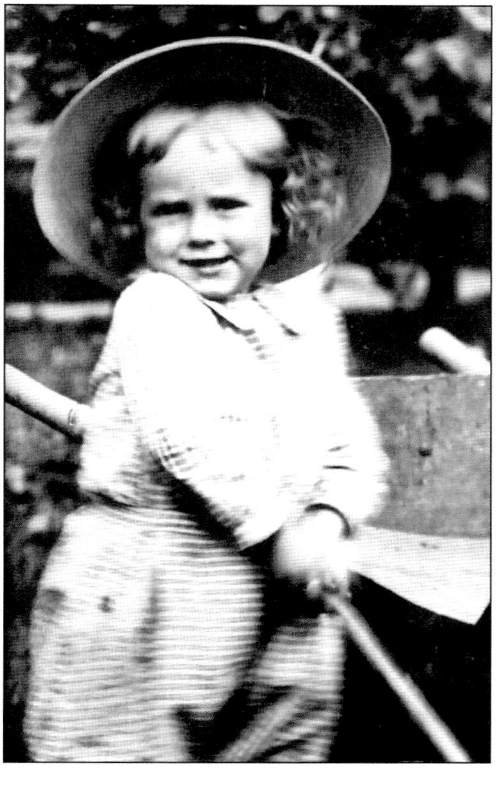

At three-and-a-half years, Kenneth helped in the garden. Back then, Lindenwald was filled with backyard gardens and fields. (Courtesy the BCHS.)

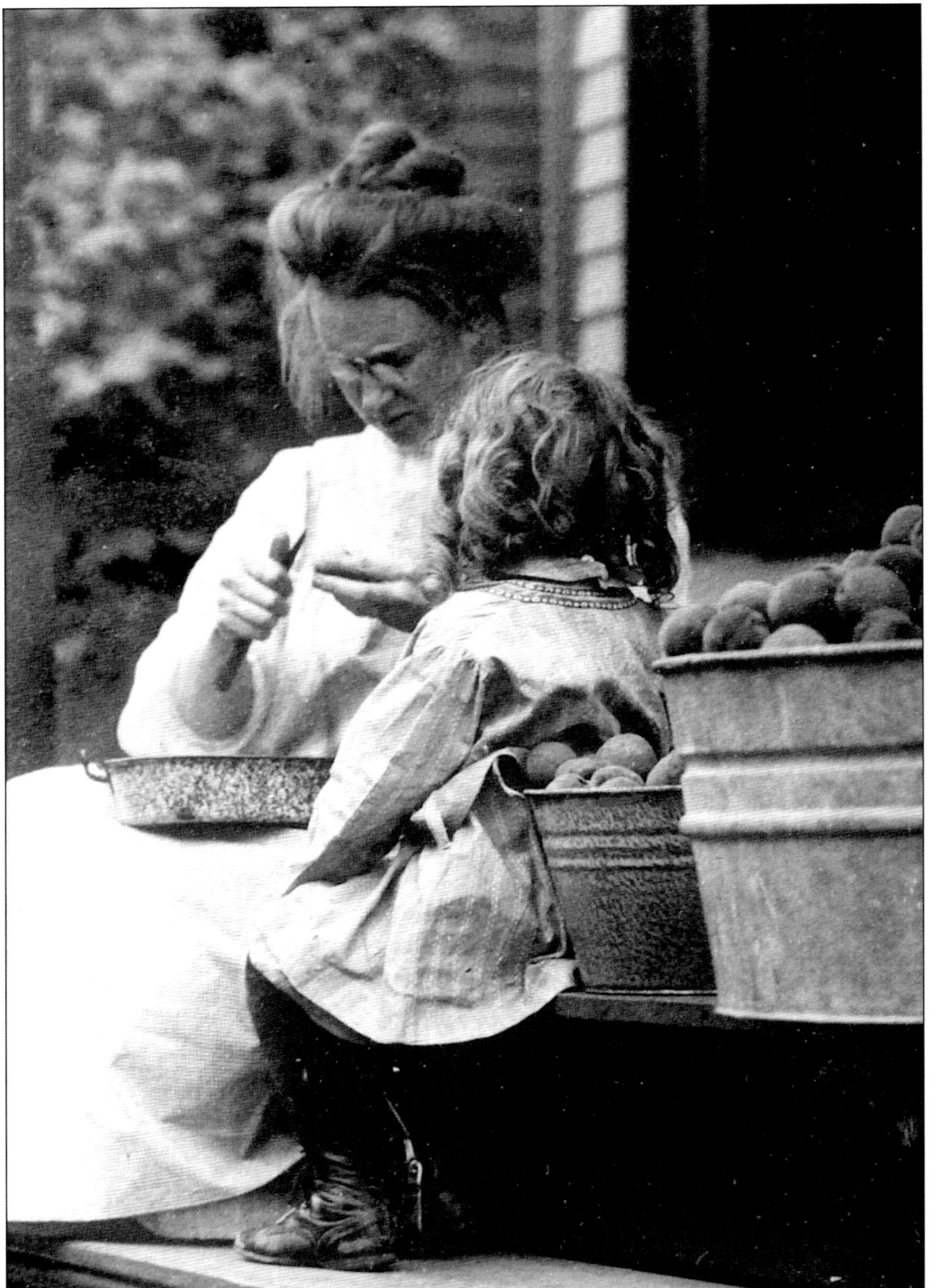

Looking like the quintessential Gibson Girl, Kenneth's mother peeled peaches for canning on the porch while Kenneth watched. His long hair resembled that of a little girl. (Courtesy the BCHS.)

Kenneth, now about four, posed with his mother in the yard of their Hamilton home. (Courtesy the BCHS.)

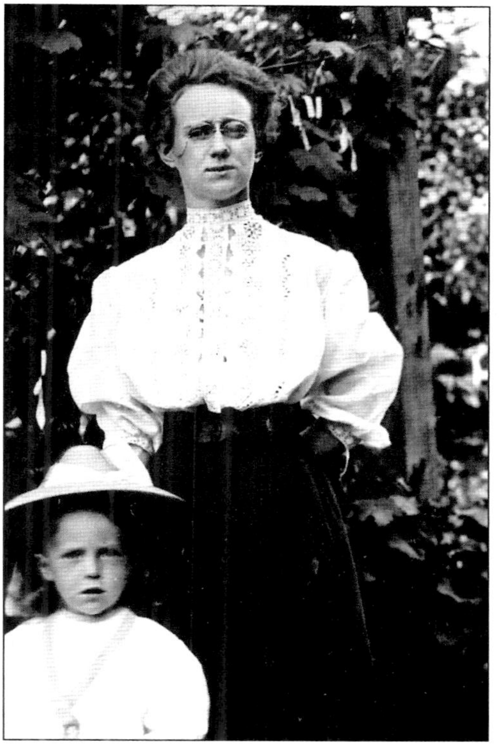

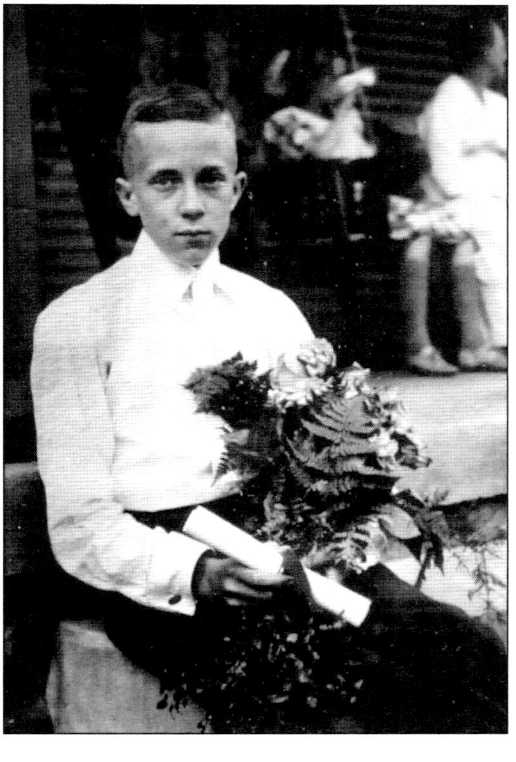

At age 14, Kenneth graduated from grade school as an honor pupil. From here, we lose track of him and his family. (Courtesy the BCHS.)

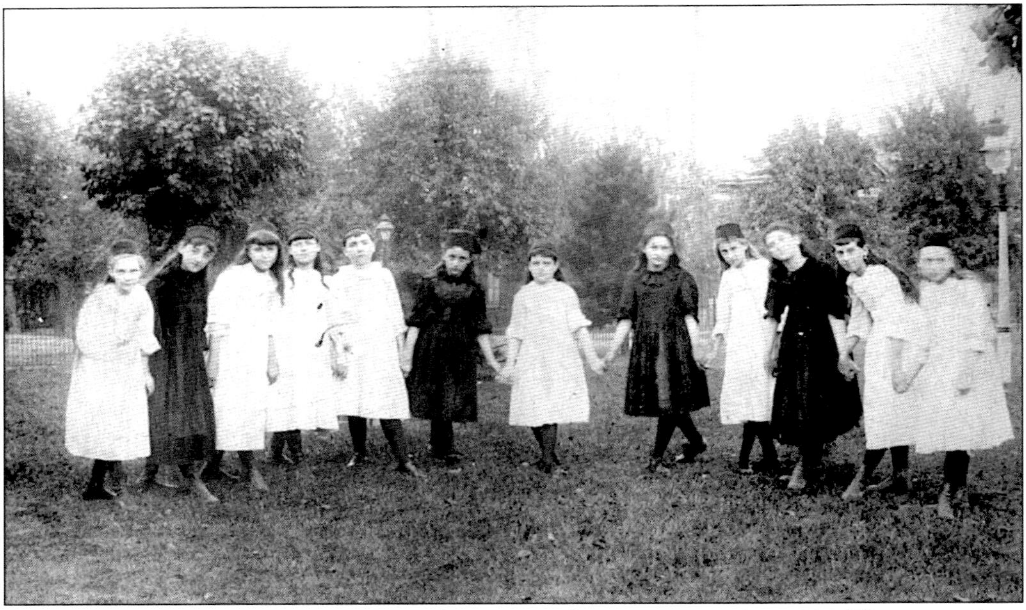

These girls performed a May pole dance during Hamilton's centennial in 1891. They were, from left to right, Jessie Price, Anna Kack, Fanny Rife, Pearl Jessup, Sarah Hayes, Nannie Shields, Mary Neilan, Cara Becker, Sadie Cary, Hattie Dreyfus, Helen Weiler, and Sue Schwartz. (Courtesy the BCHS.)

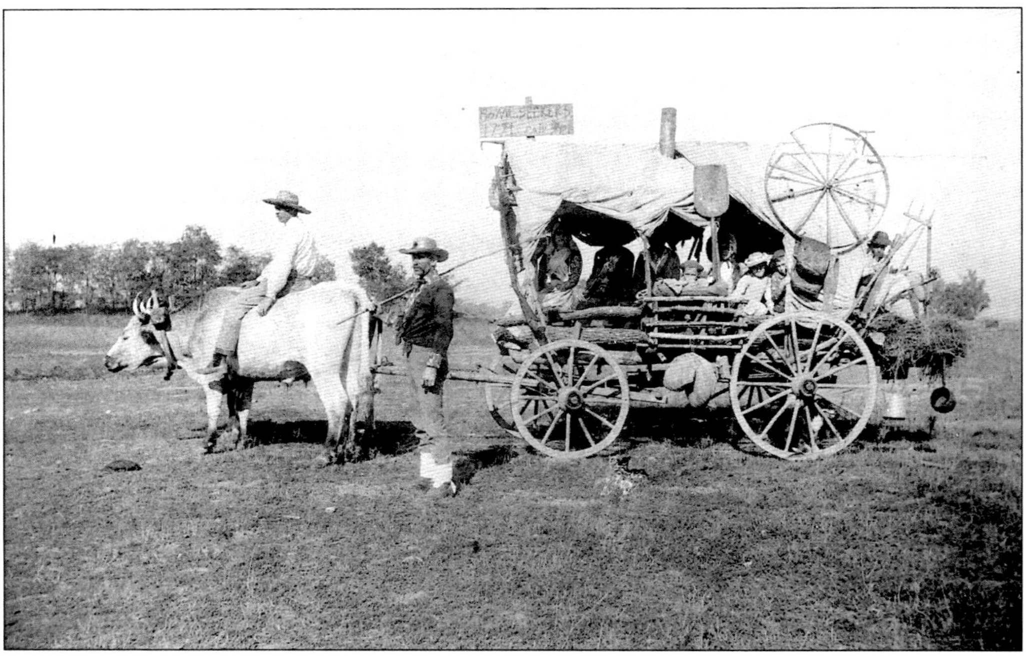

During the Hamilton centennial parade of 1891, these unidentified city residents re-enacted the pioneers' arrival to the Ohio Country by riding in a wagon pulled by an ox. They looked as though they could pass for people from 1803, when Ohio became a state. (Courtesy the BCHS.)

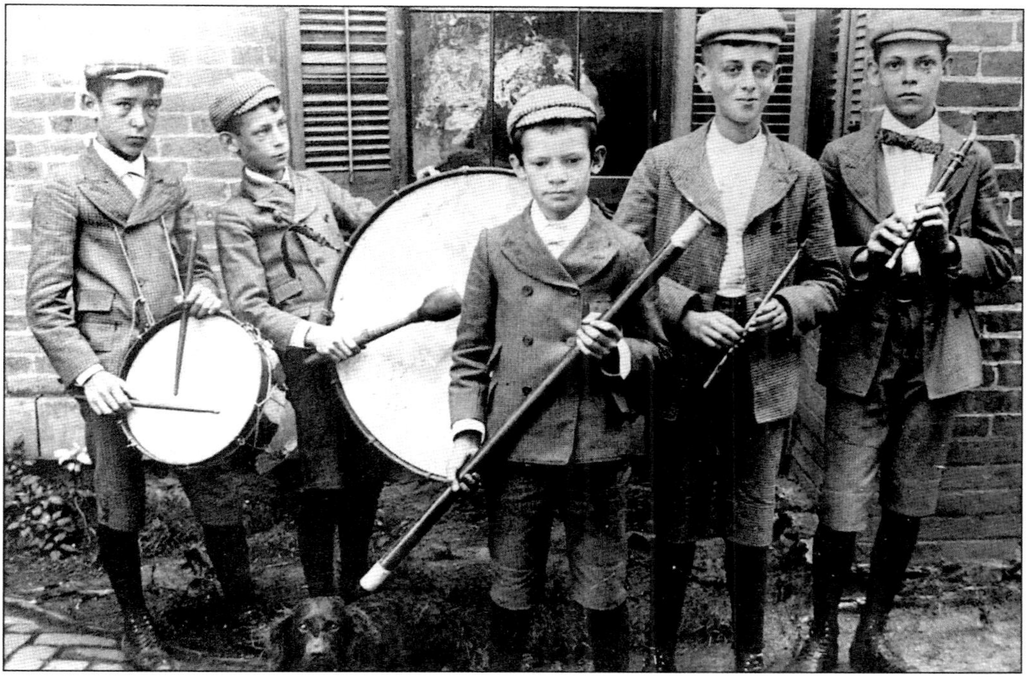

In this photograph taken in the early twentieth century, five unidentified Hamilton boys performed in a band at the YMCA. (Courtesy the BCHS.)

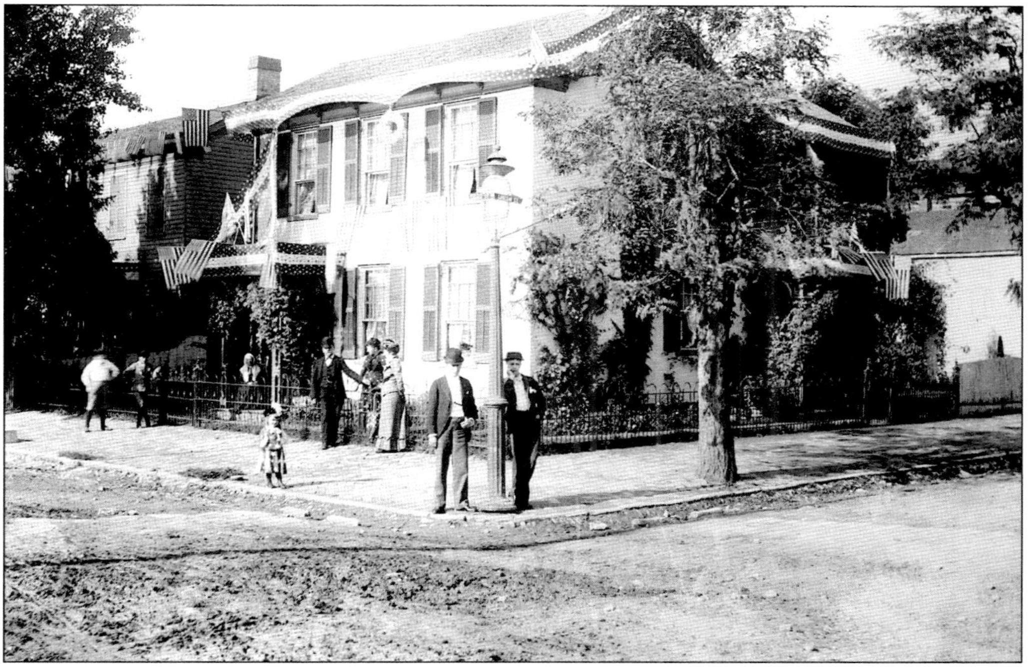

Clyde Sheehan and his family and friends stood around a house at 303 South Third Street at the turn of the twentieth century. Note the dirt street and the gas lamp. (Courtesy the BCHS.)

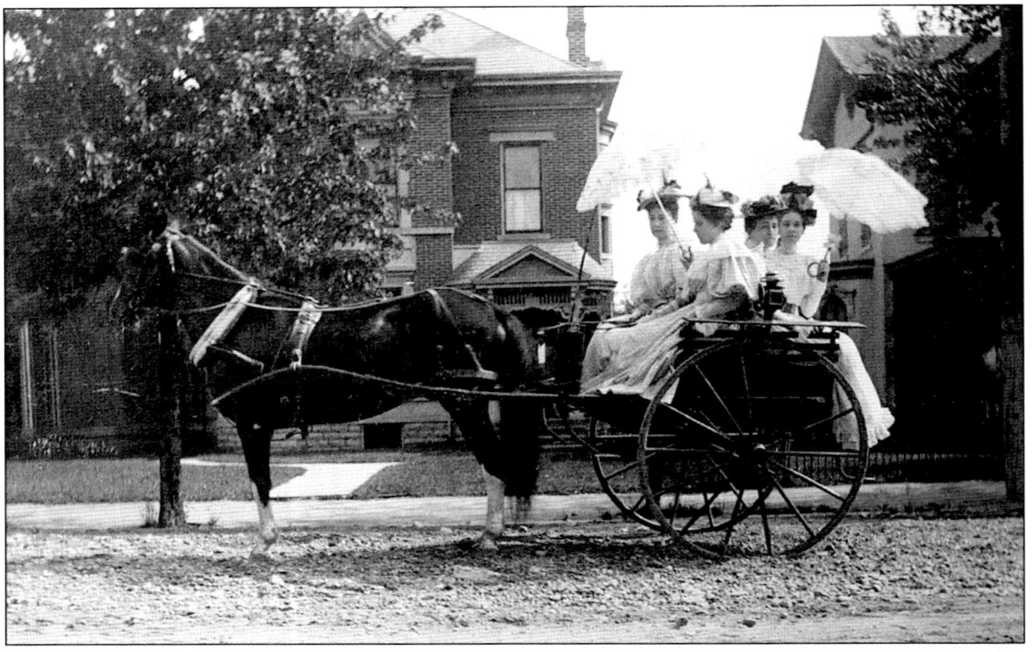

These late-1890s ladies left 730 Dayton Street for a buggy drive. They were, from left to right, Pearl Wood and Ella Hume in front, and Robin Hughes and an unidentified woman in back. The parasols kept the sun from burning their faces. (Courtesy the BCHS.)

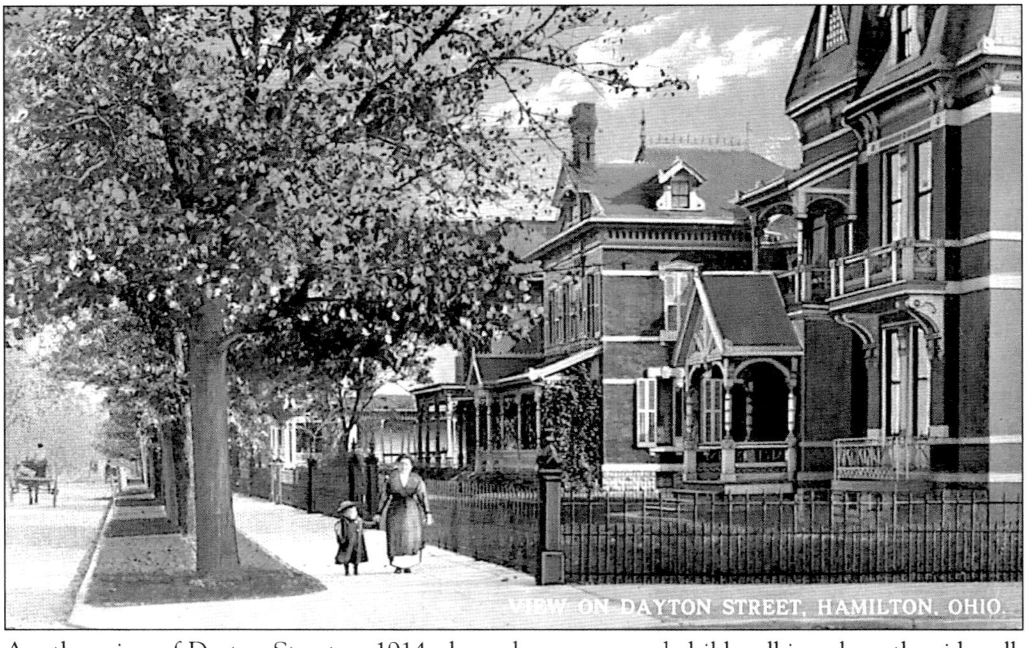

Another view of Dayton Street, c. 1914, showed a woman and child walking along the sidewalk past some large, luxurious homes. Just east of downtown Hamilton, Dayton Street featured some of the city's finest homes, built with rich woods and the finest bricks. Today, the neighborhood once desired by the city's most successful residents is restored. (Courtesy the BCHS.)

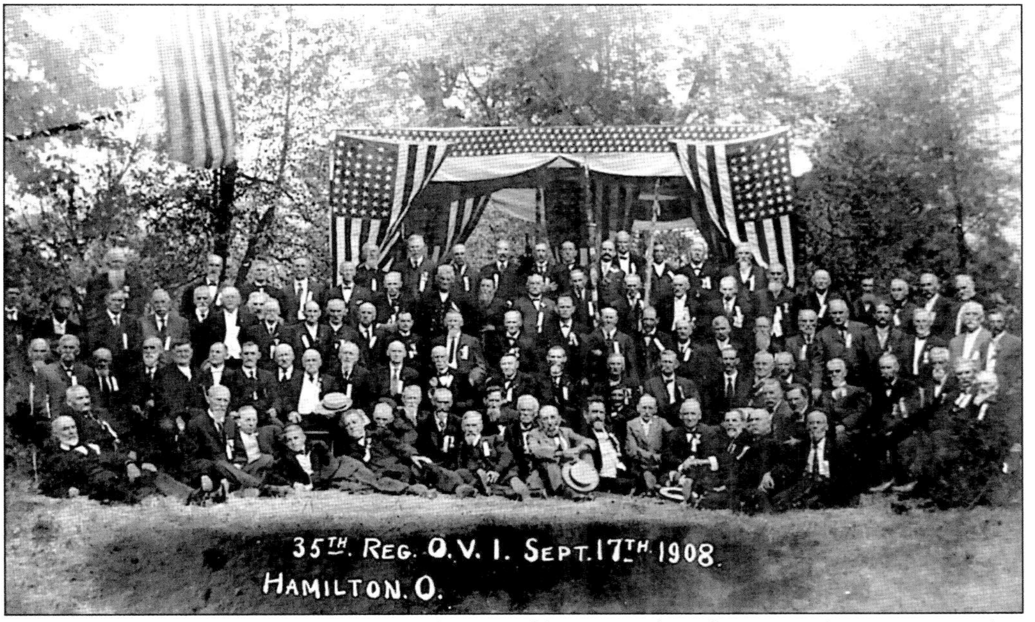

On September 17, 1908, approximately 110 old men gathered in Hamilton to remember America's darkest time—the years of 1861 through 1865. The men were members of the 35th Regiment of the Ohio Volunteer Infantry. Because many Civil War veterans had died by 1908, the unit's reunion was a big event for Hamilton and Butler County. (Courtesy the BCHS.)

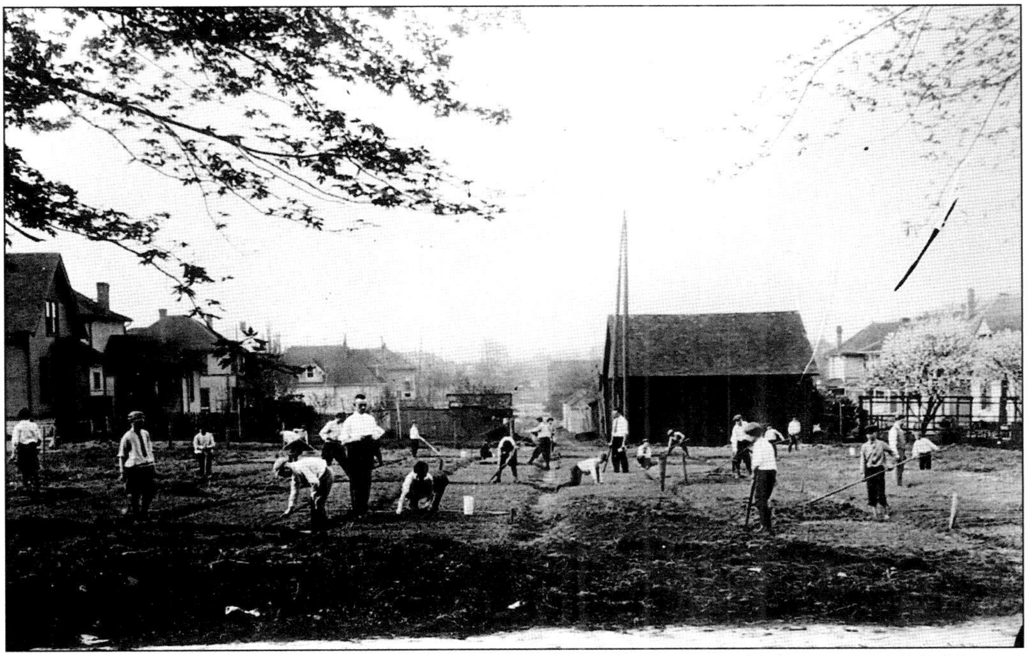

In this photo taken during World War I, Hamilton children worked in a YMCA Victory Garden in an unspecified neighborhood. During the war years, the whole city united to work for victory. (Courtesy the BCHS.)

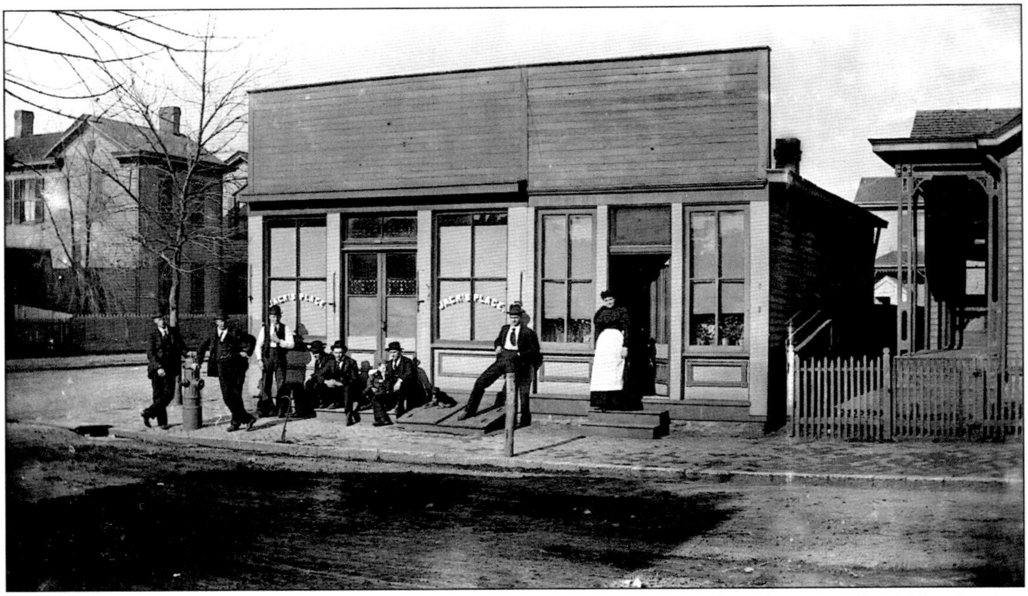

Hamilton had many more neighborhood saloons in the 1800s and early- to mid-1900s. In this picture, passersby probably considered crossing the street before reaching the crowd on the sidewalk in front of Jack's Place at Fifth and Vine Streets. (Courtesy the BCHS.)

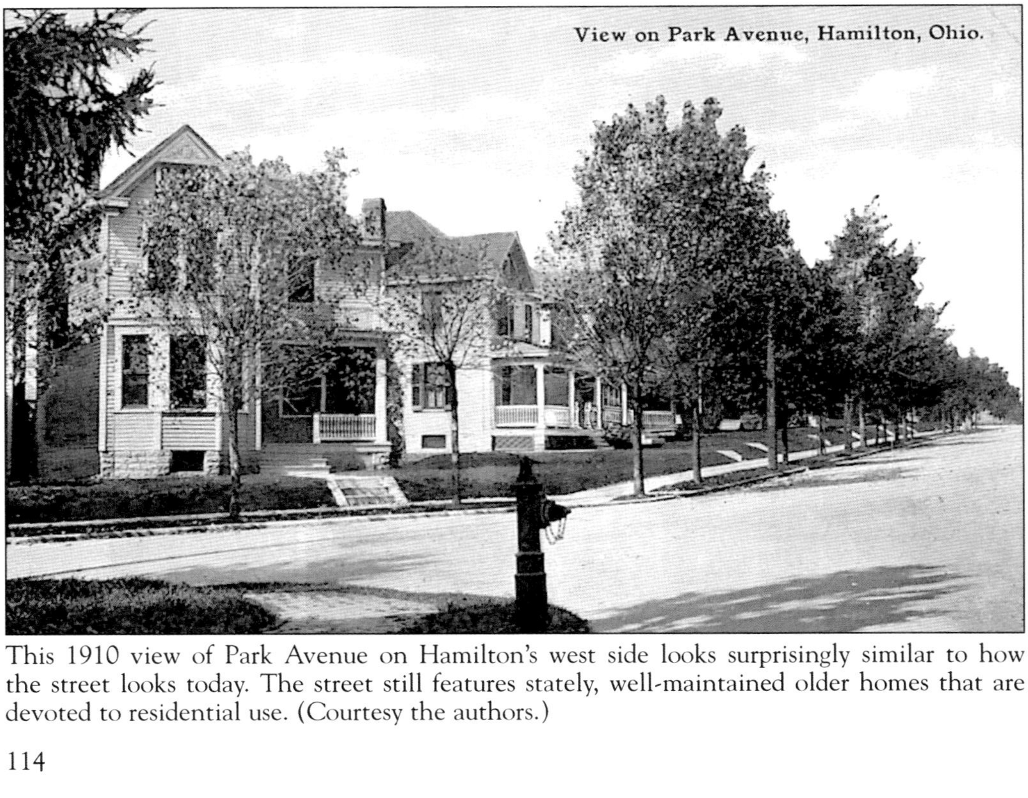

This 1910 view of Park Avenue on Hamilton's west side looks surprisingly similar to how the street looks today. The street still features stately, well-maintained older homes that are devoted to residential use. (Courtesy the authors.)

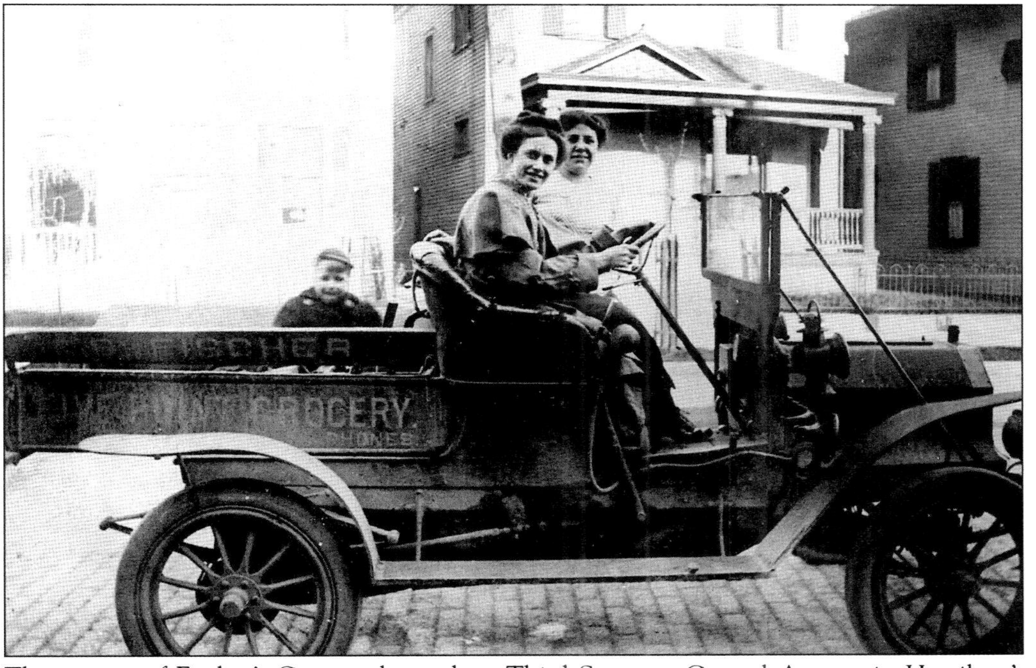

The owners of Fischer's Grocery, located on Third Street at Central Avenue in Hamilton's core, didn't wait around for people to come to it. They delivered all across town. In this 1912 photograph, Mrs. C.G. Fischer delivered groceries in a 1908 REO touring car that has been converted into a truck. Standing next to the truck were Mrs. Paul Campbell and six-year-old Donald Fischer. (Courtesy the BCHS.)

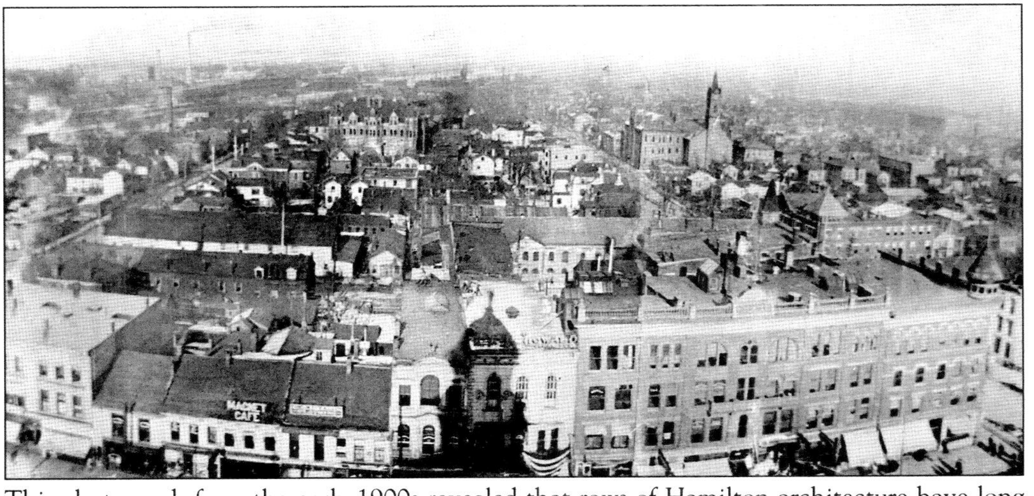

This photograph from the early 1900s revealed that rows of Hamilton architecture have long vanished or been transformed into more modern-looking places. The photographer probably captured this image by standing high in the courthouse. The tower's shadow can be seen on the High Street buildings. (Courtesy the BCHS.)

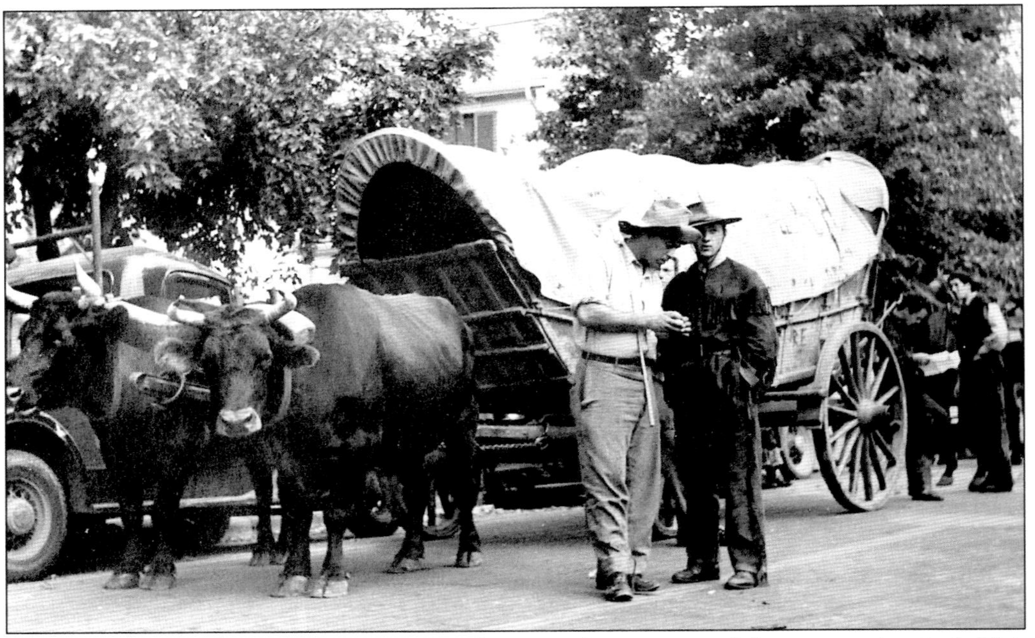

Unidentified Hamilton residents re-enacted yet another version of the pioneers' arrival. This photograph was probably taken during Ohio's sesquicentennial celebration in 1953, although it could have been earlier. (Courtesy the BCHS.)

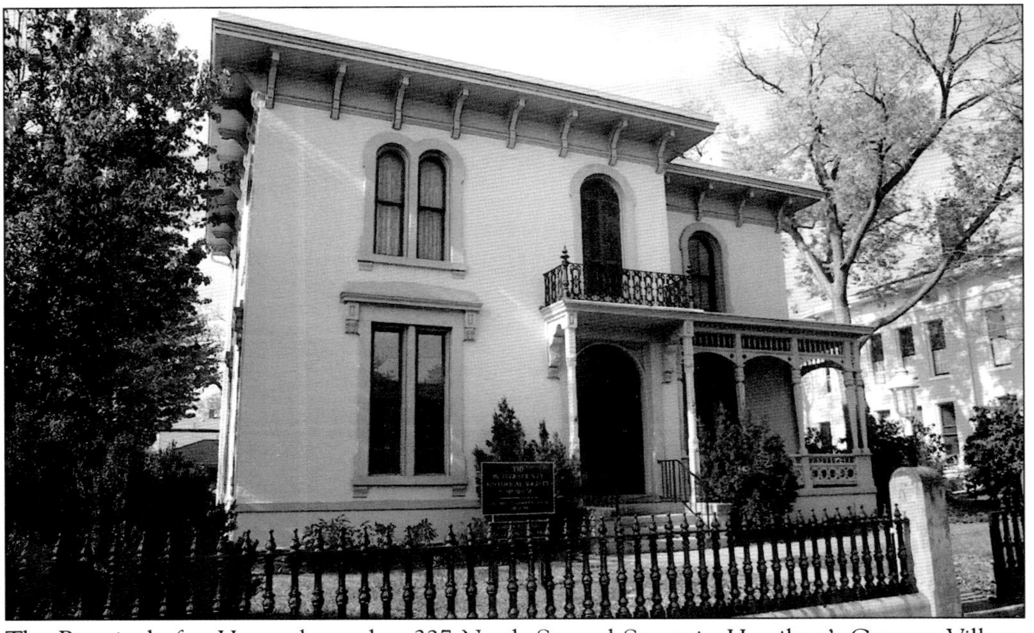

The Benninghofen House, located at 327 North Second Street in Hamilton's German Village, houses the Butler County Historical Society and Museum. The house, an example of Italianate architecture, was built *c.* 1861. The Benninghofen family, a successful Hamilton business family, lived there for 75 years. The museum celebrated 50 years of operation in 1999. It depicts the lifestyle of a prominent business owner and his family in the late 1800s. (Courtesy the authors.)

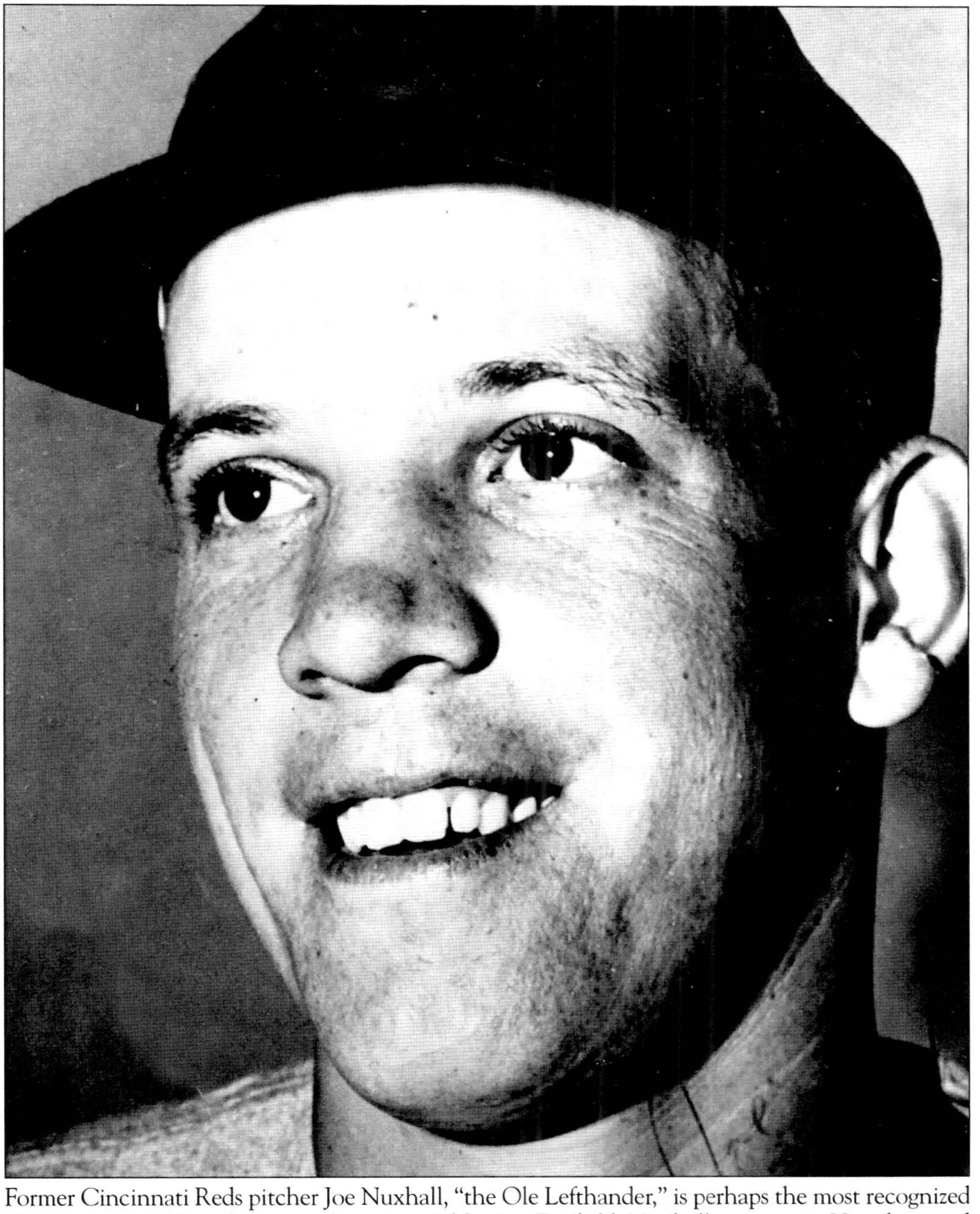

Former Cincinnati Reds pitcher Joe Nuxhall, "the Ole Lefthander," is perhaps the most recognized Hamiltonian. Although he now lives in neighboring Fairfield, Nuxhall grew up in Hamilton and pitched for Hamilton High School during World War II. He first pitched for the Cincinnati Reds when he was a 15-year-old student at Hamilton High School, becoming the youngest player in the major leagues in the twentieth century. Nuxhall later became an effective left-handed starter and reliever. He retired as a player for the Reds in the spring of 1967 at age 37. He then entered the team's radio booth as an announcer. After the 2004 season, he "retired" from broadcasting, but continues to work for the team as a goodwill ambassador and consultant. His bronze statue stands at the Great American Ballpark in Cincinnati. (Courtesy the BCHS.)

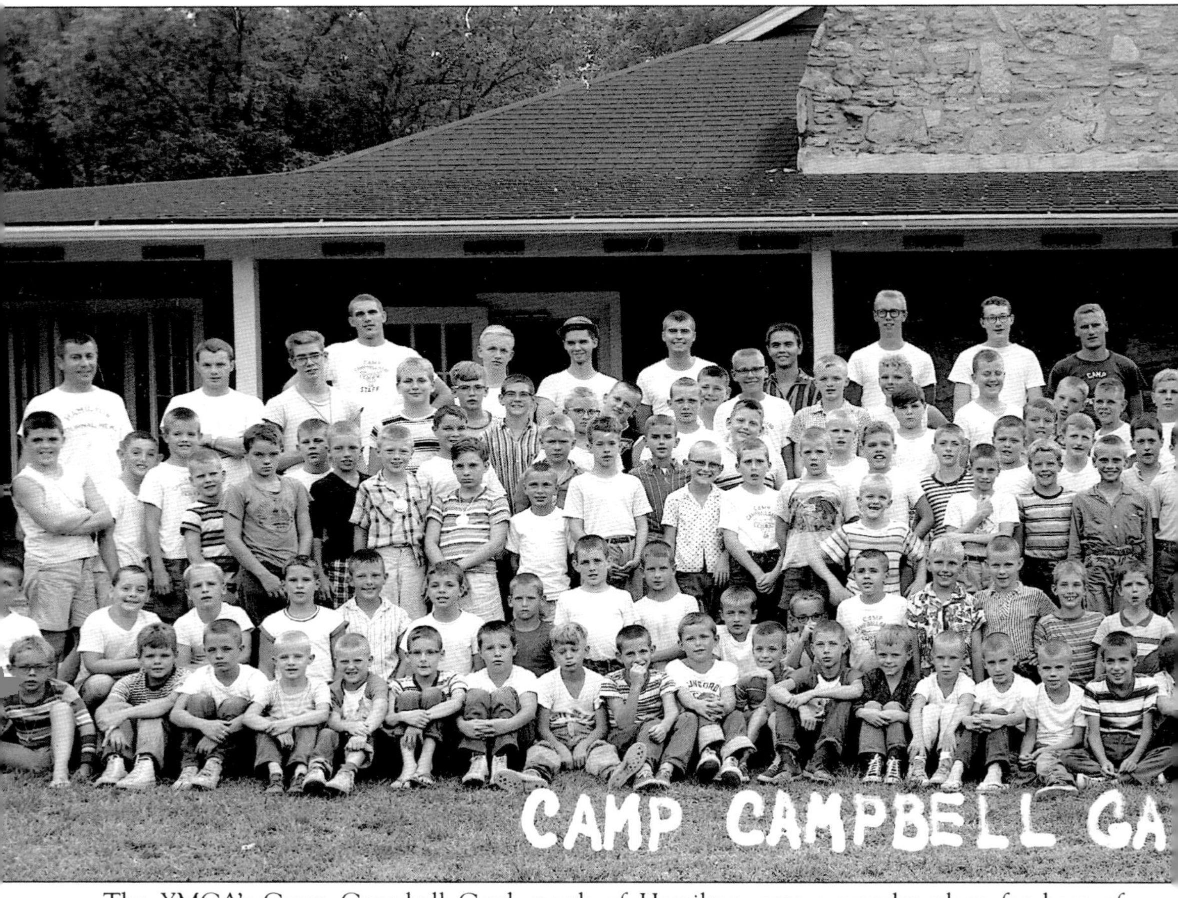

The YMCA's Camp Campbell Gard, north of Hamilton, was a popular place for boys of summer. To look at them, you'd never think the world was under threat of nuclear attack, or that polio still threatened young lives. August of 1959 was a magical time when boys left their homes for two weeks to live in rickety wooden cabins, play cowboys and Indians in the woods, hit baseballs until their hands hurt, fish in the Great Miami River, hike for miles at night and

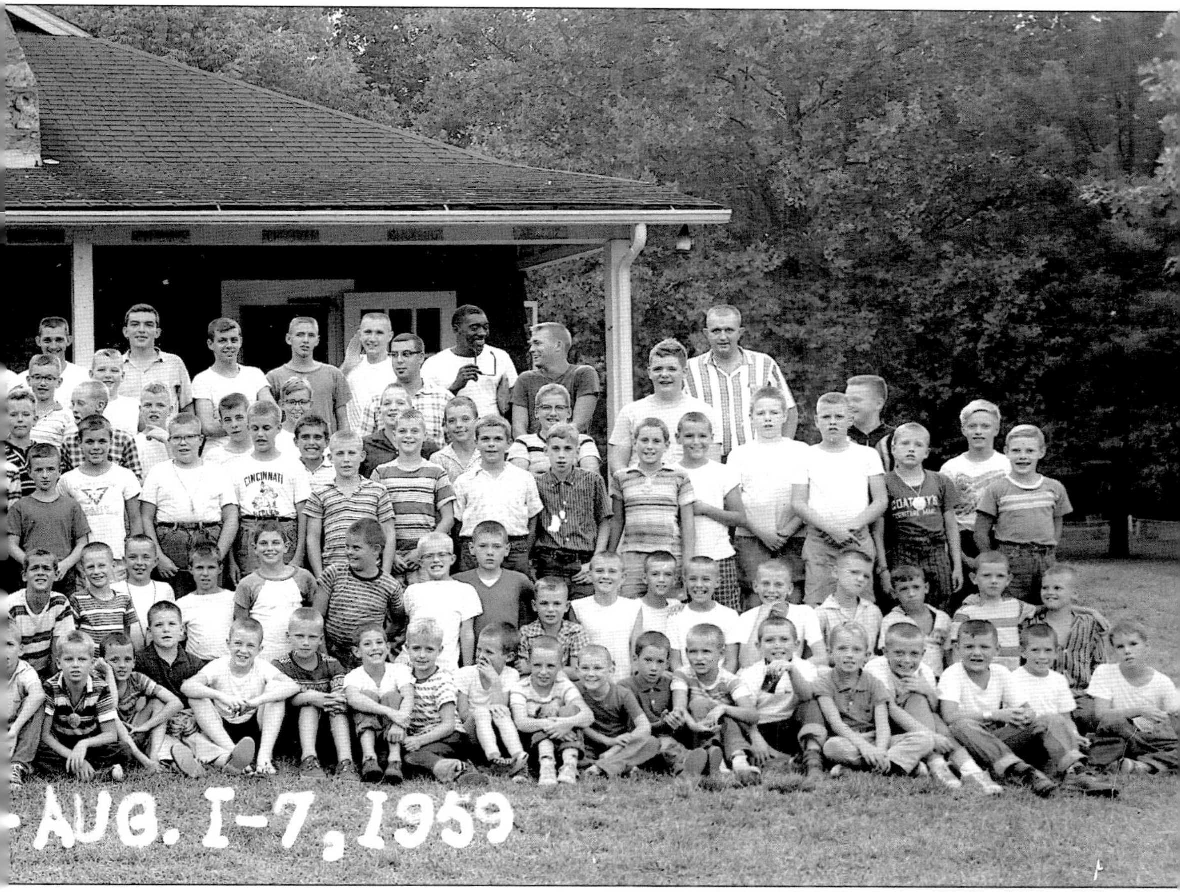

camp out in the rain, devour thick roasted ears of corn in the field, and eat thick hamburgers in the camp mess hall. The boys guzzled red Kool-Aid—called "bug juice" by camp leaders—by the quart. Coauthor Randy McNutt is the eighth boy on the left side in the first row of boys standing. (Courtesy the authors.)

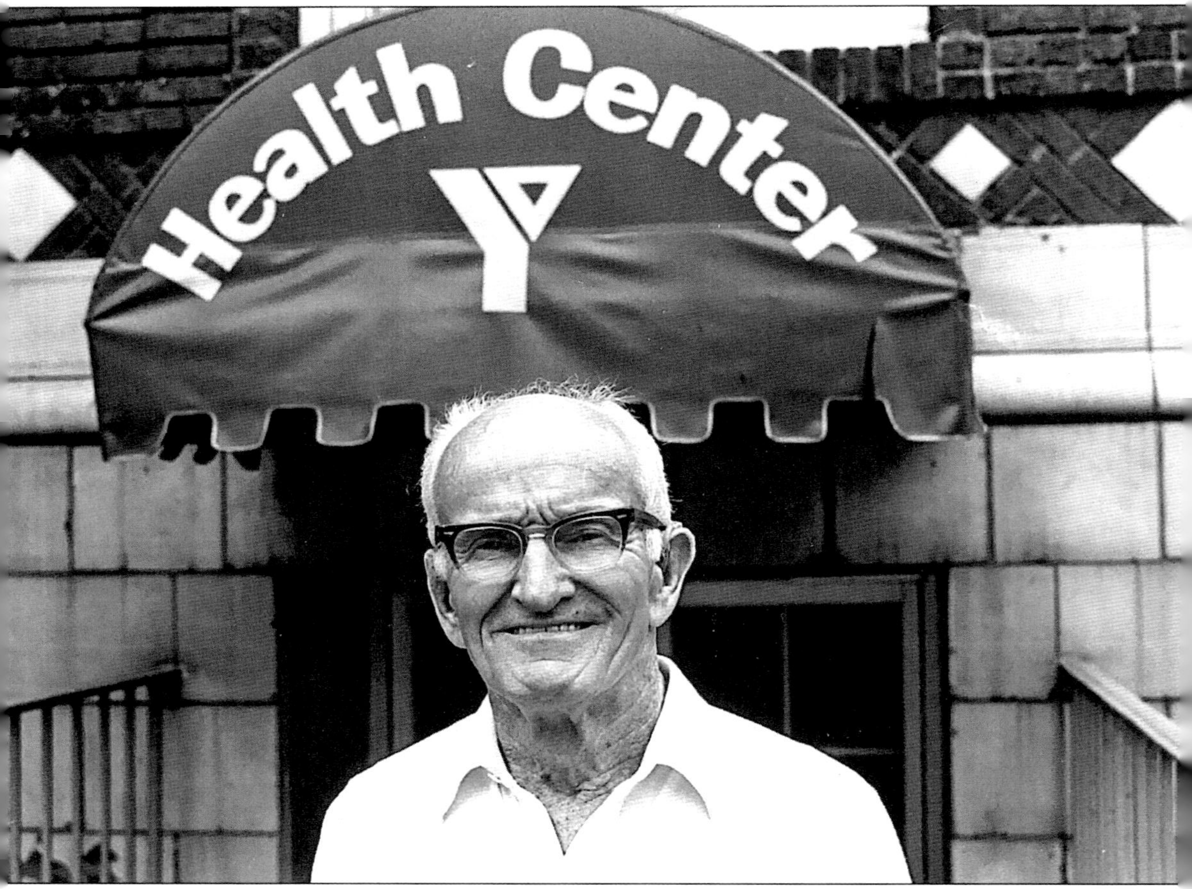

William "Bill" Sharp, one of Hamilton's most beloved educators and coaches, is pictured in this 1982 photograph taken in front of the YMCA, where he assisted in the training room after retiring from teaching. Although he was in his eighties by then, Sharp—simply called "Coach" by the thousands of men who knew him from their days at Hamilton and Garfield high schools from the 1940s through the 1970s—looked much younger than his chronological age. He maintained a muscular physique and a positive attitude that influenced everyone who knew him. He rarely forgot a name and he stayed in touch with former students. During his long tenure in the local schools, he taught much more than facts. He served as a role model and loved the city. (Courtesy Randy McNutt.)

Ten

CITY OF SCULPTURE

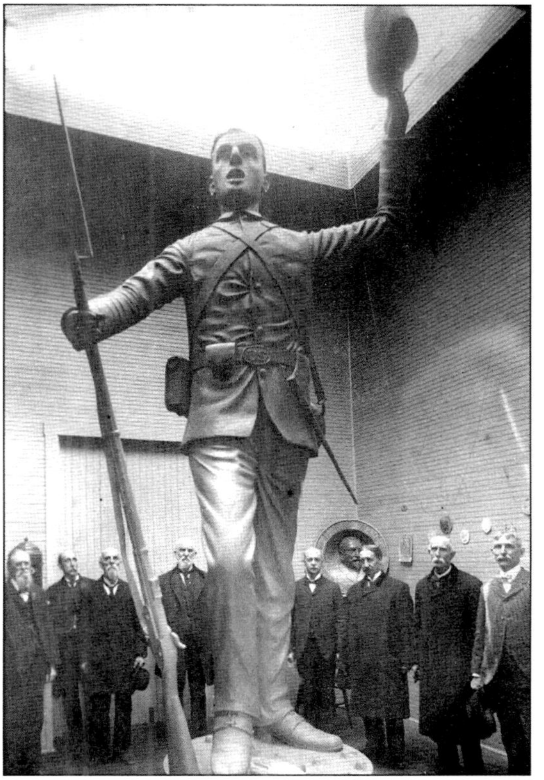

The Monument Committee, *c.* 1904, observed *Billy Yank* before he was erected atop the Soldiers, Sailors and Pioneers Monument. Hamilton sculptor Rudolph Thiem created the figure, which stands at 17 feet and weighs 3,500 pounds. Monument Committee members pictured were, in no particular order, former Governor James Campbell of Middletown, N.B. Tubbs, Captain J.W. Meyers, Henry W. Mallory, M.D., James Fitton, James Beldon, Aaron Wesco, George T. Earhart, and Dr. J.H. Roll. (Courtesy the BCHS.)

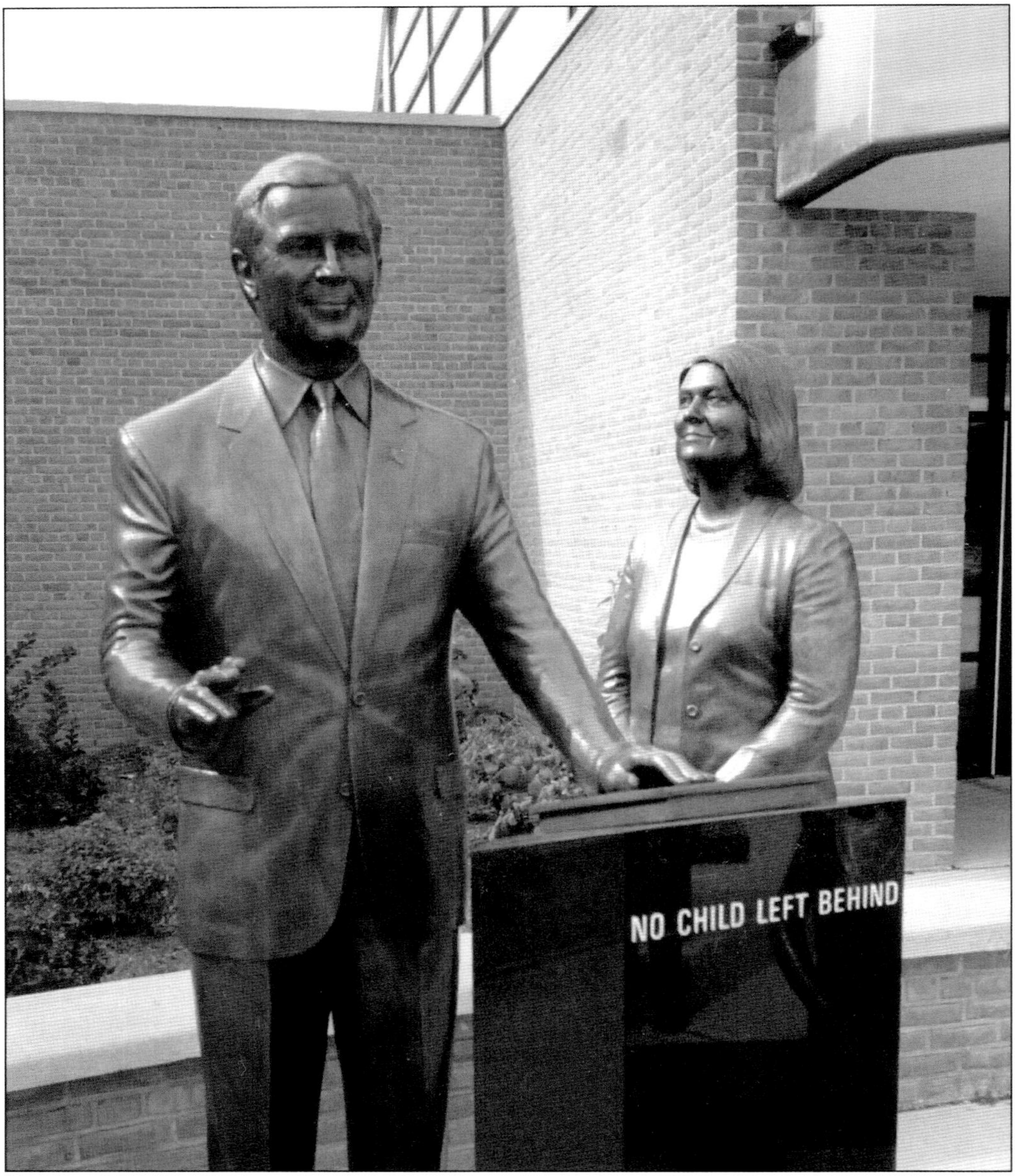

Bronze sculptures of President George W. Bush and Hamilton Superintendent Janet Baker stand in front of Hamilton High School. They commemorate Bush's signing of the No Child Left Behind Act at the school on January 8, 2002. Various national, state, and local leaders gathered that day to watch Bush sign the historic legislation. (Courtesy the authors.)

In Ludlow Park, a bronze globe from the 1840s commemorates Captain John Cleves Symmes. In the 1820s, Symmes promoted his Theory of Concentric Spheres and Polar Voids—the idea that the earth was hollow and inhabited within by a race of advanced people. Although the world laughed at him, Symmes continued to lecture and seek money for a polar expedition. He died in Hamilton on May 29, 1829. (Courtesy the authors.)

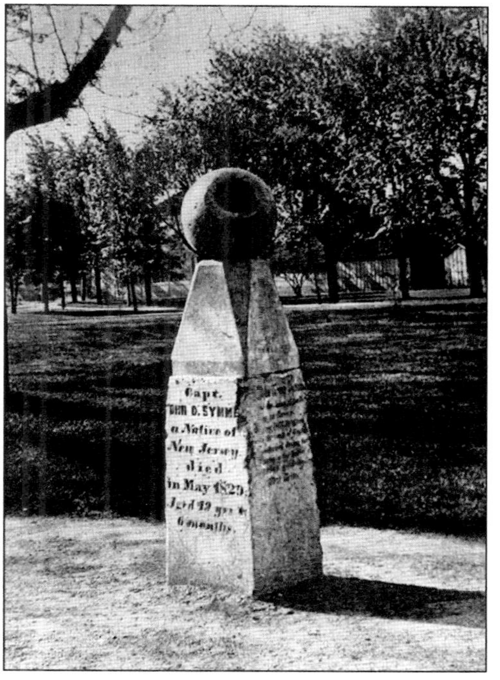

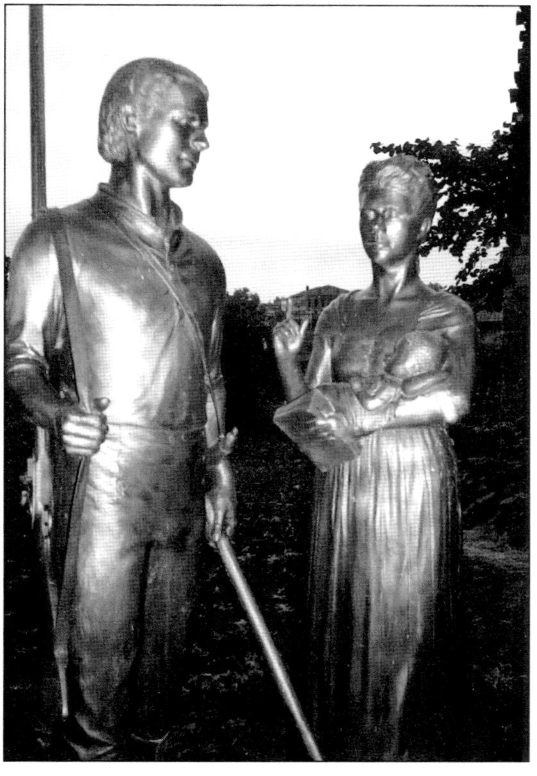

Pioneer Family, a sculpture by Jarrett Hawkins of Cincinnati, represents agriculture and protection. It was added in 2002 on Monument Avenue, where Fort Hamilton once guarded the Great Miami. The sculpture also represents Hamilton's pioneer founders. The man carries a rifle; the woman, a baby and a Bible. Their faces were inspired by that of the sculpture's donors, John A. Stewart, M.D., and his wife, Marian Vail Stewart, when they were 25 years old. (Courtesy the authors.)

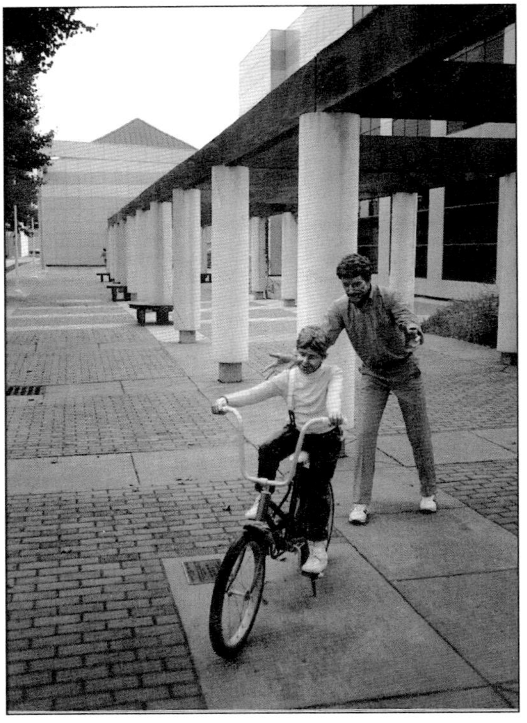

When *First Ride*, a realistic sculpture of a father and daughter with bicycle, first appeared in front of the Fitton Center for Creative Arts in 1997, some people momentarily wondered if the figures were real. One of the first of Hamilton's new sculptures, the piece by J. Seward Johnson Jr. hints at the art that waits within the building. (Courtesy the authors.)

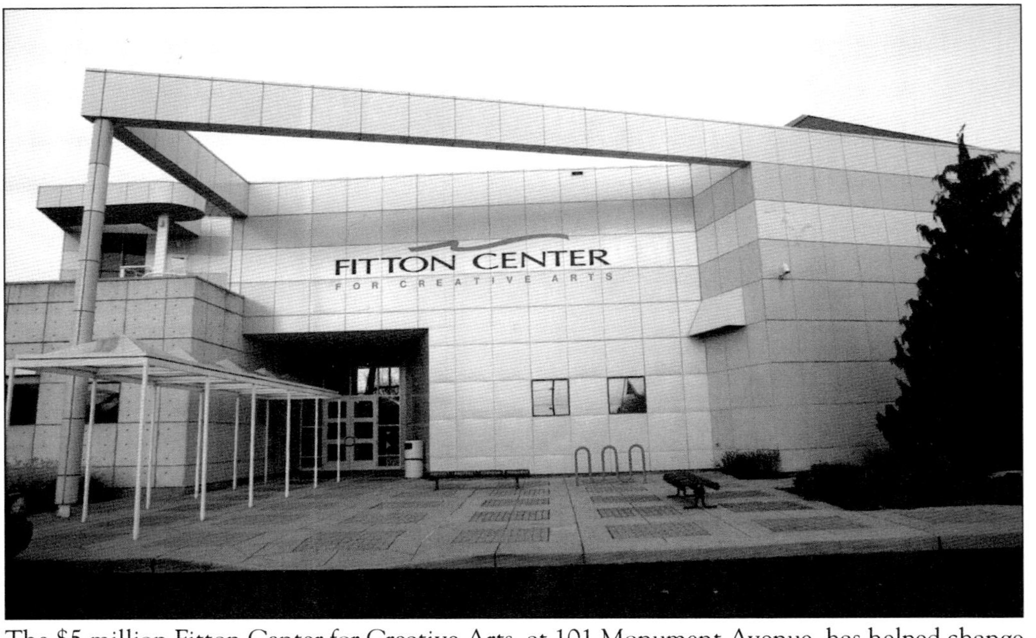

The $5 million Fitton Center for Creative Arts, at 101 Monument Avenue, has helped change Hamilton's image from a fading factory town to a center for the arts. It attracts visitors from across southwest Ohio. The center offers art classes, art exhibitions, concerts, and a direction for the future. The Fitton has also led Hamilton's move toward achieving its goal of becoming the City of Sculpture. (Courtesy the authors.)

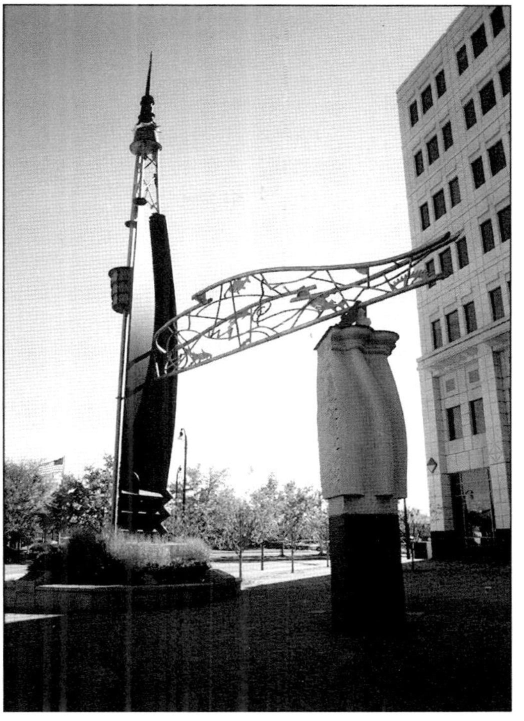

The Hamilton Gateway, a 66-foot sculpture erected in front of the Government Services Center on High Street c. 2000, greets visitors to the City of Sculpture and provides a link to other historic artwork in the city. The plaza on which it stands is the eastern focal point for Hamilton's annual ice sculpture festival. The Gateway was designed by Andrea Myklebust and Stanton G. Sears and donated by Judge John R. Moser and his wife, Shirley. (Courtesy the authors.)

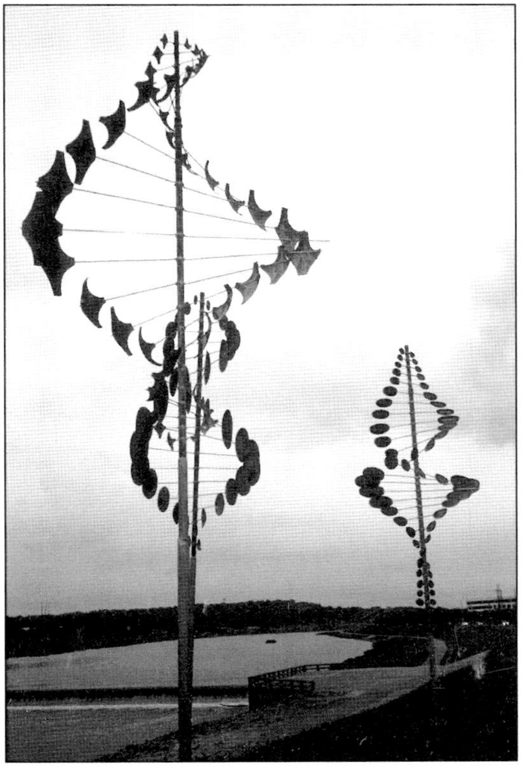

Wind Forest, by sculptor Lyman Whitaker of Utah, is at the Great Miami River dam, across from the Hamilton Campus of Miami University on Neilan Boulevard. Unlike Hamilton's fixed sculptures, this one revolves in the wind. Whitaker says wind sculptures such as this one "provide serenity in a world of confusion." (Courtesy the authors.)

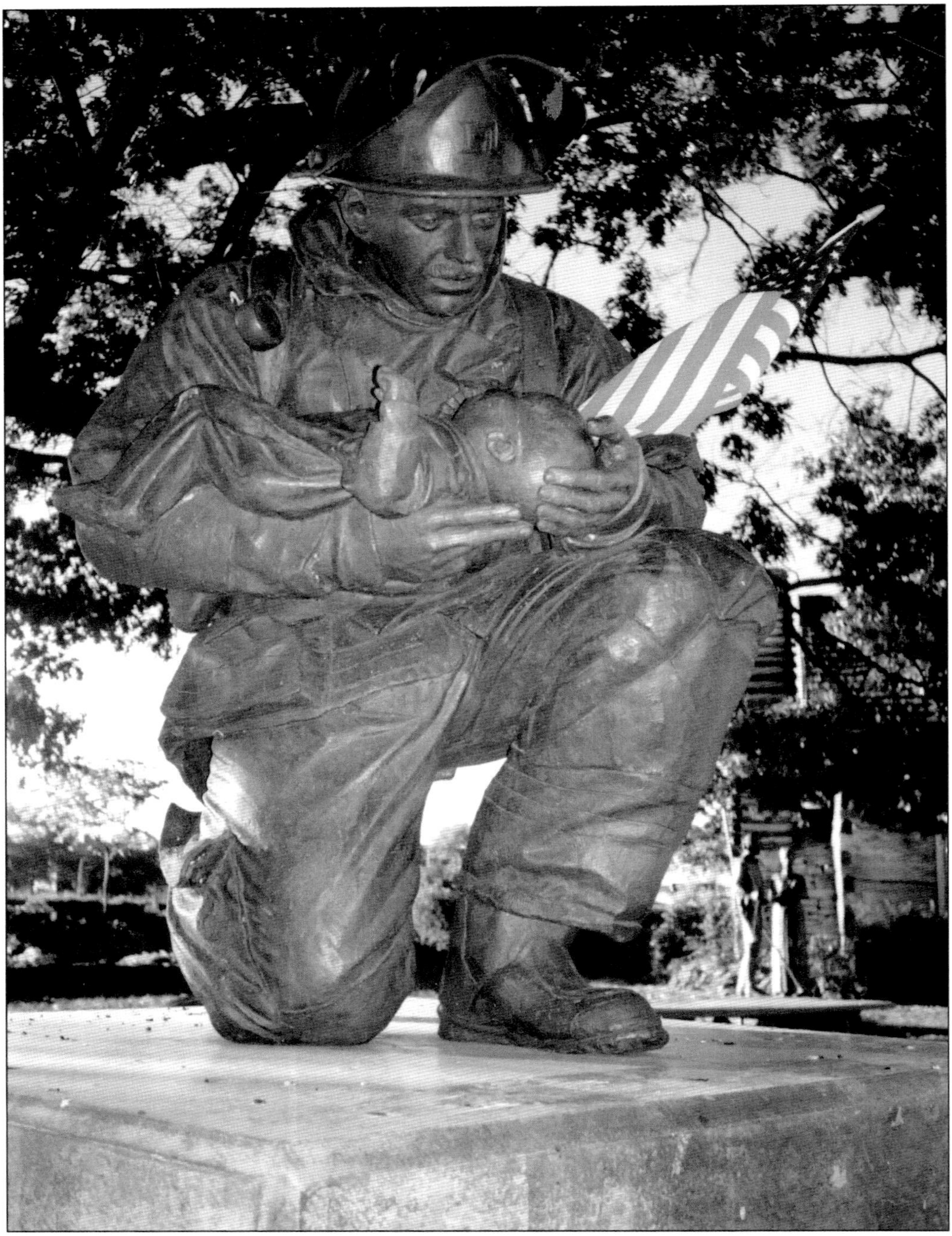

The life-size *Firefighter Memorial* sculpture, commissioned by the Butler County Fire Chiefs Association, stands on Monument Avenue near the Fitton Center. The highly detailed piece, created by George Danhires of Kent, Ohio, depicts a firefighter holding a small child. The memorial commemorates the 15 people who have died protecting the city from fires and other disasters. The piece was financed by private and public donations and erected *c.* 2000. (Courtesy the authors.)

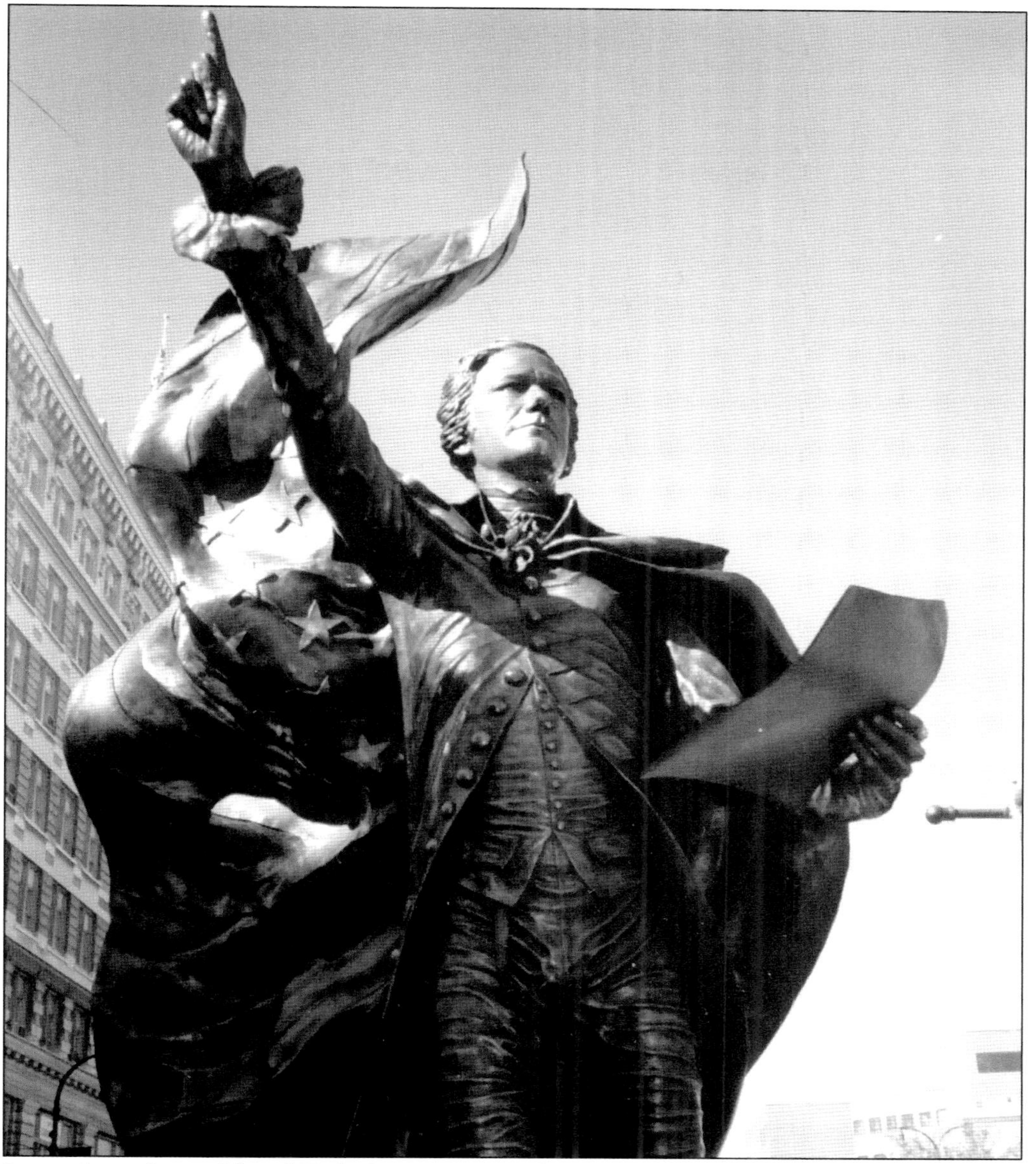

It stands in the middle of High Street at Journal Square downtown, a monument to liberty, patriotism, and history. But *The American Cape*, the world's largest statue of Alexander Hamilton thus far, makes more than grand statements. At 4,000 pounds and 16 feet in height, with a granite base, the bronze figure stands as a remarkable work of art by sculptor Kristen Visbal of Lewes, Delaware. Commissioned by Historic Hamilton Inc. and Hamilton's City of Sculpture group, the piece depicts Alexander Hamilton holding a document and pointing toward the heavens while his large cape and Old Glory unfurl behind him. At the sculpture's dedication on October 23, 2004, participants included Visbal, city leaders, and Douglas Hamilton, a fifth great-grandson of the former secretary of the treasury and an American founding father. The piece cost more than $200,000, paid for by a fundraising campaign in which schools, businesses, clubs, and other groups participated. As David Belew, president of Historic Hamilton Inc., explained, "Hamiltonians have waited a very long time for this event—213 years to be exact." (Courtesy the authors.)

BIBLIOGRAPHY

A History and Biographical Cyclopaedia of Butler County Ohio. Cincinnati: Western Biographical Publishing Company, 1882.

Bauer, Cheryl, and Rob Portman. *Wisdom's Paradise: The Forgotten Shakers of Union Village*. Wilmington, Ohio: Orange Frazer Press, 2004.

Behr, Edward. *Prohibition: The 13 Years That Changed America*. London: BBC Books, 1997.

Bicentennial Atlas of Butler County. Hamilton: *Journal-News*, 1975.

Blount, Jim. "Early 1900s years of Hamilton's industrial boom." Hamilton: *Journal-News*, date undetermined.

Blount, Jim. *The Road to Fort Hamilton*. Hamilton: *Journal-News*, 1976.

Blount, Jim. *Soldiers, Sailors and Pioneers Monument*. Hamilton: Butler County, 1988.

Boyer, Mike. "Beckett Paper mill in Hamilton to be sold." *The Cincinnati Enquirer*, December 16, 2004.

Jones, Richard O. "Statesman's likeness arrives in center of city." Hamilton: *Journal-News*, October 22, 2004.

McNutt, Randy. *Ghosts: Ohio's Haunted Landscapes, Lost Arts, and Forgotten Places*. Wilmington, Ohio: Orange Frazer Press, 1996.

McNutt, Randy. "Yesteryear's Glory Returns to Mansions of Hamilton." *The Cincinnati Enquirer*, December 25, 1981.

Our City: Hamilton, Ohio. Hamilton: Hamilton City Schools, 1968.

Visitors Guide: Hamilton! The Greater Hamilton Convention and Visitors Bureau, 2000.

"William Dean Howells." City of Hamilton, 2003.

Walking Tours of Historic Hamilton, Ohio. Greater Hamilton Convention and Visitors Bureau, 2001.

"Welcome to the Benninghofen House." Hamilton: Butler County Historical Society and Museum, 2003.